# On Mexican Time

# On Mexican Time

*A New Life in San Miguel*

*Tony Cohan*

BROADWAY BOOKS    NEW YORK

BROADWAY

Note to the Reader: In an effort to safeguard the privacy of several individuals, the author has changed their names, and in some cases disguised identifying characteristics or used composite characters.

Broadway Books titles may be purchased for business or promotional use or for special sales. For information, please write to: Special Markets Department, Random House, Inc., 1540 Broadway, New York, NY 10036.

BROADWAY BOOKS and its logo, a letter B bisected on the diagonal, are trademarks of Broadway Books, a division of Random House, Inc.

Visit our website at www.broadwaybooks.com

Library of Congress Cataloging-in-Publication Data

Cohan, Tony.
    On Mexican time: a new life in San Miguel / Tony Cohan.
— 1st ed.
        p.   cm.
    ISBN 0-7679-0318-8 (hc)
    1. San Miguel de Allende (Mexico)—Description and travel.
2. San Miguel de Allende (Mexico)—Social life and customs.
3. Cohan, Tony—Homes and haunts—Mexico—San Miguel
de Allende.   I. Title.
F1391.S2C64   2000
972'.41—dc21                                                    99-29296
                                                                    CIP

FIRST EDITION

Book design by Pei Loi Koay

00   01   02   03   04   10   9   8   7   6   5   4   3   2   1

O*ver there everything is going to be different; life is never going to be quite the same again after your passport has been stamped and you find yourself speechless among the money changers. . . . It is like starting over again.*

—GRAHAM GREENE, *ANOTHER MEXICO*

# Contents

# On Mexican Time

# Chapter 1

# Twenty-One-Day Ticket

JANUARY 1985. THERE IS NO AIRPORT
directly serving San Miguel de Allende.
Boarding a midafternoon bus from Mexico
City's north terminal, I watch the clotted
capital become desolate factory outskirts,
then dissolve into cultivated swaths of agave
cactus, sorghum, bean. The air softens.
*Música estereofónica* raises sweet laments. A
Virgin of Guadalupe pendant sways from
the driver's mirror between decals of Che
Guevara and Rambo. A tossing reverie must
have become sleep, for when I next look out
the shadows are long, the hills closing in.
Along the roadside, farmworkers materialize
out of the air, then recede back into dusky
earth. Little roadside shrines whiz by, candles lit within. Old stone walls run to nowhere. Clusters of black birds wheel, then
swerve toward the horizon like iron

filings to a magnet. I look over at Masako, her head pressed to the window.

A sudden sharp descent causes me to grip my seat. A dying sun sets ablaze a little town nestled on a hillside. We debark in a dusty clearing among stray dogs. A half dozen scruffy kids vie to carry our luggage; I wave them off. A taxi driver in a clean white shirt offers to take us into town. Anxiously I counter his figure by half; nobody's going to rip *me* off. Shrugging, he agrees, as if to say: If it's that important to you.

We step through a canopy of bougainvillea into a cool, flower-flooded patio. I enter a hotel office where earlier I'd called to ask, "Do you have a room?" and been answered with "Maybe." I'd bridled at the insouciance, with its echoes of being put on hold; but as our luggage slumps onto a tile floor in a high stucco room overlooking a shady garden, I ease, forgive.

We walk through a dimly lit town of roseate Moorish walls. A tuneless band plays somewhere. Church bells stun the air. I see a ghost or a barefoot woman walk by smiling, a bucketful of calla lilies on her head. Through the open door of a church, I glimpse a wooden Jesus in a wine-colored velvet robe. Cobbles and narrow, raised sidewalks force me to notice where I place my feet, imposing a minuet with each passing person.

In a small, thronged plaza, we sit on an iron bench gazing up at a quirky pink church, its serrated spires embedded in a full complement of stars. These strolling, chatting, laughing citizens don't seem to realize the TV they're missing at home. I war with the evening's sweet lassitude, trying to keep it all outside, avoiding eyes. I feel repeatedly for my wallet, my passport. Vainly I fish for the summarizing blurb, the snapshot, the quick hit.

*Drop it,* something whispers. *Just let it all go . . .*

Our Spanish-style house was in an area south of Hollywood known in real estate parlance as "Hancock Park adjacent," an attempt to bind it to the million-dollar neighborhood close by. We'd bought it with money made writing words and music, designing clothes, and making art. We were busy, successful, tired.

An uncharacteristically cold January, and we kept the heater on all day. A book of mine had just come out and I was trying to get a grip on the next one: a story about a dwarf writer in a South American prison and an American lawyer attempting to free him. I was spending afternoons at the Amnesty International office downtown, poring through prisoner files, reading about the dirty war in Argentina, atrocities in West Africa, slaughter in East Timor. I was bringing home books with names like *Torture in the 1980s.* Masako would look at me oddly. She herself was painting large, grim self-portraits, acrylic on canvas.

At dinners I listened politely to friends' conversation about the price of real estate, projects in development, notable recent crimes. After a cultural night out I lay in bed reviewing the drive there and back, the parking experience, where I put my keys—the event itself barely recalled. I left messages on machines; they were returned in kind. Surrounded by art, music, information, and food, I saw, heard, thought, and tasted little. A series of robberies and killings had erupted in our neighborhood: first the Bob's Big Boy murders, in which the victims were executed; then a robbery at a favorite restaurant two blocks away, the customers mugged and herded into a freezer; then a break-in at the house next door. In a moment of grave personal defeat, I installed a house alarm system with an "Armed Response" sign stabbed into our lawn, a blinking "command center," "perimeter defense," "panic button," and roving patrol cars.

We were wired for apocalypse: *Blade Runner* was no longer a metaphor.

There were days when I'd find myself hurtling down freeways toward receding destinations of evaporating worth, suspended between the fantastic and the mundane, between wide acclaim and abject defeat. Somewhere, I'd missed a turnoff.

Cold, anxious, trapped inside our house, we'd taken to bed early one night to keep warm. Masako was leafing through an issue of *Gourmet*, a Christmas subscription from a friend. I was with Bruce Chatwin in Patagonia. The *Gourmet* magazine represented to me the very complacent consumerism we'd once scorned, now breaking through our "perimeter defenses." In youth we'd both traveled widely on shoestrings, lived in Europe, North Africa, India, Japan. Now we had the money but no time. Instead we read about it, recounted old experiences, festooned our dwellings with Third World artifacts, talismans of trips once taken.

"Look," Masako said, holding open a double-page color spread.

Warm rose-colored walls, azure sky, red bougainvillea. A scalloped fountain, a courtyard restaurant, a sandstone church spire.

"Isn't that where Mina and Paul go?"

We'd known them separately in Berkeley before we met, then again in Los Angeles together. Mina makes and teaches independent films; Paul is a painter best known for his surrealistic record cover paintings for avant-garde rock bands. Years earlier they'd fled bad marriages and run off together to Mexico. They still returned there every summer. When asked about it, they always grew vague.

"San Miguel de Allende," the caption said, "in the mountains of central Mexico."

I knew the border towns, the west coast, inland as far south as Guadalajara. Masako had visited Mexico City and Oaxaca as a teenager.

"Do we have a map?"

I slipped out of the blankets, scurried through the freezing house, and returned with Rand McNally. The town wasn't on the map, though we did find Guanajuato, mentioned in the article, some distance north of Mexico City.

I glanced again at the magazine spread. "It looks warm," I said.

W e've taken a room in the Hotel Ambos Mundos, a decaying ex-hacienda a few blocks from San Miguel's main plaza. Its name means "both worlds." The rooms are ridiculously cheap, about five dollars a day: a steep peso devaluation three years earlier had emptied Mexicans' pockets and chased a generation of foreign retirees, their peso accounts now worthless, back across the border. Our little room in back, once part of a stables, faces an overgrown patch of earth, an abandoned swimming pool, the hotel washing.

The days are sunny and warm, the skies the sharpest blue I've seen since Marrakech. January nights, at 6,300 feet, are cool. We sleep in jeans and sweaters, as the blankets are thin and sometimes the heat doesn't work. Each morning a brigade of young girls swabs the tile floors and makes the bed. The hotel's dissolute, low-intensity ambience, reminiscent of youthful travels, suits us. We are content.

Most of the rooms are occupied. A barefoot Huichol Indian couple in white and red costume, visiting from Nayarit to sell their beaded masks, stays in a room facing the central courtyard. A half dozen earnest *norteamericano* students, en route to Managua to work with the Sandinistas, occupy rooms up front. There is a white-haired Canadian painter who has been coming since the sixties, an Argentine restaurateur with hopes of going into business in San Miguel, a Mexican-American couple from Oaxaca dealing Guatemalan shirts, beads, and presumably dope. Mexico City visitors check in and out. Each night a haggard American remittance man in a sombrero stumbles home, dead drunk, from a bar called La Cucaracha.

In a lobby off the entry, Rafael the proprietor sits behind an old wood reception desk, contemplating a flickering black-and-white television, accepting or turning away guests seemingly at whim. María, an Indian cook, delivers simple meals in a cavernous dining room: eggs, tortillas and beans, rice and vegetables. For the midday meal, the *comida,* she foments interesting stews. Evenings we eat out.

We sleep and wake at odd times: our tiredness, we discover, has many layers. We wander the town endlessly, speaking only to exclaim at something that interests us. While Masako goes off to explore the markets, I pace the cobbled lanes, which after some blocks become hilly dirt paths, then dissolve into raw countryside. Though the little green and white taxis are just a few pesos, I walk everywhere. When the mountain air tires me, I pause and take in a view.

From a scenic lookout above, San Miguel de Allende most resembles Spanish and Italian hill towns, its steep lanes and old houses gathered around churches and squares. Tumbling down its slopes, the town fades off into trees and scrub, a narrow lake that is a dam, then a wide plain and mountains beyond where the sun dies each day. The land is pale, dusky, dry, though I'm told daily rains turn it verdant, subtropical in summer.

Descending winding paths, I peer through open doors at courtyards, gardens, fountains: that old North African trail from the Saharan mud towns and Arab medinas up through Spain, then to Mexico and California, patterning the conquered lands, modeling the earthly paradise. The aged walls I walk beside seem like great blotters of human desire: four and a half centuries of dreams and tragedies lived in their shadows. Churches anchor almost every block—simple wood and stone, ornate baroque, severe Franciscan stucco, riotously churrigueresque—their bells tolling dolorously or sweetly, depending upon my mood. I linger around the markets off Calle Insurgentes among swaggering cowboys in new boots and hats, mothers with babies swaddled in woven cloth shawls called *rebozos.* Indian women sit in rows selling flat, handmade cornmeal tortillas in baskets. Cowboy *ranchera* music, rich with feeling, bleeds from radios in the stalls. Absently I fish in my pocket for my car keys; I find only loose pesos.

People seem calm, soft of demeanor, parting in the streets to let each other pass with a whispered *"permiso"* answered by *"pásale."* Children seldom cry. Everywhere my blighted Spanish is tolerantly endured. After a meal in a small restaurant, I realize I have no money; the proprietress laughs and says pay me later, though she's never seen me before.

Masako and I meet up in a courtyard restaurant, our eyes shining. The words tumble out, our recountings taking longer than the trips themselves. I saw a man with a stack of chairs on his back for sale, another piled high with tropical birds in cages. She saw mariachi musicians serenading the Virgin of Guadalupe under the portals off the plaza. In a hardware store I saw faces right off the codices. She followed a funeral to the graveyard, spent two hours there sketching.

How long since we've talked like this? Married a decade, we've mostly worked. Recently we've endured a succession of family crises: my mother's illness and death, my father's subsequent neediness, strains in Masako's family's business. Tangled in adulthood's web, pumping out the tasks: we've barely had time to look up.

Masako is ravished by the art, handcrafts, and clothes—things she loved in early travels in India and the Middle East. A Japanese American, child of the World War Two internment camps, she's comfortable in Mexico in ways she can never be in the States (before we'd left, angry Detroit autoworkers had beaten to death a Chinese American they'd mistaken for Japanese). Mexicans are curious at most, never hostile. On my side, I feel released from L.A.'s flat, paranoid impersonality into clean bright air, sensory richness, unforced gaiety. We've traveled together before, but this is different: in Mexico we hear the music of surprise and revelation that first drew us to each other.

Food arrives. In our nightly investigations we've left behind the California taco, the enchilada combination plate, and entered the domain of real *sabor*. We've discovered a soup called either *sopa azteca* or *sopa de tortilla:* fried tortilla strips and a smoky, dark red chile called *chipotle* combined with a crumbly local cheese, chicken stock, avocados, and sometimes pieces of chicken; with each spoonful the *chipotle* taste grows stronger. Masako has unearthed a dish called *tinga con chorizo,* spicy shredded pork with Mexican sausage. We try dark, redolent *mole* sauces spread over meats, blending dozens of spices and cooked in seemingly infinite combinations—sweet, hot, mild—different in every region, every home. The elusive, oily taste of *ensalada nopal,* cactus salad—from the same plant found in southern California but there considered inedible—grows on us. Mexicans seem to squeeze the small green lime they call *limón* over everything, a universal solvent and cure-all. *Salsas,* or sauces, are proprietary to each establishment, no two quite alike. From fresh corn tortillas we move on to the thicker, chewier *sopes*. In a bakery on Calle Reloj, Clock Street, we pass through the turnstile, grab aluminum tongs and tray, and pluck glazed donuts and *bolillos*, the all-purpose bread roll. We find chiles of varying colors and intensities—*serrano, jalapeño, poblano, habanero, ancho, chipotle*—hanging from beams, spread out on blankets, ground into sauces and soups. Tonight Masako has ordered a squash flower soup, *flor de calabaza*, which arrives in a deep brick red bowl, a color as pure and soft as the soup's flavor. My chocolate brown chicken *mole* sauce is sweeter and hotter than the mild yellow one in the restaurant off the central plaza; and the syrupy, deep brown dessert flan entirely unlike the pale spongy one I had two nights ago.

Some evenings after a long meal, or a detour through some street festival, we arrive late and find the hotel doors shut. Our pounding awakens sad-eyed Rogelio the *velador* (he who keeps the candle burning), who sleeps under a horse blanket on the office couch. He opens the massive creaking door a crack and lets us scuttle through. We fall asleep in the tiny room to church bells, devoid of thought, our "perimeter defenses" disarmed.

One night near the end of our first week I awaken from dreams, sobbing, passing off griefs I didn't know I had.

I've stopped shaving. I wear huaraches, cowhide sandals bought in the covered market, though my feet bleed at first. Masako arrives back at the hotel one afternoon wearing a shiny blue blouse she's bought literally off the back of a braided Otomí lady who sells dolls in front of San Francisco church. She's beside herself with delight.

"But doesn't she need that blouse?" I ask.

"No, she has a new red one. She's happy. Look, this one's faded anyway."

We are naive visitors, in a state of grace, taking the cure, using Mexico for catharsis. We've come for the warmth: now, warmed, I want to know where I am.

In a little bookstore off the main plaza run by a Mexican woman and a silver-haired American woman, I buy a couple of books by the writer Octavio Paz, and *Madrigal's Magic Key to Spanish* (with illustrations by Andrew Warhol—simple line drawings of a shoe, *zapato;* a blouse, *blusa*). Later I come back for a novel by Carlos Fuentes, a book on Frida Kahlo and Diego Rivera. I discover a little bilingual library a few blocks away with inscribed copies of novels by passing authors, back issues of a National Geographic–type magazine called *México desconocido,* books on Mexican history. I read in Bernal Díaz's chronicles of the Conquest, a biography of the eighteenth-century nun-poetess Sor Juana Inés de la Cruz. New names enter my consciousness: the artist Covarrubias, the politician Cárdenas, the architect Barragán.

It dawns upon me that, arriving as a tourist, I've blundered into a civilization. No, three civilizations overlaid upon each other: Mesoamerican (Aztec, Mayan, Toltec, Olmec, Zapotec), Spanish colonial, contemporary. How could I have lived so close by all my life and neglected to realize? I vaguely thought I already knew: a trick of perspective because of the border towns, the coasts, the migrant workers. Passing through Mexico City, we'd seen the open excavation at the Templo Mayor next to the great cathedral downtown: sun-stone calendars, massive human and animal statuary, entire sculpture walls. We'd visited the vast Anthropology Museum with its jade masks and ancient calendars. Civilization. Had I been oblivious to the great territories to the south, my own hemisphere? Inadvertently we've

landed in the cradle of Mexican history, the very towns
where the revolt against the Spaniards began: San Miguel,
Dolores Hidalgo, Guanajuato. The emperor Maximilian was
slain in Querétaro an hour away.

We begin to excavate our scant Spanish, buried cities:
Masako's from school days, mine from Barcelona decades
ago working as a musician. Nouns bob up: *puerta, cielo,
edificio.* Door, sky, building. Verb forms resurface in clumps,
with their euphonious conjugations: *amo amas ama amamos
aman.* So many ways to love. We try speaking only Spanish
to each other. We decode menus and signs: *exquisitos* are hot
dogs off a vendor's truck, *carnage* is one menu's attempt to
render the meat selections in English. Limited to the only
tense we know, we exist in an unbroken, sensuous present.

I read of San Miguel's Chichimecan and Otomí anteced-
ents, of its founding in 1542 by the Franciscan brother San
Miguel, its boom years as a link on the silver route. Ignacio
Allende, a hero of the War of Independence—that man
astride the bronze horse in the plaza whose name adorns
schools, museums, reservoirs, the town itself—was born
here, sanctifying the town as a national monument, a kind of
Mexican Williamsburg. A succession of fervent religious
movements since its founding has left the town with twenty
churches, countless chapels, and endless holidays and fiestas.
The population is composed of a stable bourgeoisie; a cowboy culture from the surrounding farmlands; educated, af-
fluent refugees from Mexico City; and a smattering of gringos, American and European foreigners who've settled here
since World War Two to retire or study or make art. I see
them in the central plaza, the *jardín,* each morning, clustered among the iron benches, awaiting the arrival of the
*Mexico City News.* If I walk a few blocks north or east they
disappear.

One morning, full of new energy, I decide to walk down to the lake at the bottom of the town. After half an hour in huaraches that no longer hurt my feet, I arrive at the railroad tracks where the Mexico City–Juárez train gives off the whistle we hear late at night in the hotel. This is where Neal Cassady, real-life hero of Kerouac's *On the Road*, was found sprawled dead on the tracks one morning in 1968, after setting out from San Miguel the night before with the amphetamine-fueled intent to count every railroad tie between here and nearby Celaya with his nose—or so goes the account. I watch a local train take on water. Pulling out, it reveals three brightly painted cabooses on a siding, home to teeming families, their tattered washing hung out like news. The squatter kids run across the tracks with buckets to catch the last drops from the pump.

I walk on through rich agricultural fields, past boys herding oxen, braided girls tending pigs. By the lake, an old chapel spire sticks up from the receding water. Tall organ cacti grow out of the slumped walls of a doomed resort hotel. I sit on a piece of driftwood, watching egrets follow net-casting fishermen in wooden pirogues. Turning, I look back up and see San Miguel de Allende, glimmering on its hillside.

Back at the hotel, I read in the sun, doze off. I begin postcards home but never finish them. I'd planned to write every day but so far haven't gotten to it. At sunset, hiking to El Chorro, the old waterworks at the south end of town, I realize with a start that I've been standing on a corner for a good fifteen minutes, staring at the exfoliating *pentimenti* of an eroding wall, my mind bleached of thought or language, lost in traces of history, the passage of time.

Some deeper process is being addressed here. I've become the unthinking minder of my own renewal.

Walking home after dinner one night, we follow music and arcing sparklers to a fiesta off Calle Mesones. A rickety wooden tower of fireworks has been erected in the middle of a plaza. A man lights a cigarette and holds it to a fuse: wheels of fire erupt, one after the next. Children scream with delight. Little boys dance beneath the showering sparks, pieces of cardboard over their heads. The finale is a hissing, spinning circle of fire that suddenly breaks free of its armature and mounts into the air until it disappears. I look over at Masako, her face upturned in wonder like a child's. We munch fried sugar twists called *churros* and watch couples dance to a local band. Somber in the Indian way, they don't clap when the number is over; yet their brimming pleasure washes over us.

I often hear the word *milagro*, miracle, as in the expression *"Qué milagro!"* when one encounters a friend after a long time. It also refers to the tiny charms of junk silver affixed to the bodies of saints in churches as prayers or thanks for blessings received, which Masako has been collecting and which now decorate our room at the Ambos Mundos.

We've begun taking our breakfast in the covered market, among the food and flower vendors. Working Mexicans, we notice, will have soup, *menudo*, to start out the day, or steamed *tamales* and *atole*, a thick, variously flavored hot corn drink, sometimes swilling a glass of powdered Nescafé in hot water at the end. We've found a favorite stand that serves fresh fruit drinks called *licuados* in fat soda glasses, blended to order. Afterward, wandering past the flower sellers' fragrant array of tuberoses, carnations, and gladioli, we come upon an announcement that a religious peregrination leaves for San Juan de los Lagos, a holy site several days west on foot.

We eat everything we see on the street: strawberries and cream; corn on the cob slathered with chile, lime, and mayonnaise; chicken and enchiladas from the outdoor grill under the portals off the town square. We sip fresh juices through straws from plastic bags tied with rubber bands. We munch slices of white, crunchy jicama, a root vegetable, with powdered *chile* and a squeeze of fresh lime, sold from fruit carts. Every few days one of us is ill with the *turistas;* even this seems to be part of the catharsis. Lomotil, Imodium, and Pepto-Bismol crowd the toothbrush and comb on the cloudy glass counter above the sink.

With the passing days I note the gradual departure of the frozen, strained glare in the mirror. Some vaguely human apparition gazes back.

Early in the second week we run into Mina and Paul in the market, their shopping bags bulging with provisions. We hadn't looked them up as we didn't know where they were staying and we felt shy about invading their precincts unannounced. Bemused at our unexpected appearance, they invite us to follow them home.

Paul works a key in the lock of an old colonial building a few blocks down from the jardín, and swings open a massive door. We follow him into a high, beamed entryway with yard-thick walls. We cross a stone patio with a fountain in the center and enter a tall interior room where furniture, art objects, and books commingle with film equipment, frames, paints: a disarray familiar to us. In the kitchen we examine an oval griddle Mina tells us is a pre-Hispanic *comal.* A necklace of garlic hangs from a nail. A bowl full of dried red chiles sits on a tiled counter, another of wooden spoons and whisks. We notice a water purifier affixed to the faucet. Mina pours bright vegetables, fruits, and tortillas out of shopping bags onto a long oak table. In the dining room, yellow-stamened calla lilies fill a blue blown-glass vase, right off a Diego Rivera painting.

Living in an old colonial house in a sixteenth-century town. Cooking, shopping, waking up in your own room. Wandering back through town late at night, hearing a tall mesquite door slam behind you. What would it be like?

Mina is a veteran of the old Bay Area underground cinema of the 1960s, her work now collected by the Museum of Modern Art. Tall and dark, her long black hair parted in the middle, she has a near-Indian bearing. Only now she tells me that a film of hers about a Mexican trumpet player was shot here—the same man I'd heard in the Sunday night band serenading the strollers in the jardín. Paul, moon-faced and plump, is weird, witty, oblique—like his comic, hallucinatory paintings of animals and humans blending surreal cartoon and high art. I think of Mina and Paul as links to an earlier Mexico that bore currency among artists and expatriates: the Beats, and before them Diego and Frida; the muralists Orozco and Siqueiros; Artaud and Breton and Lawrence; the photographers Weston, Bravo, Tina Modotti.

"So how do you find Mexico?" Paul asks me.

"If I smile, people smile wider. If I say 'buenos días,' they say it back, stronger. Sometimes they don't even wait."

"In Mexico," Paul says, "you put out a little, you get back a lot. In human terms at least, you could say it's a functional economy."

I look up at the domed ceiling of red bricks, arranged in an oval pattern converging at the center. Only a thin layer of cement seems to hold them together.

"It's called a *bóveda*," Paul says. "I keep waiting for it to fall down."

"And if it does?"

"*Ni modo.*"

"What does that mean?"

"It can't be helped. Nothing to be done."

Like the Japanese *shikatta ga nai*, I think, which I used to hear in Kyoto. Or the Arabic *Insha'allah.* The idea that fate is ultimately larger than human will.

"A Mexican artist named Chucho Reyes called it 'the adventure of disorder,' " Paul says.

Mina says, "There's a Mayan poem that starts out, 'The day set out from the east and started walking.' The day is on a journey. We're woven into the design of that day, though we're not inventing it."

That afternoon we drive with Paul and Mina to a holy penitent shrine twenty minutes outside of town. Leaving the two-lane highway north, we inch down an unpaved road, cross a narrow stone bridge, and enter a dusty, abandoned square. Steep shadows hang along a towering, weathered church facade. We step out into the expectant silence, our footsteps echoing on the worn forecourt stones. Three crones unfold from their rags and outstretch skinny, leathered arms.

"Atotonilco," Paul says. "It means 'place of hot waters' in Náhuatl. There are underground springs all around here."

Atotonilco, Mina explains, is a holy penitent sanctuary for rites of flagellation, automortification. When they first came to Mexico, she says, they'd see thousands of flagellants crawling in the dirt for miles, organ cactuses strapped to their backs, skin torn to the bone; women flaying themselves with scourges, tears and blood mingling in the dust. Nowadays the spiritual exercises take place inside the vast walled precincts behind the sanctuary. It was here, Paul says, that the priest Hidalgo hoisted aloft a painting of the Virgin of Guadalupe and cried "Death to the Spaniards!" igniting the revolution against Spain and launching the Mexican cult of *guadalupismo*, the worship of the indigenous Virgin.

Inside, the walls are covered with fading frescoes, fantastical biblical visions entwined with mystical poems and inscriptions. Statues of martyrs, draped in loincloths of colored velvet, hang like broken dolls. Mortified, bleeding Jesuses in glass cases drip with little tin *milagros*. Faint light leaks from invisible shafts, bathing faded colors in sudden, heightened brightness, as if seen under peyote. Everywhere, robust pre-Hispanic death fixations blend with the European Catholic baroque in some phantasmagorical alliance. Adoration, fate, mystery: we have left the endless rectilinear suburb. Wandering through this bizarre object of art, I begin to glimpse more of Mina and Paul's mysterious bond to Mexico.

An old priest shuffles to his place and commences Mass in Spanish for the benefit of a few huddled figures. Candles burn in metal racks at the foot of black, burnished wood crosses in the half-light.

Back outside, the air is pink, the shadows steep. A lone dog skulks across the square. A car accelerates in the distance, portent of return to a "normal" world.

We drive on through a grove of sorghum to a narrow, muddy river. Mina is making a film about a family who lives there. Their dwelling is little more than a squatter shack, yet they welcome us warmly, invite us in among pigs and chickens, offer food.

On the road back to San Miguel, we pass an old green pickup truck piled high with bright orange blossoms. "Marigolds," Paul says, "to feed chickens so the yolks of their eggs will come out a deeper yellow."

We arrive back at sunset, enter a town afire. Salmon skies

over the plain below. Crying, circling birds. A cacophony of
bells. In a flickering courtyard, Peruvian flutes and guitars.
We sip margaritas, eat *filete* and flan. Beneath a diorama of
stars we talk until late.

**M**asako is harvesting her hair. She sits
on the ledge of the abandoned hotel swimming pool after a
shower. Her hair is very long, very black; she collects it to
embroider with. I watch her from inside the hotel room,
which has lately filled with fresh callas, gladioli, and white
agapanthus bought from the barefoot lady we'd seen our
first night, the one who bears buckets of flowers on her head.

I sit at the desk, noting colors I've seen: green of cactus,
lime, cornstalk; red of tomato, watermelon, bullfighter's
cape; yellow of corn, *cerveza,* sunflower. Blue of indigo, water, sky. Brown of adobe, chocolate. Mango orange, eggplant
purple, white of plaster wall. Gold is the sun, an Aztec calen-
dar, a church icon, a brass band in the plaza. Silver is Taxco
jewelry, a soldier's bayonet, fish scales, an ingot from a Guanajuato mine.

The novel pages I've brought down sit beside me on the
desk untouched.

This morning I woke up laughing. This is suspect. Am I
losing it? From my window I see sun-splashed stones, a butterfly the size of my hand respiring on a jacaranda branch, a
smiling girl with a bundle of fresh, sun-dried sheets in her
arms.

Bright sunlight, sharp shadows. Unfiltered air, knife-
sharp. The sky immediate, clouds within reach. At night,
star-smeared galaxies just beyond the tip of my finger. . . .

Today a twin-engine Cessna buzzed the town. Everyone ran out to look up. I realize I hadn't heard a plane since we arrived. This rude emissary from the world I'm truant from brought panic. Less than a week left on our twenty-one-day ticket.

D uring our last days, we range farther away from San Miguel. Crossing an hour of farmland, we hike a ghost-strewn silver mining site abandoned after the revolution. The next morning we set out for the tiny village of Xichú, the westernmost outpost of Veracruz-style *huapango* music, but turn back when the car overheats. We spend an afternoon wandering the colonial redoubts of the city of Querétaro, an hour away, talk over dinner about the human costs of the hacienda culture that once thrived here.

The town of Guanajuato, moody and faceted, is a collage of dreams, a collapsed geography, a crumpled map of the soul. Lining a river valley gorge, above a cool stone labyrinth of subterranean roadways where once the river sluiced silver, it seems to shove its history in our face: as if its pale green and pink stone had been cut away to expose striated layers of memory. We shoulder through a bobbing sea of white cotton-clad *campesinos* shouting support of the governor who promises food and salvation on the steps of the Teatro Juárez, a jeweled fin de siècle opera house rising improbably out of the provincial dust.

Guanajuato's bizarre architecture, chiaroscuro streets, and somber gentility remind us of other places all at once: Toledo, a Tuscan town, a baby Fez. We stroll its stacked, serpentine lanes and little squares, idle along its pastel walls and collapsed monuments, browse its university bookshops and museums, drink espressos in a student café hung with Diego Rivera posters. We're falling in love with another Mexican town.

"Home tomorrow," I say. The words sound tinny.

"You look like yourself again."

"Is it Mexico or just being away?"

She looks out the window. "What would it be like to live in one of those odd little houses hanging over that *plazuela?* Or in one like Mina and Paul's?"

How could we? Our professions are portable, to a point. Years of work have taught us that the market's memory is measured in months if not weeks, and absence is invisibility. My daughter has left for college in New York; but now our surviving parents grow elderly.

On the way back, following a tip from Mina, we take a small dirt road on the outskirts of the town of Dolores Hidalgo in search of an obscure chapel called El Llanito. Farmers wave us onward. Finally we come upon it, in the middle of stark farmland. A lone, wizened caretaker lets us in. Piles of fresh lilies adorn niches. Simple illustrative panels of biblical scenes seem to lift off from the stone walls. Built in 1559, the same year as Guanajuato's founding, a simple purity hovers about El Llanito. Nearing the altar, we see them: life-sized effigies of favored saints in white wax, carved each year afresh by local artisans.

Our bus to Mexico City leaves at noon, our L.A. flight at six. While Masako finishes packing, I head out for a last walk. We agree to meet in the Parque Juárez, a few blocks south of the jardín, in half an hour.

Passing a luridly painted restaurant called El Infierno, where chickens turn slowly on a spit, I see a blind couple talking animatedly, plastic cups dangling loose from their fingers, begging momentarily forgotten. In front of the San Francisco church I come upon an Indian woman in a turquoise blouse and red shawl, a bucket of pink roses on her head, pausing to look at riotously colored wooden folk toys—tops, snakes, skulls—colliding on a market seller's blanket.

I take a seat on the bench in the jardín, riffle through my lone copy of my novel, rescued from a crashed diskette. I've barely addressed my story about the imprisoned dwarf this trip. I'll bring back nothing to show for my stay. Somewhere my mind bleached out; the words died in my mouth.

Bells chime. Time to meet Masako. As I head down Calle Aldama to the Parque Juárez, I feel my inner compass turning northward, the renewed pulse of return. Approaching the park, seeing Masako coming from the other direction, I suddenly realize I left my manuscript on the bench in the jardín.

Panicked, we turn back, retracing my steps. Hurrying toward the jardín, I try to embrace the idea of two years' work lost, down the drain. An obliterating thought. How could I have been so foolish as to have taken my only copy out?

We arrive back at the jardín. I rush to the bench where I'd left it. It's gone.

I have no idea where to begin looking. I rummage through nearby trash cans. I rush to the only place I can think to go, the bookstore off the plaza. Maruja, one of the proprietors, suggests I go to the radio station. This makes no sense to me. People take lost things there, she says. Why not the police station? I ask. She shrugs. As you like.

I cross the plaza to the station, where three armed youths

in blue outfits with carbines regard me blankly. A stack of papers? No, *señor.* I make another fitful tour of the plaza. Finally I head for Radio San Miguel, a block up from the plaza in a courtyard off Calle Sollano.

Inside a glassed broadcast booth, a man with thick black spectacles and a fifties-style crew cut is talking into a microphone. The call letters on the window read *XESQ.* There's nobody else around. I turn to walk away when the man sees me and waves. He punches a cassette into a player, takes off his headphones, and comes out. He eyes me expectantly.

*"Me olvidé las páginas de mi libro,"* I blurt, deploying my rehearsed phrase.

He strokes his chin. If I have them, he says, it'll cost.

Here it is: the bite, the *mordida,* the *baksheesh. "No importa,"* I say. "I'll pay what you ask."

The man laughs, extends his hand. *"Señor Francisco Zavala, a sus órdenes."* He is at my service. I'm growing irritated.

Sr. Zavala turns and walks back into the broadcast booth. He brandishes my manila folder through the glass.

Grinning, he comes back out with it in his hand. Someone had found it on the bench and turned it in, he says. The loss had been broadcast throughout the entire community fifteen minutes ago. What took me so long to get here?

*"Mil gracias,"* I gush, overcome with gratitude, reaching for my wallet. "How much do I owe you?"

Sr. Zavala waves me off, his eyes crinkling. *"Una broma, señor.* A joke. Be careful. Literature is hard to find, easy to lose."

Late that day, as the Flecha Amarilla bus rumbles across Mexico City's quake-riven landfill taking us to our plane, I feel myself tightening, donning a mask, girding for return to my homeland: that place where, in Octavio Paz's words, people "wander in an abstract world of machines, fellow citizens, and moral precepts." I feel dismayed yet newly awakened.

# Chapter 2

# T he Return

JUNE. WE'VE ASTONISHED OURSELVES.
We've sold our house in California, put our
remaining things in storage, and returned to
San Miguel de Allende.

*"Qué milagro,"* Rafael says pensively,
watching us stumble back through the Ambos Mundos entry, bags in tow. He must see
this regularly, I think: return voyagers, refugees from personal Arctics, faces plastered
with tired grins. When he asks how long
we'll be staying, it's my turn to shrug.

Rafael has a second-story unit in back
with a kitchen he rents by the month: a
white stucco rectangle lodged against the
massive stone walls of the military barracks
next door. A narrow stairway leads up to a
small room with red tile floors, brick ceiling,
double bed, and rudimentary kitchenette:
motel fridge, two-burner stove, sink. Arched
windows offer a northern view over the

curved tile roofs of the old stable rooms where we'd stayed in January. The gash of cracked blue cement that was once a swimming pool is still empty of all but weeds and a little rainwater (hatching ground for mosquito larvae, we quickly discover). The washing area, with its daily flap of drying sheets and pillowcases, ends at Rafael's ice factory—a metal shed off the dusty parking lot that emits a shuddering industrial growl every twenty minutes. Below our room, a rusted metal table and chairs perch on a cement foundation slab. It's cool there in the mornings among the twisted rebars, the sun still low behind the barracks, the pigeons burbling in their crevices in the wall: a good place to write.

Since January the hillsides have mutated from ocher to moss green, the gardens brightened with blooms. No jackets or shawls in the evening. Clouds gather after siesta, releasing violent, cooling squalls that tamp the dust, soak the ground; then they draw back like curtains to reveal long, modulated sunsets.

Dawn is announced from the bell tower of the nunnery, La Concepción, three buildings away: muted, velvety tocsins summoning sleepyheads to mass, escalating across the hour to a clangorous "Get your ass up!" A guidebook confidently explains the bells' exacting patterns of religious and clock time—only they fail to obey. I try running these inscrutable tollings against my watch but this quickly breaks down. Something happens each quarter hour, more or less, maybe. I remove my watch and put it back in my suitcase. We're on Mexican time now.

T he sky is silvery pale, the hotel still asleep. I slip into the jeans, light cotton shirt, and huaraches

I'd worn last visit and have since kept in my suitcase like holy vestments. I close the door softly, tiptoe downstairs, and pad through the hotel precincts. Dewdrops quiver on the spiky tips of barrel cacti in the glimmering dawn. A pale green agave, bursting from its pot, snags my pant leg. An iridescent green hummingbird probes the black stamen of a yellow hibiscus bloom. Ripe oranges cluster among the deep green leaves of a giant citrus in the courtyard.

*"Hola!"*

I wheel, my heart racing.

Pedro, the hotel parrot, chomps the metal bars of his cage with his beak. *"Hola!"* he shrieks again, his greeting waking up the world.

I pass the sleeping night watchman on the lobby couch, gently let myself out, and fall in among the early-morning crowd trudging up Calle Insurgentes toward the market: peddlers lugging grain sacks and rope-tied cartons, blue-uniformed school kids, Indian women bearing baskets of food. Scruffy burros I'd seen hauling firewood up the steep lanes in winter now bear bags of soil to the town's gardens. The summer air holds new fragrances: jasmine, tuberoses, citrus. Above the churchs' tiled domes, the sky deepens to blue.

On the corner of Calle Hidalgo, a lean, weathered farmer in a sombrero thrusts three live, red-wattled chickens at me. A woman invites me to weigh myself on a bathroom scale for a peso. A grinning man in a baseball cap walks a bicycle past with fresh-woven grass *petate* mats strapped to it. A tiny ancient trudges by with stacked wooden cages full of warbling tropical birds on his back: canaries, mynahs, toucans. I pause by the entry to the canvas-roofed outdoor market, where a painted statue of the Virgin of Guadalupe looks beatifically down upon the kneeling peasant Juan Diego, who first saw her in a vision.

Elbowing my way among the fruit and vegetable stalls, it dawns upon me that I can shop for food. The hotel fridge has room for a tiny rack of provisions, and an ice tray that works when the electricity does. The stove burners light with matches as long as there's gas in the patio tank, though the tiny oven, which might just accommodate one of the pigeons nesting in the wall behind us, doesn't seem to work at all.

People carry their goods in bright-colored plaid plastic shopping bags, *bolsas.* Plaid doesn't seem very Mexican to me, yet people find ways to blend things in, turn them Mexican: plastic buckets, cotton clothing, old cars. The plaid bolsas of thin woven mesh, which seem to fray but seldom break, are used to carry almost anything about: in January I'd seen a mechanic carrying a crankshaft in one, a butcher chicken parts in another. Open your bag, the market seller fills it for you. No checkout counter, no paper bags. The first time I'd seen Mina and Paul in the jardín, their bolsas bulging with provisions, it had signified residency.

I find a seller with an assortment of plaid ones on a nail hook and buy a red, green, and orange one for two pesos. Gripping its bright blue plastic handle, I swing it a few times. I've entered the life of the town.

*"Mamey,"* the woman says when I point into a cornucopia of strange fruits. *"Pitahaya."* She offers me slices of each. I pick a couple of paisley-shaped orange mangoes, drop them in my bolsa. At a crowded vegetable stand, a woman splits a black, rough-skinned avocado with the turn of a knife and holds it up to me. *"Parahoy?"* I look at her blankly. Then the words float apart: *"Para hoy?"* "For today?" I nod. Yes, today. I have no life beyond today. She selects by feel of her thumb one for today, neither too hard nor too soft.

One avocado, two mangoes. Three tomatoes. What else? Coffee. We must have coffee for the room. And eggs. Six

eggs are tied in a clear plastic bag and laid gently in my
bolsa. Coffee is nowhere to be found. Milk. Where to get it?
I've seen pickup trucks driving the streets in the early morning, honking in front of houses, ladling it from metal containers into the waiting pitchers of the women of the town.
Here, among endless displays of fresh fruits, vegetables,
flowers, colored beans and powders in baskets, utensils of every description and variety, toys, curative herbs, spices—
even virginal white confirmation dresses—I find no coffee,
no milk.

In a shaded area behind the covered market, I pass Indian women with long braided hair, their wares at their
feet or in aproned laps. I notice white disks on dark green
palm fronds. Cheese? *"Queso?"* *"Sí, señor."* Smiling, the girl
hands me one on a wet green leaf. An old woman unwraps
handmade blue tortillas from her lap, counts out a dozen,
covers them with a sheet of brown paper, and hands them,
still warm, up to me.

Morning light bathes the rooftops. My bolsa fills. Some
vendors have nothing but a few quivering cups of gelatin to
sell, a bit of embroidery, a lone carved pickax handle. Reason enough to come and sit all day? Maybe I miss the point. I
think of a story by B. Traven, *Canastitas en serie.* It tells of
an Indian man who brings a few woven baskets to market.
Approached by a rich American who wants to buy in volume
to export, the seller turns him down. The American natu-
rally thinks him a fool. "Señor," the basket maker tries to explain, "I weave these baskets in my manner, with songs and
fragments of my heart woven into them." It's not about volume but participation.

In the States my aversion to supermarkets nears the
pathological. Here in open air and natural light, moving
among pyramids of tomatoes and avocados and onions,

brushing hands with sellers, exchanging words, I feel alive, a participant. Cortés's chronicler Bernal Díaz spoke in awe of the sprawling, fecund Aztec markets, the sensory profusion, the merchandise from all corners of the Americas, the mixture of intimacy and spectacle. It's here this morning, and I'm in it. To my bulging plaid bag somebody has added a sprig of cilantro, another a chamomile blossom I can't remember buying.

In the jardín, an elderly sweeper is dusting the stones with a twig broom. Early risers take shoeshines along the benches. Street curs sniff trash cans. The clock in the tower next to the parish church, the Parroquia, says nine, confirmed by a sudden burst of bells whanged by a boy visible in the tower. The food store next to the Presidencia, the town hall, is just opening. There I find milk in an unrefrigerated carton, a jar of powdered Nescafé, *salsa picante* in a can. It's the best I can do this morning.

Back at the Ambos Mundos, Masako is emerging from the shower, a sign the gas heater, the *calentador*, is working. I hold up my multicolored bag swollen with provisions. "You bought a plaid bolsa!" she exclaims delightedly.

We cut and prepare the vegetables and fruits, warm the tortillas over a sputtering burner flame. Outside at the metal table by the empty pool we eat our tacos, slurp weak Nescafé. Our first homemade meal in Mexico.

"I saw so many different-colored corns in the market. One had this alarming black fungus bubbling out of its husk."

"*Huitlacoche*," she says. "It's a summer delicacy. You should have bought it."

"Do you know how to make it?"

"No, but I'll bet Rafael's wife does."

"You first."

We laugh, mango juice running down our chins.

W e know nobody here. Each morning, exempt from whatever unconscious semiotics guided our choice of appearance in urban America, we choose a shirt or blouse out of pure whim, eat what and when we wish, speak whatever comes to mind. We've come to recognize a few vendors and beggars and mariachis around town by sight, and the people around the Ambos Mundos. Mina and Paul haven't yet arrived for their summer. We trade pleasantries with Maruja and Billie, who run the bookstore on the corner of the jardín. Mostly we are strangers, moving through a world of color, light, and aroma, the language a pleasing tangle of alien sound, the whitewash of the old walls flaking off in our hands, the canopy of night stars ours alone.

The Hotel Ambos Mundos has accrued a new cast of characters since winter—a weird mélange of those who, as the saying goes, are either not wanted where they came from, or are. Slowly their little dramas emerge. In the dining room where María the cook serves up her simple meals, a hulking, taciturn American with thick spectacles and an army haircut sits at a table alone, shoveling in platefuls of rice and beans, jaws grinding, tension pouring off him in waves. Teresa, a jewelry designer from Monterrey who stays in an azure-walled room off the front courtyard, tells us the American, "Jeem," is popping over-the-counter amphetamines he buys by the bagful at the pharmacy a block away, determined to lose 100 pounds fast and "get me a Mexican wife." Every afternoon Jeem huffs and groans over his barbells in the courtyard; at night he stalks the cantinas. Conchita, the flouncing sexpot daughter of Ramiro the gardener, had incited Jeem's interest when fortunately her Mexican *novio* stepped in and snagged her. They're to be married next Saturday in the Parroquia.

Gabriela, the daughter of a prominent local family, and her boyfriend, Gustavo, a flamenco guitarist in a restaurant in town, act out a tormented relationship each night: screams, flying vases, *mescal* bottles. A lecherous, doddering painter of vague nationality known as Emil sits in a rocker beneath the courtyard eaves in skullcap and robe, discussing his imminent demise to anyone within earshot or cackling back at the parrot. An angelic-looking German photographer named Heinz and his teenage Mexican wife stay in a tiny room near the kitchen, busily starting up a Mexican postcard business.

Rafael's sister Ofelia lives in a separate house off the rambling garden. The real owner of the hotel, according to Teresa, Ofelia emerges late afternoons in loose blouses, capri pants, exaggeratedly large Italian sunglasses, and with a small white poodle on a leash, to stalk the property, feed crumbs to the irritable ranging geese who consume Ramiro's plants and vegetables, and browbeat Rafael. Then she disappears back inside her house and draws the curtains.

This is our home for now. We have no other. We've planted our flag in this crumbling ex-hacienda hotel in the Mexican mountains, with no future plans beyond living and working here until fall.

In late January we'd returned to flat, tepid L.A.: nobody on the streets, answering-machine voices, staring straight ahead at stoplights. I felt dangerously opened: warm, sincere, sentimental. I didn't *want* to rearm my perimeter defenses. Even as weeks passed and Mexico's fulsome *sabor* faded into a mere concept, our thoughts moved inexorably toward extrication. We began to examine the hinged sets of permissions, opportunities, and obstacles that defined our life: work, family, friends, money. Once we'd broached the idea of getting back across the border, our actions reduced to a series of compact, finite gestures. We put our house on the market. It might have been smarter to rent it, only we didn't want to be there anymore, in that spot in space. It sold in three days to a French horn player in the Los Angeles Symphony Orchestra. Let him grapple with the drive-by shootings, the midnight helicopters, the armed-response panic button. I made an arrangement with a friend to pay some remaining bills and take care of the small arts publishing company I'd founded and maintained for years. At a weekend garage sale we sold off years of objects, treasures, encumbrances. We described our exodus to friends as a "sabbatical," time off, though we suspected we had something stronger in mind.

"You're really leaving," an incredulous screenwriter friend said at our garage sale.

Yes, we are.

"So is it a quality-of-life issue or what?"

His very choice of words seemed to encode the reasons we were getting the hell out of there. At what point do you stop doing the same thing over and over? Sooner or later, windows turn into walls.

On a sweltering smoggy day, in a kind of operatic climax of stress, we piled our remaining things into a U-Haul truck and drove off to a storage facility in Glendale. The truck broke down in 104-degree heat; we began shouting at each other. Later back at the house the burglar alarm went berserk, flashing its lights and siren wails, bringing squad cars and security officers, guns drawn, barking into two-way radios, to protect us from our own paranoia. L.A. meltdown, the city rearing up and throwing obstacles in our way at every turn as we tried to leave. I didn't know it cared.

The next afternoon, hurtling across Mexico City in a taxi to the San Miguel bus, I looked over at Masako. Her eyes were moist. "I'm so glad we're here," she whispered.

The meter was off. Our cracked smiles on the bus as the tangled city gave way to open road lasted through late dinner under a low-slung San Miguel moon. We collapsed onto the creaking bed at the Ambos Mundos, mariachi singers' plangent howls echoing in our bones.

**M**asako has begun painting in the long, narrow hotel room she uses as a studio. Each day a barefoot Otomí Indian flower seller comes to model, her ragged daughter in tow. Masako draws them both for a few pesos an hour. Mornings I work at the table outside our door until light and sound leech me away into the town. Today I saw an Indian woman sitting on a plaza bench, nursing a boy who must have been at least nine or ten. Nobody disturbed her. Only a passing man looked at me and screwed his finger to his head, indicating they were both crazy. Last night I saw a man carrying his aged, shriveled mother on his back up the stairs of the Temple of La Concepción, the nunnery. Each day people bring armloads of flowers to the public fountains, clean and cut them. Vendors bear twelve-foot-high, bamboo-handled feather dusters through the streets like spears. People have names like "soul" and "heart," call their children "my life." Couples lurk in doorways for hours, kissing and murmuring, oblivious to passersby.

Nature is still strong here: extravagant birds of eye-popping color, insects of surreal size. Weather is vivid, immediate: bright fervid sun, steep cooling shadows. Intense daily rains cool the town. When the first fat drops hit the stones, vendors break down their displays or drape them in plastic and scurry for cover. Disdaining umbrellas, people hover cheerily beneath arches or in doorways while the savage downpour hammers roofs, smashes foliage, turns streets into impassable creeks. Just as quickly the clouds pass on, leaving the land cleansed, the sky released into blazing sunsets and star-flung nights.

Patio restaurants and cafés I hadn't noticed in January have opened their doors. One called Corto Maltese, run by an Italian named Paolo on a street called Calle Flor, features fettucine dishes, an espresso machine, and live music on weekends: salsa bands, percussion ensembles, Veracruz harpists. We dine late there, sometimes dance among young Mexicans and foreigners whose faces are becoming familiar. Afterward, walking slowly home, we slump onto a bench in the jardín, watch the moon dodge the spires of the Parroquia. Each night ends with the same ignominy: me jumping around our room with a rolled up newspaper, embedding mosquitoes in the stucco walls until the buzzing and bloodletting cease.

I t's Day of the Locos, the yearly Corpus Christi festival, and San Miguel de Allende has gone completely mad. Crowds line the street from San Antonio Abad church a few miles south of town all the way to the jardín. On Calle San Francisco, giants in bizarre papier-mâché masks bob into view. Bands tootle. Hundreds of celebrants dance deliriously down the street, dressed up like members of the opposite sex, or IMF bankers, or ghouls, or gringos (Hawaiian shirt, cigar, shorts, silly hat, camera). Devil-horned, rubber-masked Uncle Sams leap about. Whores dance with rum-swilling priests. I spot four Hitlers, three Fidels in fatigues and cigar. Here comes a flatbed full of "Mexicans" parodying themselves: white campesino outfits, bullet belts, tequila bottles, fake cacti, and the huge floppy sombreros nobody wears anymore. Reagans grin vacuously, Kissingers look malevolent and predatory.

Suddenly I'm being whirled down the street in the arms of a hooker in red lipstick and fake tits. She says my name in a deep voice. Shocked, I peer through the makeup and drag and make out the soft-spoken teller at Bancomer who changes my money. Laughing, he flings me back out among the onlookers. Miguel de la Madrid, the president of Mexico, wanders stiffly by, carrying a briefcase stuffed with dollars. Another flatbed tableau reveals a backyard scene with washing hung out and a fat Mexican woman ironing. The locos snake around the jardín, fling candy to the crowd. Bands blare out *norteño* tunes, Sousa marches, Beatles hits.

I draw away from the parade, my stomach sore from laughing, and head for Calle Umarán, the street running below the Parroquia. This morning Irma, who is fourteen and works at the Ambos Mundos, told me that San Antonio Abad, patron saint of Locos, is my namesake saint. What does that mean? I asked her. This is your day, silly! she said. In other words, I'm crazy, too. This sent Irma and her friend into stitches.

A wedding party has gathered in the forecourt of the Parroquia. Conchita, Ramiro the gardener's sexy daughter, stands in an improbably virginal white dress beside her handsome new husband, the one who rescued her from the predations of Jeem the speed freak. Ramiro looks like César Romero today in blue suit and bright tie; and the corpulent woman beside him with the orchid bouquet pinned to her dress would be Conchita's mother. The honeymoon car, a blue Nissan coupe, sits in front of the church with its hood raised while the parish priest waves a censer over it, blessing the engine.

By the time I get back to the Ambos Mundos, Conchita's

wedding reception is going full steam in the courtyard. A mariachi band laces the air with sweet lament. Watching Conchita dance with her new husband, I notice for the first time the bulge in her tummy beneath the white-lace dress. Still she flashes dark-eyed looks over her shoulder at the men. In a corner of the garden, crazy Jeem, shirtless and sweating, grunts over his barbells, glowering at Conchita's new husband. More stragglers from the Locos parade arrive, still in costume. The scene is Fellini, Jacques Tati—or Luis Buñuel.

Later that night, Masako, Teresa, and I follow firecrackers and crowds to the atrium in front of the Oratorio church, where a few dozen tireless locos dance and bob to a local ranchera band in a marathon trance of delight.

That night in bed I say to Masako, "I couldn't get the grin off my face today."

She reaches over and flicks off the light. "Remember lying in bed listening to the helicopters? You'd say, 'There must be something after L.A.' "

"Maybe what's after L.A.," I whisper, "is what was before L.A."

# Chapter 3

# Lost in the Day

DEEP IN JULY. WHAT DOES IT MEAN TO internalize the sound of church bells, fireworks at six in the morning? Burros' braying, Mexican curses and words of praise? The days and weeks gain rhythm, unfold in time. The cobbled paths we tread become inner landscapes.

In the hotel garden, geese chase each other in the keen afternoon light. Pigeons burble in the barracks walls. Around me lies the littered evidence of our stay: magazines and books in English and Spanish, old Penguins with their faded orange spines from the sale rack of the little bilingual library on Calle Insurgentes: Greene, Lowry, Carlos Fuentes, Lawrence. A tiny yellow Langenscheidt dictionary sits atop a bigger red and yellow Signet one. *Madrigral's Magic Key to Spanish*'s bookmark has advanced to the

middle: I've broached the past tense. So has my reading, for
there is time and space now for more of Bernal Díaz's chronicles of the Conquest, Fanny Calderón de la Barca's nine-
teenth-century memoir of life in Mexico, and Stephens and
Catherwood's *Incidents of Travel in Central America, Chià-
pas, and Yucatan,* which leaves me hungry to visit Chichén
Itzá, Palenque, the Mayan South.

Bits of village folk art adorn tables and walls: papier-
mâché dragons, a black wood mask from Guerrero with a
twisting green snake for a nose, a gaily painted ceramic tree
of life. My sandals sit on the straw petate mat beside the bed.
Masako's red and white handwoven Guatemalan jacket
drapes the back of the carved wood chair. A blue vase filled
with white gladioli adorns the kitchen table; oranges, ba-
nanas, mangoes, limes fill a green ceramic bowl. On the low
pine desk by the window, new pages gather about them the
order of finality.

The painting hanging over our bed is of a black-and-
white agave plant, its spiky leaves waving like undersea ten-
tacles. Interesting that Masako chooses to render Mexico
monochrome: the result is radical, unmediated light and
form, extremes of sun and shade. Like Edward Weston or
Tina Modotti's 1920s photos, all shadow and light; or Mina's
Mexico films; or Sergei Eisenstein's *Que Viva México,* which
we saw on video at Mina's house the other night, a film I
hadn't known existed.

Yesterday at lunch in the hotel dining room, old Emil announced with great ceremony that he was leaving for Sri
Lanka to die among Buddhist monks. Nobody believes he'll
go, but if he does, Masako has laid claim to his huge studio,
the ex-hacienda's master bedroom. Meanwhile she etches
mornings at the Bellas Artes building, the national arts center on the other side of the military barracks. Tempestuous

Gabriela and her guitarist Gustavo have decamped for Puerto Vallarta, alleviating the hotel of their stormy *amor.* Jeem, the teeth-grinding, speed-popping weight lifter, has lost an alarming number of kilos. Two nights ago he broke into Teresa's room: she woke up to find him standing over her demanding sex until finally her screams drove him off. The next day Jeem broke up everything in his room— stereo, desk, chairs. Negotiations are under way for his deportation, though there seems to be more to it than simply disturbing the peace or violating local laws; the American embassy will repatriate citizens only under special circumstances. We speculate that a family somewhere is using its influence to prevent Jeem's return. Rafael and his wife seem to have infinite tolerance for the human wreckage infesting their ex-hacienda.

We see less of Mina and Paul these days. Like us, they work mostly—Mina finishing a film, Paul painting toward a fall exhibition. Gradually our Mexicos diverge. Still every Friday we meet at El Caribe, a seafood restaurant down Calle Canal. Maruja and Billie from La Golondrina bookstore join us, sometimes others.

In this part of Mexico, nothing happens between two and four in the afternoon. Businesses close, drivers pull off the road, towns go dead for *comida,* the day's main meal. Nominally shops reopen at four; but if it's a good lunch or the conversation is rolling or the proprietor could use a little siesta—any excuse will do—it might be closer to four-thirty, five even. Yet the same store might stay open past eight if there's a stray customer, or nothing special waiting at home.

Whitefish from the lake at the bottom of town is sold in San Miguel's markets, but as local reservoirs and streams are outlets for human waste and refrigeration is often primitive or nonexistent, people tend to stick to fresh *carne* from the nearby ranches. On Fridays, though, when the delivery truck arrives from Tampico with fresh fish on blocks of ice and pulls directly up to the door of El Caribe, a table beneath the florid marine mural on the east wall is the place to be.

"Today I finally figured out the bells," Masako is telling Maruja over *tostadas de ceviche,* lime-marinated scallop salad on a crisp fried tortilla. "One gong for each hour. Then a pair of different-tone clangs for each quarter hour. Plus calls to prayer."

Maruja smiles patiently, wiggles her flattened hand: *más o menos.* More or less. Lately we've begun to ape Mexican body language: the pinch of thumb and forefinger signaling "in a minute," the sideways waggle of the index finger meaning emphatically "no," the good-bye wave with the back of the hand rather than the exposed palm.

"Sometimes, though, the bell rings at seven-nineteen," Masako says. "Or two-oh-eight. What does that mean?"

"It means the bell ringer is late," Paul says, deadpan.

Gringos, obsessed with time. We want it all perfectly clear—on the dot, by the book. What's with us? We arrive at an eight o'clock dinner at eight, not ten or ten-thirty as Mexicans do. We stand vigil in front of a store that's supposed to reopen at four, nervously consulting our watches.

*Cóctel de camarones* arrives in tulip glasses, the Gulf shrimp plucky, white, and tender. We talk of local characters and scandals. Last Sunday there was a large wedding reception at El Ring, a disco on Calle Hidalgo where kids go to dance. The groom was a son of one of the town's better families; Maruja had gone to school with the parents and knows them all. The bride was the alleged former mistress of the governor of a nearby state, a notorious bag man for the ruling party, the PRI. Enraged at his mistress's marriage plans, the governor sent a hit man to knock off the groom. The thug had blundered into the party, gun drawn, sending everyone screaming in all directions, then shot the best man by mistake, killing him and injuring the bride (her beautiful white lace dress splattered with blood, by all reports—an image out of García Lorca). The groom and his party chased the assassin into the night and caught him. They beat him to a pulp, then dragged him off to the Presidencia, where he languishes in jail. In this peaceable town, the shooting qualifies as a major scandal. Maruja says everybody understands that nothing will happen to the governor, the crime's "intellectual author" (as they like to say in Mexico), and that after a suitable amount of time it will be duly noted that the hit man mysteriously "escaped" from jail.

After lunch we stumble up Calle Canal, heavy with food, thinking of flagging a cab but too much enjoying the walk and the talk. We arrive back at the bookstore as the clock strikes four-thirty. Gringo customers mill around the door, fretfully checking their watches.

Tuesday morning I head into town in search of paper for my printer. The light is keen, the cool air smelling faintly of a mesquite fire. Along Calle Hernández Macías, maids wet down the stones in front of the old buildings. Caretakers swing open the massive doors of the Bellas Artes Institute where Masako studies etching. Pigeons cluster in the forecourt of the cloister, where the nuns sell a sweet drink they make called *rompope* from a side door behind the confessional. Up along Calle Canal, a crone's leathery hand accepts the peso I've dredged from my jeans pocket. God will reward me, she croaks, though I really don't require such divine recompense.

At the intersection of Canal and Hidalgo, a brown-uniformed traffic cop toots a silver whistle, languidly waving on a car or two. There are no streetlights or stop signs in San Miguel, though in recent years traffic has built up (old postcards from the 1940s show horses, burros, pedestrians, only an occasional vehicle). According to the local weekly *Atención*, a citizen's group is urging the mayor to ban traffic permanently from the streets around the jardín, not just on weekends and holidays, as at present. The *taxistas* are against it because it would be bad for business; others argue there's no other place to park in this hillside labyrinth built four and a half centuries ago.

The central plaza draws the walker toward it by the shapes and rhythms of the streets, but at one's own pace, and with digressions en route, finally to that center which then flings you out again along one of its arms. The stationery store, the *papelería*, lies down Calle Hidalgo to my left; but as it's a few minutes before stores open, I continue on up Calle Canal. The sun splits the tips of the jardín's trimmed laurel trees as I pass the Presidencia building, which serves as police station, jail, and town hall. Clever those Spaniards, to have built Church on one side of the plaza, State on the other, obliging the populace to gather under the twin gaze— though I suppose it could equally be seen as a protective arrangement for the citizens themselves. Certainly it doesn't stop people from using the plaza as an outdoor living room: to sit, stroll, court, listen to bands, even launch protests against the Presidencia.

At Calle Reloj—named for the clock tower on the jardín whose bells mark that fluid, beguiling time—I turn left. Halfway down the shaded block I come to La Colmena, a bakery named after a beehive, whose blue doors open in early morning, the aroma of freshly baked *bolillos* flooding the street. I pass through a turnstile, grab a flat aluminum tray and tongs, and select from among racks of breads and pastries an *empanada de queso,* a turnover with cheese inside.

I walk back to the jardín, where it's 9:30 by the clock tower, still no guarantee that the papelería is opening its doors. On a bench in the warming sun I eat my empanada, consider the drift of people across the plaza, watch the light advance down a red stone wall—reduced for the moment to the simple decision of whether to get up or stay put.

Rousing myself at last, I walk down Calle Hidalgo to the papelería, a dim, narrow shop set several stairs below the street. Behind a chipped yellow wooden counter, glassed shelves are crammed with cheap pens, colored papers, school notebooks. A copy machine, surely one of the first ever built, groans out smudged, barely legible copies on legal-sized paper. The señora greets me with the same compassionate smile and pinched-finger gesture she made yesterday: *ahorita,* soon. Your paper will be here soon. *Ojalá,* God willing, the truck from Mexico City will get here this morning. Ten-thirty, señor. *Por supuesto.* For sure.

I'm less upset by this further delay than I might be. Maybe I'm catching on. Mexicans don't seem to have time anxiety, in our sense. If the day, as in the Mayan poem, sets out from the east and starts walking, wisdom suggests one fall in step with it. If there are infinite causes for things, and everything is interrelated, bound inside this walking day, then there must be a reason why the truck is late from Mexico City. This was advice given me by Teresa at the Ambos Mundos, who told me one day: in Mexico *there's always a reason.* In the States I expect things to work, quickly and well; often they don't. Here, expecting little, I find things generally do function, and at the end of the day things get done, more or less, *más o menos.* If not, there must be a reason, however inscrutable to me. My narrow need, inset in this day that started out walking from the east, is deferred, or revised, or revealed to have not been all that important. These pages I need to print out will arrive in New York a day later: as if agent and editor were drumming their fingers on the table waiting—a convenient fiction I use as a goad. I may be a little late with my delivery, but then I may be a little late for my own death as a result. Is that so bad?

Heading back to the hotel, I run into Vicente Arias, the portly painter with the studio next to us at the Ambos Mundos, coming out of the dry cleaners on Calle Mesones. His plaid shopping bag now emptied of clothes, he intends to fill it with provisions at the Tuesday market and invites me to join him. My muttered reply in the mélange of Spanish and English I use about needing to work strikes a sour note on this bright July morning. It does seem sinful to coop myself up.

"Maybe you'll find printing paper at the Tuesday market," he inveigles. *"Quién sabe?"*

We cut through the Ambos Mundos parking lot to a steep unpaved lane called Indio Muerto, which spills directly onto the *mercado de martes*—that teeming, traveling bazaar and guerrilla flea market that materializes once a week in the blocks around San Juan de Dios church, turning the sedate neighborhood into a hallucinatory Beirut. Buyers and sellers arrive at dawn by truck, car, taxi, horse, burro, and bicycle, and spread their wares—from tacky to elegant to illicit—on blankets and improvised tables. Prices are rock bottom, and there are goods unavailable anywhere else in town: Third World dumping at its finest.

We plunge in, laughing. Vicente calls to me to hang on to my wallet. Hawkers shout, ranchera music keens. Hordes shoulder us along in the shadow of canvas awnings. Old women half my size jostle me as if I were a bale of straw. Vicente is after an electric screwdriver for his studio. I follow him through a sea of hardware, saws, machetes, knifes, and bicycle pumps. At last he spots what he's looking for on a seller's blanket. While he bargains, I gaze at a display of mudguards for trucks, cars, and bicycles, their fluorescent motifs rich with open male sentiment: *"Mi Vida Mi Amor"* ("My life my love"), *"Para Siempre Mi Corazón"* ("Forever, my heart"), *"Yo* (red heart icon) *Guanajuato."*

*"Escójale!"* "Pick something!" cry the sellers.

We've wandered into a food area. Vendors thrust samples at us on the edge of knives, fruits whose very names are colors. Vicente bites into a bright, radish-colored cactus fruit called *tuna.* I gaze down at a profusion of salsas, each with different ingredients and colors. Among a pile of green calabaza squash topped by orange flowers, a flopping red fish's glassy eye looks balefully up at me. Happy eaters gather around a sizzling grill of *carnitas,* tender cooked pork parts. An Indian woman sells raw chocolate, as in the Aztec markets Cortés first beheld.

Vicente brandishes an uncooked cob of corn, its pale green husk torn back to expose a bubbling, moldy black fungus— that same alarming growth I've seen in the town market. Put it down, I want to tell him, before you contract some scrofulous affliction. But Vicente, grinning beneath his mustache, shouts *"Huitlacoche!"* which sounds like "wheet-la-ko-chay." *"Sabrosito! Riquísmo!* Delicious!" He vows to cook it for us. A promise or a threat?

*"Barato!"* ("Cheap!"), the sellers cry. *"Qué le doy, Señor?"* "What can I get you?"

Shoppers stampede us into an alley of clothing vendors, past acreage of T-shirts splattered with American slang: "I'm a Cool Gal." "Are We Having Fun Yet?" "AC/DC." Calvin Kleins: knockoffs or the real thing? Next to beautiful leather boots and saddles from the Spanish era, a display of cheap aluminum bracelets. We pass through stalls of radios, televisions, CB units, electronic games from Japan. A man with a tape-to-tape cassette will dub off anything for you. Forget copyright laws: here, the customer rules.

I turn and look for Vicente but he's gone. Bustled on by the crowds, I find myself in front of a display of herbs and curatives: magical soaps to hex your lover, inscrutable herbs and potions, weird amulets and charms. A tiny human fetus floats in a jar with words taped to it exhorting mothers to avoid this sad fate. Worms fifteen-feet long, allegedly extracted from human intestines, float in bottles with labels proffering cures. A small, stout woman with one milky eye, her silver hair tied in a bun, smiles and says something I don't understand. She holds up a small pyramid made of a clear plastic gel or compound. Suspended in it—like little snowflake scenes inside a Christmas diorama—are auspicious charms and symbols from everywhere: a horseshoe, a shamrock, a sitting Buddha, a cross, a Star of David, an Arab crescent. The ultimate eclectic talisman: Masako must have it.

Reaching into my pocket for pesos, I realize Mina is standing beside me. Preoccupied, she holds a small box with occult symbols on it. She looks up, equally surprised to see me. Her dark eyes are troubled. Paul is ill, she says; they don't know what it is. Weakness, quivering in the limbs. Maybe amoebas; they're awaiting lab tests. She's come to buy packets of herbs from the *bruja*, the *curandera*, the medicine woman. She jots down the woman's exact instructions: boil, decant, combine with other foods and herbs.

Mina's worry lingers with me as I work my way on down the busy lanes, eager to find an exit from the market. Brilliant, odd, cheery, Paul. What's wrong with him? They've been coming to Mexico for decades and would be comfortable with indigenous medicine; still I take her visit to the curandera as a sign of deep concern.

Emerging at last from the Tuesday market off Calle Canal, well below the town, I find myself inside a small parade. Dancing kids follow a neighborhood band. I have no idea what the occasion is. Maybe the merchants hire them on market day, maybe they just feel like being a parade today. I follow them past the Puente Guanajuato, where the hillside levels. The ragged band—saxophone, tuba, trumpet, clarinet, snare drum, bass drum—begins to peter out, as one by one the musicians disperse into the surrounding neighborhoods. Finally only the bass drummer and a tuneless clarinet player are left.

Ejected from this small twister, I find myself alone on the road leading to the train station and the lake where I'd walked on our first visit. I turn and look back up the hill toward the town. Above the tip of the Parroquia, just visible over the treetops and ascending roofs, a sunbeam shoots through a crack in the cloud, hitting the spire. I suck in my breath.

Trudging back uphill toward town in heat softened by the cooling clouds, I realize I'd forgotten all about the paper I'd set out to find. I pass through blocks I don't know, peering through doorways into gardens. In an abandoned ruin I come upon an old man living among weeds, cooking by fire, carving odd, surreal animals out of wood scraps. A monarch butterfly lands on my wrist. I watch its huge black and orange wings open and close. A crow struts brazenly at my feet, cawing.

When I was a boy, my family moved from crowded

Manhattan to a southern California of abundant spaces: a fecund terrain of intrigue and discovery, unpopulated canyons
and abandoned dwellings, flowers and animals—coyotes,
deer, great monarchs like these—before DDT and tract developments. Mexico, forgotten by time and commerce, run
roughshod over by successive revolutions, languishing in
backward politics and economic straits, still breathes that air
of possibility. Buildings lie unused, awaiting the restorer's
hand. Threatened species survive here. Dreams range, hidden from the global advance of capital that erases culture
and difference.

It won't last. Population pressures build, Mexican industry advances. Migrant workers return home to develop their
lands. These old towns will become tourist meccas, like central Italy or Provence: exquisite, expensive, gourmet sites.
But standing in the ruins of what must have been a bath-
house (*"Balneario,"* the faded letters read), cactus growing up
through its adobe walls, I savor it while it lasts: *México
olvidado,* forgotten land.

The clouds pass on, the midday heat returns. A couple of
blocks below town I realize I've just passed a tiny neighborhood papelería. I turn back and enter. Inside, a girl behind
the counter is reading a comic by dim light. She turns and
feels along the dusty shelf behind her, pulls down a lone
ream of Zellerbach paper.

I arrive back at the Ambos Mundos, hot
and dirty. Masako is standing at the kitchen table, examin-
ing her first completed etching: mosquitoes against mesh
netting.

"That was a long trip," she says. "Did you find printing paper?"

"Look," I say, removing the pyramid from my bag.

She takes it, turns the all-purpose charm in the light, examines each talisman. "It's perfect. It has everything."

We set it on the kitchen table so the light can catch it. Gazing at its concatenation of fetishes, I think of Mina at the curandera's stand, her worry over Paul.

"Paul is sick," I say.

# Chapter 4

# *L*arga Distancia

IT HAS BEEN RAINING FOR DAYS. THIS happens some Augusts, I'm told. At first the clashing thunderheads in the mountain skies and the sudden blue spits of lightning over the Guanajuato plain were welcome, inducing a cheery shipboard camaraderie at the Ambos Mundos. But now as the days wear on and the power lines fall, as roads turn into rutted ditches and mold erupts along the walls, a melancholy settles over the hotel, the town. The human jetsam that gathers in the hotel dining room to gibber of small scandals, peso devaluations, and drug deals run amok has come to resemble a salon of the damned. I'm ready for the rains to abate, the skies to clear, the roads to open.

A week ago old Emil left for Sri Lanka to die—though someone claims to have sighted him in nearby Celaya yesterday.

Masako has taken over his studio, with its great soaring white walls and green-tiled bathroom as big as our room. Crazy Jeem has become involved with a small, abject Indian woman who scrubs the hotel paving stones on her knees, and has moved into her thatched-roof shack with kids, chickens, and pigs. We all feel relieved he's gone but fear for the woman.

This morning, standing under the eaves in the hotel courtyard, I fell into conversation with a French-Canadian city planner en route to Venezuela. He told me a story about Venezuela that might equally apply to Mexico, or almost anywhere in the Third World. In Caracas the government allocated oil money to build a huge new neighborhood of high-rise public housing on the outskirts of the city. Thousands of workers, brought in from villages and towns all over Venezuela to complete the project, built tent cities for themselves surrounding the work site. Soon their wives and children came; other makeshift communities grew to serve the workers in the tent cities. The high-rises went up—ugly, sterile, overpriced—and when they were done nobody wanted to move into them. Meanwhile the workers' communities that had grown up around them were teeming with children, families, life. Today the high-rise buildings remain unoccupied, crumbling, scheduled for demolition. Ringing them is a large, vital shantytown city. Jacques the city planner is on his way to consult with the government about this dilemma. I told him what I'd seen in Hong Kong, how the boat people didn't want to move into the public high-rises the authorities had built for them but preferred to remain on their boats without running water or electricity. We agreed that the Third World's vibrant unruliness, not central planning, may be what will save it in the end.

Today in town, driven to cover by a downpour, we ducked

into an ornate colonial building on Calle Pila Seca. Once home to the town Inquisitor, it's now a home-furnishings store. Certainly the church functionary lived well in his day while quelling heresy in these parts. Looking up at the great carved oak cross beams, the massive mesquite doors, the scalloped niches in the meter-thick walls, the iron balustrade winding through the three-story dwelling, we imagined living in such a place. People do such things here: buy seventeenth-century buildings, fix them up, live in them. The thought charged our conversation all afternoon back in the tiny, dank hotel room. For the price of a down payment on a modest home in L.A. we could buy a two-hundred-year-old home here. But invest in unstable Mexico? Foreigners can't really own anyway, but must buy property through a thirty-year bank trust instrument, revocable come the revolution. And there is talk of such things, as Mexico's economy languishes, capital flees to Zurich, unrest grows in the southern states.

Friends from New York write they're coming for a week in September: our first visitors. We hope the rains will have let up. Meanwhile the markets fill with food but the restaurants with few customers. With tourism down, there's little else to sustain San Miguel but the surrounding produce ranches and light industry: glass, tinware, papier-mâché.

We've stopped eating off the streets—not an easy renunciation, but we're tired of the turistas. For now, no more visits to the toothsome little *taquerías* that spring up out of nowhere at night, or the stands off the plazas selling corn on the cob laced with chile, lime, and mayonnaise slopped from an unrefrigerated jar. No more drip-sweet strawberries in plastic cups with lethal dollops of whipped cream, or spears of sliced cantaloupe, mango, jicama. We miss the food stalls off the jardín that serve enchiladas, then rinse the dishes in a bucket of standing tap water. Back at the hotel, we take pains to soak our vegetables and fruits in purifying drops, run our drinking water through a filter. Whenever I'm tempted in my wanderings to eat off the streets, I recall the curandera's jars at the Tuesday market displaying twelve-foot-long worms allegedly yanked from human intestines. I worry about Paul's mysterious affliction, which still dogs him. There is a lab a few blocks away from the Ambos Mundos that will be happy to test you for amoebas or worms, though the cure is said to rival the disease: weeks on some chalky antidote of questionable efficacy. So far we either show no symptoms or don't admit to them. Has our own bacteria count now reached equilibrium with the environment—like the church bells and the fireworks at dawn we barely notice now—while little devouring creatures bore their way through our intestinal walls?

Music is everywhere. Each night La Mama's courtyard restaurant off the plaza alternates a Peruvian band of flutes, guitars, and drum with an intense, flaying German flamenco player—while in their club annex a quintet of Veracruz harp virtuosi in white sailor costumes strums pulsating versions of "La Bamba" (originally, and still, a sea shanty). Last Saturday a Senegalese Afro-beat band passed through town and we danced until all hours at Pancho y Lefty's bar. *"Está bien así?"* chanted the lead vocalist. "Do you like it like this?" *"Está bien así!"* we shouted back. In the courtyard of the Bellas Artes, the former nuns' cloister where Masako etches, music pours out of every room, bounces off the grand murals, echoes along the vast colonnades: here for an annual chamber music festival, earnest Korean virtuosi, Russian string trios, and Mexican prodigies saw at cellos, pound on spinets, whistle through woodwinds.

At night we visit half-deserted restaurants. At La Bugambilia, an enclosed courtyard eatery that had begun as a street stall, we discover *ensalada chicharrón,* a mixed vegetable salad garnished with low-rent fried pork rinds and a squeeze of lime to become a delicacy. At El Matador, a modest restaurant a few blocks away run by an ex-bullfighter, Masako digs into *pozole* made with hominy, a soup that's a virtual meal. Other days we simply stop by El Infierno, buy a chicken off the spit barbecued in a tangy marinade, with salsa, tortillas, and a soft drink thrown in, and eat outside by the old Ambos Mundos pool.

The town is ridiculously romantic. Street musicians wail of stones that speak, women and towns known and lost. Lovers lurk in shaded doorways. A smiling, mustachioed man in a clean white shirt walks among the restaurants and cafés each night selling fresh red roses. Petals of bougainvillea cling to our jacket sleeves, float down into our soup. Some nights the stars and the moon veer so close that, pausing on the cobblestones walking home, I'm tempted to reach up and stir them about with my hand. The bells—incessant, overlapping (there are fifteen churches in the town, three hundred in the province)—at first a distraction and a mystery, are now a sensory balm, an invitation to contemplate time's passing. After dinner we walk back through the night drizzle to the Ambos Mundos, full of food and music, arms about each other. In bed we are happy. How much we needed this place.

Friday night we arrive a little late for a birthday party at La Fragua, an old bar next to the Parroquia. In a side room at a long wooden banquet table, forty-odd people raise toasts to Elenita, our celebrant. She and her husband, Carlos, have a store near the post office

specializing in folk art and artifacts from around the hemisphere: Mexico, Guatemala, Peru. Carlos, florid and
longhaired, has a fondness for philosophy and drink. Elenita,
pretty but plain by choice, her hair drawn back severely, has
an almost saintly sweetness. In California they'd read as gentle, educated, sixties idealists; in fact, through them we've
learned more of the epochal events of 1968, when just before
the Olympics police shot at demonstrating students in Mexico City's Tlatelolco Plaza—Elenita and Carlos among
them—killing many. Merchants now, they still vote for the
PRD, the opposition party that never wins, and read *La Jornada*, the paper of the left. They champion the preservation
of indigenous cultures through their work at the store, ex-
hibiting yarn paintings and masks beaded by Huichol peyote Indians living in the deserts to the north.

I slide into an empty seat at the far end of the table,
Masako up near Elenita and Carlos. Margaritas seem to be
the drink of choice, and a meal of corn soup, *carne asada*
(beef with *tomatillo* sauce, avocado, potatoes, lettuce, carrots), and flan. I fall into conversation with a silver-haired
gringa sitting next to me.

She is pleasant enough, well-spoken, not untypical of
other retired foreigners I've met here. Some bear surprising
résumés not always evident from their appearance: diplo-
matic corps, doctor in Ghana, ex-director of Versailles. There
would be something a little odd or different about them that
they'd end up late in life in this rather remote, unprotected
mountain town of such unusual beauty but with few medi-
cal facilities. Some remind me of Tennessee Williams's or
Paul Bowles's people: sad, touching, a derelict gleam in their
eyes. I surmise from this woman's red rebozo shawl and the
turquoise ring on her right middle finger that she frequents
Carlos and Elenita's store.

She lives alone, she says, in a small house on Calle Aldama. Her two American children are grown—one a doctor, the other the owner of a restaurant. They call occasionally, never come to visit. Her husband passed away seven years earlier. She finds herself quite alone, an American woman in Mexico, trying to meet the challenges of each day. She volunteers at the local library, helps at the orphanage on Calle Zacateros, speaks some Spanish. Her maid, Luisa, an Otomí Indian from the countryside nearby, often comments on her solitude, she says, and seems to feel sorry for her. The woman resents this, feels misperceived. How can her maid, poor and overburdened with work and too many children, with a husband who is never there but across the border in Texas and sends scant money home, pity her, an independent woman of means with options and the wherewithal to make her life comfortable?

The week before, Luisa her maid had invited her to a birthday party for one of her seven children. It was for today, Sunday, out on the communal ranch, the *ejido* where she lives. The woman politely declined. Every day the maid asked, and again the woman said no. It seemed inappropriate somehow, *la patrona* going out to some poor ranch somewhere in the *campo*. But the maid wouldn't let up, and finally the woman agreed to go, if for no reason other than to silence her maid.

"This afternoon," she tells me, "I had a taxi take me to this ranch about five miles out, off the road to Guanajuato." At the head of our table there is laughter, another toast to Elenita, more margaritas. The noise dies down, and the woman continues. "There must have been sixty people, all relatives or friends of some sort—old people, nursing infants, ranch hands in boots and hats. They were poor, but there were tamales to eat, and pork and tortillas all cooked outdoors, and corn drink, and beer. Everyone seemed so comfortable together. A little band played the sweetest music—an accordion, I think, and that big thumpy bass guitar. . . ."

"*Guitarrón.*"

"Yes. And an out-of-tune fiddle player, yet so marvelous and lively. Some nephew of Luisa's who couldn't have been more than eight played the drum." She laughs and brushes back her hair, seeming to liven at the thought. "Adults held the infants who never cried, not a peep. The old people spoke among each other, and younger ones sat with them and listened. There was so much . . ." She turns to me, her eyes shining. ". . . warm, simple love." She fishes in her purse for a handkerchief. "It was the best time I've had in years," she says, dabbing at her eyes. "There's something . . . *criminal* about that, don't you think?"

Around us, the table is emptying as people get up to dance to the *norteño* band in the other room. We remain in our own quiet space.

"Where have we gone wrong?" she says suddenly. "Alone in our houses with televisions and newspapers and books, crowing the whole time about how much freedom we have. The sexes are either terrified of each other or at each other's throats. We're frightened of commitment. We marry then divorce, preferring our private satisfactions, our careers, to enduring with one another." Her eyes earnestly search mine. "We've gone off track somewhere, don't you think?"

She looks away, flushing.

"I'm sorry," she says. "This is supposed to be a birthday party for Elenita. There, you see? Selfish. Taking your attention."

"It's all right," I say, grateful for the confession. I want to say something in return but don't know quite what. She romanticizes, I think. Mexican campesinos' lives are hard: the grind of poverty, babies needlessly lost to dysentery, women to abuse, men to drink and joblessness. This woman wouldn't dream of trading lives with her maid. Her position here, like mine, is one of utter privilege. Yet she's cut to the quick of something. The Parroquia's big bell tolls, deep and sonorous. Through the window beside our table, I can see the crowds emerging into the forecourt from evening Mass. In the next room, the band's two-beat *corrida* cuts across the bell's aftertones.

"Maybe it's why we come here," I say to the woman. "To try to tend to the part that's missing."

The party is dispersing around us. We stand to go.

She looks at me doubtfully. "But it's too late, isn't it?"


I awaken to bright unfamiliar light, the chirping of birds. Outside, sparkling cumuli race north across a clear azure sky. The stones dry quickly in the sun. The rains are over at last.

Our friends arrive in a couple of weeks. Paul and Mina have returned to the States for the fall term. Paul's nameless condition persists; Mina has flown him to see tropical-medicine specialists in Atlanta.

Fall looms. What will we do? We'd projected no further than September, an experiment. Now we can't imagine yielding this new territory, with its sufficiency of days. Our former L.A. life seems unimaginably remote, lusterless. Another truth lies between us unspoken: Would our life together survive the strains of return? Perhaps it wasn't only position and place that had driven us out but love's erosion.

Wanderers in youth, veterans of different earlier relation-
ships, neither of us was a candidate for a long marriage. Yet
here in this country, this town, this run-down hotel, we like
our life together again. Yesterday morning in bed Masako
said, "We're happy *for no reason.*"

XESQ, Radio San Miguel, is the only sta-
tion available on the dial without a shortwave. It plays music and news and serves effectively as the town's lost and
found, as I'd learned in January when I'd lost my manuscript. It's also a bulletin board and message relay center:
"Silvestre Ramírez, your brother will be calling from Texas
at eight-thirty at the *larga distancia caseta* on Calle
Umarán." "Doña Amalia López passed away last night at the
age of seventy-three. A Mass will be held for her today at the
Parroquia at three, followed by a procession to the cemetery. . . ."

I sit with Silvestre Ramírez and other waiting campesinos in the larga distancia office on a Sunday night. The
stout, imperturbable woman who runs the phones from behind an old desk negotiates lines with operators in Monterrey, Chihuahua, Houston, a fat black receiver to each ear.
There are a few rickety stools for those of us awaiting our
turn in one of the three booths; the rest of us stand or sit on
the floor. The Caseta El Toro is constantly busy, one of the
few places around town with long-distance capability. The
telephone company is disastrously corrupt, and private
phone lines can cost thousands of dollars on the black market. I always bring a book or a magazine to Caseta El Toro,
allowing a good hour for my Stateside calls. My father is

two hours earlier in California, my daughter in New York an hour later.

I tend to tighten up the day of the weekly phone calls. I suppose it reminds me of distance from family and friends and colleagues, hence my own uselessness to them, and my lingering unease at our "precipitous departure," as one friend called it, from the life we'd lived.

The woman beckons. I step into a stuffy booth and close the door. "Hi, Dad," I hear. I'm close to my daughter, wildly fond of her, and we usually speak freely about things; but tonight Maya, in her second year at Barnard, sounds tense, distant. She's stayed on in the city this year for summer school and a job. Her apartment on 110th Street has rats and roaches. Bums and muggers, rappers and dopeheads hover at the edge of her days and nights. Her roommate got molested up by St. John the Divine. She was in an antiapartheid demonstration on the Columbia steps. Her flat, affectless descriptions of life in New York disturb me. I look out at the soft red wall of the antique store across the street. My quotient of environmental menace reduces to near zero while hers escalates. Yet she wouldn't want me there. Of what more use would I be to her even if I were in California, not here? Yes, Dad, money's cool. No, Dad, I don't need anything. In September we'll visit her in New York. Yes, she'd love to visit Mexico at Christmas if we're still here.

Back out in the long distance office, I feel emptied, agitated by the call. I leaf through a new issue of *México desconocido.* Flamingo-filled tidal estuaries along the south Pacific coast, snowy mountain peaks of Popocatépetl, flower-flecked mountain glens filled with old Franciscan monasteries, verdant jungle ruins along the Usumacinta River in southern Chiapas. I cobble meanings out of the Spanish captions beneath the photos. I want to go to all these places. I think: We're just starting out here in Mexico.

A sweet, chubby shop girl I know clusters in a booth with her mother, sister, and daughter, talking to Daddy in Texas. They all shout loudly at once into the bad line. Some nights you lose the connection and have to start over; I've spent two hours here in Caseta El Toro trying to get through. The phone lady waves me into the next booth.

"Son? Is that you?" Dad, widowed several years now, is entering his eighties in good health, still golfing; but tonight he sounds querulous, repetitive. In L.A. I call more often, make visits for what animal comfort they provide, though we find little to talk about. Hardly reason to be there all the time, is it? The twinge, the push-pull, as parents age. What do we owe each other? What is expected? What is important? I think of the American lady at Elenita's birthday party.

Out in the street, the night air is soft with jasmine smell. I walk to the plaza, blocked off from car traffic tonight. Boys and girls throng the jardín for the Sunday night promenade, the *paseo*, as the concert band from nearby Atotonilco exuberantly murders a John Philip Sousa march to a salsa beat. Balloon and toy sellers drift through the crowds with their colored enticements. Babies burble, kids lick icy fruit *paletas*. I buy a bag of fresh, warm *palomitas* from the popcorn maker, circle with the crowds, think of my daughter. Someone is testing a loudspeaker on a riser in front of the Parroquia, where shortly the mayor will announce this year's Miss San Miguel from among the local beauties whose snapshots have been posted on the wall outside city hall for the last two weeks.

In what separate chamber of the soul does this place reside? Have I tumbled out of reality or into it?

# Chapter 5

# The Visit

SEPTEMBER. THE CRESCENDO OF
patriotic festivities gathers force. Fireworks
shatter the dawn, explode in the midnight
sky. School drum-and-bugle bands trudge
noisily down the *calles*. Drunken youths
stumble through the night streets singing
and shouting *"Viva México!"* The toy sellers
in the jardín have doubled in number, adding Mexican flags to their inventory, flags
that now festoon nearly every building in
town. Restaurants offer the seasonal delicacy *chiles en nogada*, with its colors of the
national flag: whole green chile peppers
smothered in a white cream sauce of meats
and fruits and spices and nuts, topped with
red pomegranate seeds.

It was Colonel Ignacio Allende, born in
the house facing the Parroquia I pass daily,
who conspired with the priest Hidalgo from

the nearby town of Dolores to ignite the revolt of 1810 against the Spanish Crown. Both paid dearly: hunted down and executed, their heads were hung from pikes in Guanajuato's granary as public rebuke. Their exploits and unhappy ends are endlessly memorialized in song and speech and mural, consecrating San Miguel de Allende as the "Cradle of Mexican Independence." Every September 16 the president of Mexico recites Hidalgo's cry of independence, the *grito de Dolores,* from the balcony of the National Palace, beamed to every corner of the country over radio and television. Our mayor follows this with a mini-grito from Allende's balcony to the throngs that pour into San Miguel from all over Mexico. Before the month is out there will be more music, marathon races, fireworks, a *pamplonada* (running of the bulls), bullfights, Indian *conchero* dancing—and, on the twenty-ninth, San Miguel Day, a celebration in honor of the Franciscan friar who established the town around 1542.

In the eighteenth century, San Miguel was formally charged by the Crown with the crime of having "an excess of fiestas." Citizens fought the charge and won. Now it seems there's a fiesta nearly every day in San Miguel—civic, Indian, religious, patriotic, pagan. I like the patriotic ones least, nationalistic fervor tending to be the same in every country—parades, bands, speeches, flag waving. Still I want to hear the famed grito spoken right here where the revolution began. At La Golondrina, Maruja and Billie regard my interest with benign amusement: they're closing up shop and going to Puerto Escondido. Billie counsels laying in provisions, staying off the streets, getting earplugs, and curling up with a good book. "Why all the revelry?" she says irritably, fishing a fresh Marlboro from her shirt pocket. "What has the Revolution done for anyone in a hundred seventy-five years? The same Spanish-descended families still hold most of the power."

"It's better than being a colony," Maruja says. "And there've been changes. You exaggerate, Billie."

Tomorrow our friends Janet and Richard arrive for five days. They'll stay through the festivities on the fifteenth and sixteenth, then return to Manhattan. We'll be leaving two days later for a few weeks: a novel of mine is coming out in England and France, and while I have no idea if it will help, it seems I should go. On the way back to Mexico we'll stop and see my daughter in New York. Rafael has promised to hold our rooms at the Ambos Mundos.

We've booked Janet and Richard, her new husband, into a complex of former colonial homes two blocks above the jardín. The rooms, at around fifty dollars, seem pricey in Mexico's flattened economy, but they can afford it; and we have some doubts about Richard's tolerance for humbler quarters.

Janet, a museum curator in Manhattan, is an old friend— open, ebullient, warm. We've met Richard, a professor of art, once. Older than Janet, he seems a cultivated, somewhat fastidious man who prides himself on his discernment in art, books, wines. What is it that draws fresh, exuberant Janet to these mentor types? We wonder how Richard will respond to Mexico's unruliness, its rough edges.

The evening before they arrive, Álvaro, a new friend, stops by to take us to a fiesta at a communal ranch outside of town. A thoughtful, delicate man with limpid brown eyes and a gray mustache, Álvaro grew up in the California lettuce fields and worked with César Chávez's farmworkers movement before coming to Mexico to teach printmaking at the Bellas Artes.

A few miles above town we turn onto a dirt road and pass

through a low open gate. Álvaro parks in a clearing beside a barn. Stepping out, I smell hay, animal feces. Horses are tethered to the barn, pigs and chickens roam free. Short, brown men mill about in clean cowboy outfits, women in bright dresses. A boy shoots off flares in the clearing, summoning people from the surrounding ranches. There is an open fire and a table with beer and tamales.

People arrive, greeting each with quiet gentility and the soft handshake Mexican men use. "The fiesta will go all night," Álvaro says. "This has nothing to do with the national celebrations. It's about the harvest. Most of these guys go to Texas or California twice a year to work, then come home for spring planting and fall harvest."

"How do they cross the border so easily?" Masako asks.

"It's not easy. They pay a *coyote,* a smuggler, two or three hundred dollars. The *coyote* will try three times to get you across. If you don't make it you're out of luck. Even when you do, you often get caught and sent back, or beaten or jailed. Some die."

"But they have land here. Why go?"

"These are *ejidos,* small plots given out to peasant farmers after the 1910–1920 revolution broke up the big land holdings. It's below subsistence. Small farmers still can't get loans or decent machinery. So they make the trip. They're branded criminals for entering the States illegally, even though the American bosses welcome the cheap labor."

The campesinos talk softly among themselves beside the barn. I visit their country by choice; they visit mine because they have to. Here in Mexico I come to know the places that fill their dreams when they're lying in a Texas bunkhouse, washing dishes in Chicago, bending over a hot central California strawberry field; the families they long for on the other end of the phone line in a larga distancia office.

On a wooden platform stage built against the back of the barn, young men and women begin a slow, circling dance to their own singing accompaniment. There are no instruments. The dancers repeat the lines of the song again and again, moving in the same shuffling circle. The singing is out of time, the dancing awkward; this is not the Ballet Folklórico. Yet everyone seems to know what to do. The near-tuneless, six-line Spanish ditty is oddly haunting, entering my head and lodging there. Something about corn and the moon, but so encoded in idiom I can't sort it out. Neither can Álvaro. It appears neither glad nor sad, this song, but empty of readable emotion entirely. The performers' expressions are blank, deadpan, as are the gathering audience's. When the performance stops or peters out from time to time, there is no applause or recognition. Yet Álvaro assures me this is a festival celebrating the corn harvest and everyone is happy.

I think of D. H. Lawrence's troubling description of Indian dancers at Lake Chapala, tamping the earth again and again, and his charge that the people had no developed consciousness and lacked the spark of reason. Mexico had overwhelmed the fussy, neurasthenic Lawrence, who deified the primordial but was terrified by the slightest encounter with it. In Mexico City he fled the bullfights in horror. He accused serene Indian babies of being flat-eyed and dull. Huxley's Mexican writings read similarly, as do Graham Greene's: full of distaste for the heat and dirt and dust, the untamed sights, smells, and customs. Paul Bowles discerned in pre-Hispanic life the same maw of emptiness he finds in the Maghrebi deserts. Strange, the judgments of these western writers about a people who've constructed ornate languages, vast cities, systems of mathematics and astronomy; who can be so graceful and sensitive in their human relations; whose extravagant, ironical arts speak volumes about existence. Cartesian "reason" is confounded by what it finds here. Watching the ritual dance, I think how gringo commentators fail to grasp what Pascal surely meant when he said, "The heart has its reasons that reason does not know."

The celebrants carry on the tireless dance, undisturbed by sprinkles of rain that drive us under a pepper tree, a *pirul*. It will go like this until dawn, Álvaro says, only drunker. Finally we climb back in the Ford truck and leave the ejido ranch.

Back in town, Álvaro pulls up on Calle Insurgentes before a makeshift stand outside the Oratorio church where an aproned woman ladles hot corn atole drink from a metal pot into ceramic cups, hands us steamed chicken tamales on a paper plate.

At nine-thirty the next morning we meet Janet and Richard at their hotel. They'd arrived the night before in the American Express van from Mexico City. Walking them into town for breakfast, I notice how enraptured Janet is by the bright morning, the old buildings, the fountains. Richard seems wary. As Masako and Janet walk on ahead, he leans close.

"Digestively speaking," he says, "I'm, frankly, sensitive. So's Janet." I happen to know she has a cast-iron stomach. "Water, for instance. What do you advise?"

"Bottled water. And stick to the tourist restaurants."

"Good. I brought a suitcase full of Evian. We brushed our teeth with it this morning. And one doesn't order the ice, I know."

"Probably wise, Richard."

After consulting various New York physicians, Richard has brought along a private pharmacopoeia worthy of a trip to remotest Borneo. It's easy to laugh; yet I think of Paul, who remains mysteriously ill from something we can only assume he contracted here eating or drinking.

"Kidnapping, rapes, murders," Richard says.

"What?" I say, looking around.

"It's all we read about. How bad is it really?"

"I think you can feel safe in San Miguel. Most of Mexico, for that matter."

At breakfast in La Mama's courtyard, among dappled light and birdsong, Janet feasts on *huevos rancheros* while Richard spills pills from vials into his palm. Masako and I trade glances: it's shaping up to be a long couple of days.

Richard, eager to start touring around, has already inquired about a driver at the hotel. We advise a day walking the town first to acclimate, reminding him that we're over a mile high. Well, then, what is there to see? he wants to know. I find it hard to answer. No Parthenon, no Louvre here. Richard is strung tight as a wire.

"Did you get some rest?" Masako asks.

"Hardly, with the fireworks at dawn," Richard says. "Don't they have laws?"

I explain that the patriotic holidays have begun. "It's like our Fourth of July. Or July fourteenth in France. San Miguel is one of the old historical towns."

That's possibly interesting, Richard concedes.

After breakfast we walk up to the plaza and find a seat on the benches facing the church. The sky frames the Parroquia's spires, casting its faceted surfaces into shadow. Pigeons flutter down from the bell towers to the forecourt to troll for crumbs.

"It's restful just to sit," Janet says. "We've been going like maniacs. Everything seems so vivid here, heightened. . . ."

Richard spots the truck unloading newspapers onto the street. I walk him over to buy a copy of the *Mexico City News,* the English-language daily, from Rogelio, who sells them right off the pile. After a glance at the headlines to reassure himself that he hasn't fallen off the edge of the earth, Richard stuffs the paper in his pocket. With his salt-and-pepper beard, tweed jacket, and fussy ways, Richard seems old, though he's younger than I am.

We head down Cuña de Allende, the street beside the church, passing La Fragua Bar where we'd celebrated Elenita's birthday, then the Posada Carmina with its towering, vine-latticed red walls and curling balconies. We march our guests through the Hotel Taboada lobby and up the stairs to the roof, which affords a rare view of the town. Every block of San Miguel, I realize, is textured with private associations to me now. Are these affinities communicable? Objectified through Richard's impatient, critical eyes, the place suddenly seems flimsy, without compelling attraction.

We drift down Calle Sollano toward the French Park. Willowy, athletic Janet delights in everything her eye falls upon. Richard, picking his way among the cobbles, pauses to consider the old buildings with their odd, extravagant doors.

"How do you get around without a car?" he asks.

"Like this. There are taxis, buses. Or friends give you rides. After California it's a relief not to drive." I'm not about to tell Richard other reasons I don't enjoy driving in Mexico: old unsafe cars, two-lane roads traveled by speeding buses and trucks, predatory cops.

In the French Park, kids shoot hoops on the asphalt court, a tai chi practitioner parts the air like water. Banks of pink lilies spread down to the slightly malodorous stream. By the outdoor public wash area where women come to scrub their clothes, Richard asks, "What interested the Spaniards in this region?"

"Silver. Over a quarter of the world's supply was mined around here." We climb slowly up to the Chorro, the old waterworks. At the top we turn and look back over the trees. "You'll see when we visit Guanajuato. Over there, beyond those mountains."

Idling back toward the town center, we pause by old walls, peer into courtyards, linger by fountains. The jerky, demanding quality of time we'd started out with untangles into a more human shape. In Carlos and Elenita's folk art store we wonder at a beautiful *quechquémitl* cape woven in Chiapas. Richard takes interest in a Huichol yarn painting showing the cycle of the seasons, and a riotous ceramic tableau of a truckload of skeletons. Janet tries on a Guatemalan blouse. Roaming the grand Bellas Artes building, once part of the nunnery, Richard becomes curious about an unfinished mural by Siqueiros.

We head for the market to gather ingredients for a lunch at our place. At El Infierno we select a barbecued chicken hot off the spit, then after promising Richard extreme acts of purification before ingestion, we select vegetables and fruits in the indoor market. Janet buys so many tuberoses, red roses, and irises that we buy her a plaid plastic bolsa of her own to carry them in. "In New York, a single rose would cost more than this entire bouquet," she says.

We lug our bolsas to Lucha Contreras's pharmacy to buy disinfectant drops. Anxiously Richard pores over a *Physician's Desk Reference,* trying to find Mexican names for American drugs. He wants a list of local doctors in case he and Janet get ill or need more prescriptions. Most drugs are sold over the counter here, I tell him. In fact he could get a vitamin or flu shot in the back of Lucha's pharmacy. He's horrified.

"Without a doctor? What about infection?"

I start to tell him they use disposable plastic syringes, then think: What's the use?

At the hotel we immerse the vegetables and fruits in a bowl of water treated with disinfectant. Richard watches intently. Over lunch, Janet talks effusively of our morning walk and new places she'd like to see. Richard struggles mightily to get a verbal fix on San Miguel—"I mean it's a bit like an Italian hill town. But then not. Southern Spain. Granada, say. Completely charming. Goes back to the Moorish . . ."—until finally he talks himself into silence, and there is only the sound of doves cooing in the stone walls, the clinking of silverware, the occasional bell from the nunnery. Sparkling fruit, mint tea, the afternoon's languor.

"Delicious," I think I hear Richard murmur.

We walk them back to their hotel for siesta, arrange to meet for dinner.

The Nissan van bursts out of an underground tunnel into bright midday light. We pile out into Guanajuato's Jardín Unión, with its stately Indian laurel trees and kiosks. Posters advertise the yearly Festival Cervantino beginning in a few weeks: theater troupes, string quartets, and dancers will come from all over the world. We guide Janet and Richard through the dense, moody streets, the steep lanes that curve suddenly upward then come to dead ends, the cloistered alleyways that spread into little flower-filled squares called *plazuelas.* Dense, cultivated, mysterious, tucked in its narrow valley cleft, Guanajuato has all the chiaroscuro drama and interiority of a walk through an Arab medina.

We walk up the wide steps of the Teatro Juárez opera house. A velvet rope leads us through an ornate art nouveau lobby into the hushed, deserted theater. A colossal curtain of plush red velvet falls to a hardwood stage floor. Soaring balconies overhang a sloping ocean of bright painted wood seats, silver and gilt filigree, brass fittings imported from France, Italy, Germany.

"It's like being inside a little music box," Janet says breathlessly.

"Such extravagance, in these remote mountains," muses Richard.

"The dictator Porfirio Díaz commissioned it at the turn of the century," I say.

"They tried turning it into a movie theater in the 1960s," Masako says, "but dirty jeans and popcorn and *chicharrones* were ruining the velvet seats."

Back outside, billowy clouds, dark at the center, prefigure afternoon rains. We climb twisting paths among stacked, brightly colored houses. In the narrow, four-story house where Diego Rivera was born (only recently opened as a museum: for decades the painter was disowned by the conservative town for having been a communist), we take in a small collection of his early work. I imagine the gargantuan painter literally bursting out of the little house, the provincial city, into the larger world.

We eat lunch at El Retiro, a restaurant up from the opera house with an invariably good, fixed-price *comida corrida*.

"I can see why you like it here," Janet says over dessert.

"What do you see?" I ask.

She laughs. "This bite of flan. Here, in this place." She looks across at Richard.

Richard puts his teacup down, a wild shine in his eyes. "Okay, I admit it. It's great. What's the catch?"

We all burst out laughing—even Richard.

**B**y the time we get back to San Miguel, the town is a madhouse. Horns honking, traffic is at a standstill. Most stores are already closed. *"Viva México!"* echoes off the walls and through the cantina doors. Climbing out of the van, we're drawn into the hotel bar by a group of celebrants from Mexico City. To resist is out of the question on this of all days. Tequilas are proffered, toasts raised, backs slapped. Richard tipples José Cuervos with the flush-faced, grinning *chilangos.* We leave Janet and Richard with their new friends, agree to meet later in the jardín for the chanting of the *grito.*

Working our way through the crowds on Calle Correo, Masako says, "You were a little like that."

"Like what?" I shout.

"Like Richard. Before we left L.A."

"Thanks a lot."

"How nice that you don't remember."

Back at the Ambos Mundos, we close the hotel curtains against the noisy revelers in nearby rooms. Our suitcases lie open on the floor. What to take on our trip? Europe seems unimaginably distant.

Just after nine we work our way back to the jardín. The crowd has become a surging, shoulder-to-shoulder mass. From the second-floor window of the Allende house, above the white statue of the brave Colonel in his cape, the words of Mexico's President Miguel de la Madrid—formal, lugubrious, carefully enunciated—spit from a loudspeaker, live from the balcony of the Presidential Palace in Mexico City. One by one he announces the names of Mexico's heroes, each answered by thunderous response in Mexico City's great square, and here in our little plaza. *"Viva Hidalgo! Viva Allende! Viva México! Viva! Viva! Viva!"*

We raise our fists and shout along with everyone else: *"Viva! Viva!"*

Feeling a hand on my shoulder, I turn around. It's Janet, looking dazed, worried.

"Where's Richard?"

"I don't know. He kept drinking with those Mexicans, then they wandered off somewhere."

"I'm sure he's fine," Masako says. "How far can he go?"

Pinned in place, we can't possibly go looking for Richard in any event until the *"Vivas"* abate. Our mayor appears on the balcony of the Allende house and launches into a fulminating, overlong speech until finally the noise of the crowd drowns him out.

Slowly people disperse into restaurants and cantinas, houses and cars. We stand worriedly in the jardín, uncertain where to begin looking for Richard.

"Look," Masako says.

Richard comes lurching up Calle Umarán, a Mexican flag in one hand, a plastic cup in the other. His jacket is off, and there's a bandage on his left temple. Janet rushes to meet him, with us in tow.

"Richard, what happened?"

He slumps onto a bench. Janet tries to dab at the bandage but he waves her away. "They took me to a cantina," he says woozily, his chest heaving. "Afterward I fell down on the street." He points to his bandaged head. "Everybody stopped to help. They took me to a doctor—all of them. They patched me up for free, then helped me back to the hotel." He starts to sob into his hands. "As if they *cared.*"

Janet rubs his shoulder, looks helplessly at us.

We walk them back to their hotel, Richard singing snatches of a double-entendre song his Mexican friends taught him, and leave them at the entrance.

Walking back through town, Masako says, "We should have thought of tequila earlier."

The next morning we arrive at their hotel to see them off. Janet emerges trailed by Richard, doubled over with a hangover and a galloping case of turista.

"Oh, no," Masako whispers.

"Montezuma's revenge!" Richard exclaims, hugging us each good-bye. "Worth every miserable, dribbling bit of it!"

Janet says her good-byes and thanks us.

*Adiós*, Richard. *Adiós*, Janet.

They wave out the back window as the van bounces off down the cobbles.


In the open entry of the Church of Santa Ana, on Calle Insurgentes next to the library, a lurid, bleeding, purple-robed Jesus greets passersby. Townsfolk always cross themselves and kiss their fingers when they pass. Humble by comparison to its neighbor churches, Santa Ana is a simple building with no niches or side chapels along its straight walls, no reliquary of particular value or art that would draw a price. Still there's something vibrant and welcoming about its mix of Catholic morbidity and pre-Hispanic playfulness. After picking up a gift for my daughter in the covered market, Masako and I veer into Santa Ana on the way back to the hotel.

It's cool and quiet inside, near empty. An old woman, her head covered in a rebozo, murmurs prayers up front. A caretaker on a ladder is changing a display. Birds chirp outside. We take a seat in back.

In Mexico, where the invisible counts for so much,

Masako and I, refugees from the techno-future, sometimes seem to gain glimpses of a wordless, sacral world. We don't understand it but feel its resonances continually, wending through Mexican Catholicism but not remotely contained by it. Maybe, as Carlos Fuentes has suggested: "In the land of need that is Mexico . . . the impossible distance between desire and the thing desired has given both yearning and object an incandescent purity."

"What were you thinking?" I ask Masako as we stand to leave.

"Just a wish for a good journey and a quick return."

# Chapter 6

# *El Temblor*

IT'S EARLY MORNING, BEFORE MEXICO
City awakens to the tumult of the day and
traffic tangles the streets. There's little at
dawn for the thieves who nip at the city to
steal, and the lung-flaying smog is still at
bay. Leaving the Hotel Guardiola, I catch a
glimpse of the volcano Popocatépetl—
white-tipped, eternal, like Fuji. A dawn
wind has cleared the basin, affording a rare
sight of the mountains ringing the city,
where from a pass in 1521 Cortés and his
conquistadores first saw floating, canal-
veined, resplendent Tenochtitlán. *Mexicas,*
the half million residents called themselves.

In Café El Popular, a block off Mexico
City's central square, the Zócalo, it's not
early but late for most customers: night-shift
laborers, bleary insomniacs, off-duty cops,
chattering hookers in flaming red mini-

dresses sipping *café con leche* after a night's work. A rotund, beehived waitress who might have once fit into those slinky, frayed red dresses slides a platter of fresh *pan dulce*, sweet pastries, before me, then pours steaming coffee and milk from separate pitchers to the consistency I choose. One more day in the city before we leave—a pleasurable prospect in spite of the headache-inducing pall that has settled into my brain and behind my eyes. The Imeca reading, the city's pollution meter, has exceeded 200 the last few days, begetting news reports of birds falling out of the sky, asthmatics slumping on the pavement as if felled by snipers. Twenty million inhabitants, unofficially—a paradigm of urban disaster—yet the city teems with art, archaeology, culture, life.

Outside on Calle Cinco de Mayo, a khaki-clad organ grinder emits a broken-winged Viennese waltz, his instrument's innards half gone. His shill edges up El Popular's narrow aisles, his sweaty head bent in a permanent, abject *gracias*. Pesos shower his upturned hat. They pay to chase him away, I think. Mexicans are afflicted with charity, the curse of a brimming heart. A man who spends his day blatantly raking money from the public till lavishes it on his church or a neighborhood fiesta. A drug dealer responsible for untold deaths lavishly outfits his town's soccer team. Money moves along different channels here. Beggars along the *calles* tend to be young Indian mothers, old, poor women, blind people. Anyone less afflicted is expected at least to bang a tambourine, respirate an accordion, whack a tuneless guitar to proffer the hand or the cup. *God will reward you*, they whisper back.

The waitress replenishes my coffee, deducing how many pastries I've eaten (two) by how many remain on my tray. I could have ordered *huevos rancheros* (eggs on tortillas with tomato sauce) or *huevos divorciados* (two sunny-side up with green sauce on one side, red on the other), but today the thickness of the air will make me feel I've already eaten, drunk, and smoked too much.

Two daily papers, the English language *Mexico City News* and *La Jornada*, sit before me. I buy the Spanish one because a Japanese friend of mine learned English reading newspapers, and I've taken up the habit for my Spanish. The problem is that the stories seldom coincide. The *News*, a mélange of U.S. wire service stories, government press releases, and astrology charts, could be reporting a different day entirely than *La Jornada*, a Mexican daily of leftist intellectual commentary, fulminations over U.S. imperial antics, and rants at Mexican governmental impunity. A good dozen dailies represent all sides of the Mexican political spectrum, whereas in the States, a single homogenized "news" prevails. But things are not all they seem: the government, it turns out, subsidizes every Mexican daily. Paternalism: the politics of inclusion.

Two days ago when we arrived here by bus, our taxi driver at the north terminal was so upset at having gotten a fare to the city center at rush hour that he took a tire iron out and banged on his trunk in rage. Welcome to our city. Docilely we got in his cab anyway. Around the corner he picked up a woman who, by the evidence of shoes, blankets, makeup, and food on the cab floor, lives with him in the taxi. By the time we'd passed through the shanty neighborhoods leading downtown, this temperamental taxista, belly bursting from his shirt, was laughing and talking as if we were the best of friends. My city's *jodido*, fucked, he said, pointing to the red, green, and white flags and decorations still up in the Zócalo from the fiestas patrias. Our government is a sack of *mierda*. You guys are always screwing us.

And you know what?—pounding his chest, tears welling—I am proud to be Mexican. We have *la virgen,* Hidalgo, Juárez. A warm handshake, a gracias for the tip he didn't even look at but handed to his woman. *Que le vaya bien,* he says, wishing us well.

It's a crazy city, its barely concealed madness erupting in strange ways.

I ask the waitress for the *cuenta* (in Mexico as in Europe, they never bring the check until you call for it), pay for my coffee and pastry, and step up to the street.

While Masako spends the morning feasting on the city's *mercados,* I'll explore downtown. Along Calle Isabel la Católica, the light is bright, the traffic thickening. Sweepers brush the sidewalks with flanged twig brooms. The morning dailies shout from kiosks. Barefoot Indian women from the South nurse babies against the chipped cornices of the once-grand colonial buildings. At the Tacuba metro station, sellers on blankets hawk combs, wallets, cassettes, gum, hair dryers. The subways, designed by the French and built during the oil boom years of the seventies, quickly began to crumble soon after the French engineers left: blown tires, sudden stops in the tunnels, power outages. Mexican workers and officials were patching old tires instead of replacing them, using recycled engine oil, pocketing money earmarked for spare parts. The French technicians had to be called back—a scandal even Mexicans laugh at.

Mexico's contemporary identity seems unformed at times, half in shadow, as if constrained by a past that paradoxically feeds it—leaving Mexicans inwardly rich, functionally vague. Their revolutions, more symbol than substance, failed to bind society in a meaningful civil contract. Police and army are seen as predators, not protectors, the government as corrupt custodian of privilege. Twenty million people need work. Fifteen million are hungry in a country of ninety million with rich farmlands, abundant natural resources. Milk and even corn, that most indigenous of staples, has to be supplemented by imports. The Catholic Church, officially illegal since the Revolution—it can't own property, and priests and nuns can't wear their habits outside church precincts—unites Mexicans more than the state.

From the rooftop of the Hotel Majestic, I look down upon the sprawling Zócalo square, locus of the nation. Three massive complexes lie exposed, like layered striations at a geologic dig, encoding whatever it is that makes Mexicans Mexican. The National Palace runs practically the entire east length of the vast square: if you include Montezuma's palace, built in 1502, it's the oldest seat of government in the hemisphere. To my left, the Gothic spires of the Cathedral of Mexico, Latin America's first and largest, loom darkly. Behind it crouches the monumental site where in 1978 Mexico's past suddenly erupted into the present: workers digging underground for the light and power company came upon a huge Aztec votive stone sculpture, a circle measuring ten feet across depicting the moon goddess Coyolxauhqui. Later they unearthed the enormous pyramid of Huitzilopochtli itself—the Templo Mayor, ceremonial center of old Tenochtitlán: heart of the Aztec kingdom. This sudden eruption of Mexico's buried unconscious into modern time produced excitement, guilt, activity.

Aztec, Spanish, Catholic. Pre-Hispanic, civil, religious. A triple cosmology, founded upon the sun god and human sacrifice, rape and conquest, Christianity and the Napoleonic Code. No wonder being Mexican is complicated.

The sun's rays bleach the tips of the buildings. The first stinging air settles behind my eyes. I take the Hotel Majestic elevator down to the square and cross the Zócalo among families and pigeons and photographers. Passing through the National Palace's immense portals, I turn left and come quickly to a vast mural beginning at the bottom of the main staircase and running the entire north wall of the first-floor corridor. Uniformed school kids ponder Diego Rivera's ambitious visual history of Mexico: a fecund pre-Hispanic society; "la Malinche," the Indian woman who gave herself to Cortés or was taken; the brutal colonization and conversion; the violent overthrow of Spanish rule; the 1910 revolution's attempt to redistribute wealth—and Rivera's projected finale, a Leninist utopia. What messages of identity do the kids extract? An inset panel lists crops indigenous to Mexico: corn, squash, chocolate, tomato, potato, *cacao* (coffee), *chicle* (gum), tobacco.

Yesterday Masako and I spent hours in the city's vast, thrilling Museum of Anthropology among gold statuary, Toltec clay figures, obsidian-glaze ceramics, and funerary masks. Finally, feeling a need to resurface into our own century, we caught a taxi to Frida Kahlo's house in Coyoacán, a suburb of poplar-lined streets, and slipped behind its walls of *azul añil* (a vivid blue said to ward off evil spirits) to savor the rambling spaces and Frida's folk art collection.

"We could live like this," Masako said.

"We do, sort of," I said. "In the Ambos Mundos."

"A house, I mean."

I cross the Zócalo north to the old cathedral. Tradesmen squat out front with cardboard signs advertising their services. Vendors of holy images cluster at the great church doors. Inside, it's dark and somber, built to inspire awe not affection. Metal scaffolding shores up a collapsing apse, the shifting foundation sinking further into the old lake bed. In the subterranean marble crypts beneath the main chapel, it occurs to me that where I'm standing used to be under water.

Back outside, I walk a few hundred yards east, pausing to examine a maquette of old Tenochtitlán, its canals and boulevards all feeding to the great pyramidal center. Nearby, barefoot Indians in Aztec garb stomp the stones, ankle shells hissing, headdresses flashing. Behind them loom the excavated ruins, a city block square: the Templo Mayor.

Both sacred site and marketplace, it once contained more than seventy temples, schools, and related buildings. Entering the excavation, I walk past serpent statues, glyphs, a stone wall of skulls lying against a pyramid step. Over a hundred offerings have been found here, including an Olmec mask dating from before Christ. Pre-Hispanic arrowheads and pottery shards are unearthed daily all over Mexico by farmers ploughing fields; but the Templo Mayor is an unparalleled find. I try to envision the original bright ochers and cerulean blues covering the dark, forbidding stone.

Mexico's layered history is a well of time. Impossible to imagine an ancient pyramid sleeping beneath Times Square, downtown San Francisco, the White House. We've obliterated pre-European realities, truncating continuity with land and memory of what went before, imprisoning ourselves in a fretful, unreadable present.

I cross back across the Zócalo, reenter the shaded *calles* where my morning began. At the Bar Opera, I sip fruit juice at the old-fashioned mirrored bar beneath gold filigree cornices, gaze at the bullet holes in the wall dating back to the revolution. The heretical Mexican anthropologist Alexander von Wuthenau postulated that numerous oceanic migrations preceded the Europeans' arrival here: that those broad-faced, thick-lipped Olmec statues along the Veracruz coast are in fact African, that many South American "Indians" are Polynesian. Early Chinese anchors have been found in Acapulco harbor, communities of black Mexicans live in southern Mexico. Eighty different Indian tribes still exist here, each with its own language. I've met Asian-Mexicans, Lebanese-Mexicans, Jewish-Mexicans, German-Mexicans. I begin to see the Americas, from the Arctic Circle to Tierra del Fuego, as fathomlessly rich *terra incognita*, and living in Mexico as the filling out of my American self.

In the cool sanctum of La Profesa church, a wedding is in progress, the priest dressed in rich vestments, the wedding party in tailored Armani dresses and suits, Ray-Bans, jewelry. At a side chapel, as if in a parallel universe, humbly dressed petitioners kneel before a glassed-in statue of the Virgin Mary drenched in *milagros*, the little gold and silver votive charms Masako has lately taken to using in her art.

Back out on the bright street, I practically bump into her, bearing booty from the markets. Delighted to have come upon each other by chance, we head off for lunch at La Casa de Los Azulejos, the House of Tiles.

In the tile-encrusted restaurant, Masako is trying to spot some political insiders of the sort she's been reading about in Carlos Fuentes's mystery novel *Hydra Head;* allegedly they breakfast here. A cluster of cronies in a cloud of blue cigarette smoke looks plausible, we decide. Masako begins revealing her morning's yield. She found a store behind the old cathedral that sells milagros by the kilo: arms, lungs, cars, cows, hearts—every imaginable object that one might offer to be blessed, either for relief from an affliction or thanks for its easing. At a folk art store she came upon a ceramic tableau of a skeleton mother giving birth to a skeleton baby with the aid of a skeleton doctor. Riotous, bizarre.

Masako lives in a vibrant world of things, objects, artifacts. Child of importers of folk art from Japan, she traveled around the world at nineteen for two years squatting in bazaars, bargaining in unknown tongues. If my idea of a good morning is gazing into the middle distance, pen in hand, at a café table, hers is excavating treasures from a pile of discarded garments on a seller's blanket at Lagunilla, Merced, Sonora, or Tepito market. Only in India, she says, has she seen such fertile living arts. From a bag she lifts a beribboned woven *huipil* blouse from Oaxaca, a wool cape from Chiapas, a painted wooden noisemaker decorated with lottery cards.

Where will we put these things? We have no home anymore, only a couple of hotel rooms and an L.A. storage unit stuffed to its corrugated metal ribs. In the morning we leave for London. How to get this stuff back to San Miguel? Masako, unfazed, says she's arranged with the desk clerk at the Guardiola to store it until we get back.

We drag her purchases across Avenida Madero to the hotel. Taking the elevator to our room, we realize we haven't yet booked rooms for our families, whom we've invited to Mexico for Thanksgiving. We plan to put them up in the city overnight before whisking them on to San Miguel. We'd discarded the Guardiola, as its faint poetics would undoubtedly be lost on them: in 1929 Diego Rivera concluded a deal in its former coffee shop, the Lady Baltimore, to paint a mural in Cortés's old house in Cuernavaca for a then-unheard of twelve thousand dollars; in 1937 the writer Jane Bowles, after having disappeared for three days, turned up here to the great relief of her new husband, writer and composer Paul. We've rejected the nearby Monte Carlo, where Lawrence stayed, as far too funky; the Majestic on the Zócalo too noisy; the Isabel too bohemian; the once-posh Ritz too run-down.

Instead we walk a block north to the Del Prado, a commodious, fifties-style hotel across from Alameda Park and within sight of the Palacio de Bellas Artes, nexus of the city's cultural life. Entering the broad hotel lobby, we pass Rivera's mural *Sunday Afternoon in Alameda Park,* more illustration than work of art, with its cast of contemporaneous characters: the ubiquitous Frida, Diego as a boy in shorts holding a balloon, various forgotten political figures, all standing in the park opposite. We book rooms for late November, then head for the block-long art nouveau central post office to mail postcards.

T he next morning at seven we're out on Calle Madero flagging down a taxi. We've been advised to get to the airport early, as the peso is falling hourly and our ticket prices might be revised upward, taking extra time. The streets leading away from downtown are clear, and in twenty minutes we're at the Benito Juárez Airport. Our fare price holds and check-in goes quickly, leaving us time for breakfast.

The restaurant is midway down the long terminal, reached by way of a public exhibition space that—amazing to me, if typical of Mexico—shows the work of major artists right in the middle of the airport. We study a haunting set of etchings by the Oaxacan artist Francisco Toledo—mythological turtles, rabbits, shamans—then haul our carry-on bags up stairs into an American-style coffee shop. A hostess seats us along the back wall in a pink leatherette booth beneath floral-patterned stained-glass windows and hands us laminated menus.

Soon after coffee arrives, it begins sloshing on the table. I grip my cup, but it's the table that's weaving. I look at Masako. Crooked Mexican table. Let's call the waiter, have him slip a matchbook or a shim under it.

No, the entire room is undulating. *Earthquake.*

I look up at the stained-glass windows. "If they crack, slide under the table."

We're from California; earthquakes don't intimidate us. There, they tend to be short, and jiggle like a camera shaking. This one is long and heaving, like being in a tiny skiff in the backwash of a ship—a bilious rocking that doesn't stop. I hear stucco, cement, and steel shifting behind the walls.

The lights go out, leaving only the cathode screens of the arrivals/departures monitors glowing eerily off some generator. A woman in another booth giggles improbably. We clutch the table, prepare to slide under. This quake won't stop. Only yesterday morning in the Zócalo I'd gazed at the maquette of old Tenochtitlán's canals and floating gardens. Now contemporary Mexico City is pitching like a drunk on the lake it was built on.

At last, the shaking stops. The room settles for a moment. Then an aftershock pitches us drunkenly sideways. Pieces of plaster hit the table. Stillness again.

The lights seep back on. Nervous conversation breaks out. I look up at the pink stucco wall, mapped with small cracks, wide ones where it meets the ceiling. In the next minutes I hear three new Spanish words: *temblor, terremoto, sismo.* They all mean the same thing.

A waiter gamely brings coffee refills, but customers are hastily rising to leave. We join them, pay for our coffee, and hurry out of the low-ceilinged restaurant.

In the terminal corridor, people walk dazedly past, their visages drained. Long cracks vein the soaring pink walls. We clear passport control and head for the waiting area, having no idea what to expect; but the idea of getting up in the air and off the earth appeals. An airline employee announces in Spanish that our departure will be delayed—something about checking for broken fuel lines. We sit as far as possible away from the long windowpanes facing the runway, waiting. Small aftershocks ripple through the airport; they feel like riding a bus over rough road. An hour later the call to board comes.

As the plane rises aloft, the pilot announces we'll be making an unscheduled stop in Tampa to take on extra fuel. From a window seat as the plane circles the city, I look out and see billowing reddish dust covering the metropolis like a shroud.

"That's the worst smog I've ever seen," I say.

It isn't until we're changing planes at Dulles that we see the first headline: KILLER 8.1 QUAKE HITS MEXICO.

That wasn't smog over Mexico City but the roiling red smoke of apocalypse.

A t Heathrow, waiting for baggage, we read the first accounts. The quake hit at 7:50 A.M., its epicenter somewhere southwest of Mexico City. The capital has suffered severe damage: deaths, injuries, hundreds of people missing, scores of buildings destroyed. Crews digging in the rubble, rescue teams flying in from the United States, Japan. Aftershocks continue, some almost as strong as the original quake. Entire sections of Mexico City have been leveled, the downtown area around the Zócalo hit the worst. The American ambassador, flying over the scene, has estimated 10,000 dead.

Leaving the airport we glimpse another headline: MEXICO DESTROYED. A photo shows downtown Alameda Park, and a pile of rubble where the Hotel Regis, home to retired theater folk, had stood. All residents presumed dead, the caption says. We'd passed it only the afternoon before, had coffee in the old café next door. Now it's a crater in the ground. In the cab into London, Masako says, "We'd better call our parents. They probably think we're dead."

What remains of Mexico City? Is the Guardiola still standing? The Bellas Artes? The depth of our worry surprises us: "our" country suffers. Has San Miguel been hit? Sick at heart, we try to call but all lines into Mexico are down. We reach our families in California: indeed they'd feared the worst.

In days to follow we track the devastation in the European papers. The quake's epicenter had been 230 miles southwest of Mexico City, damaging Acapulco and other areas as well. Aftershocks as high as 7.3 continue to shake the country. Over 100,000 people homeless, countless numbers injured. Football stadiums are turned into morgues (unnerving echoes of Chile's political temblor a few years earlier). Editors and publishers, gallery and museum people we visit, all want to know about the Mexican tragedy. Information is scarce. Confusion between the word "Mexico" and "Mexico City" gradually clears up: no, the whole country hasn't been destroyed, not even the entire city. Mexican officials castigate the American ambassador for overestimating the number of dead—though the number fast approaches his figure.

For days, survivors are found among the ruins. A baby dug up alive six days after the quake is deemed a miracle. In the papers and on television we see images of ruined buildings, grief-stricken relatives, rescue teams around the Zócalo and Alameda. We read stories of heroism, people who dig in the ruins for days at great risk for no recompense.

On the day we arrive in Paris, the front page of the *International Herald Tribune* runs a photo of the cracked façade of the Hotel Del Prado, where we'd booked rooms for our parents. Its windows are shattered, boarded shut. We wonder if Café El Popular is still standing, La Profesa church, the Bar Opera. Our whole trip is haunted by news of *el temblor.*

Two weeks after the quake we fly back to Mexico on the emptiest plane I've ever taken: a dozen passengers at most, mainly Red Cross workers. As the plane flattens onto the Benito Juárez Airport runway, we wonder what we'll find.

In the airport building, masons on tall scaffolding spackle rifts in the walls. The restaurant where we'd endured the quake is cordoned off for repairs. From the window of the taxi taking us downtown, we look out at gutted buildings, slumped houses with only chimneys left standing, metal beams dangling from structures like cracked branches. The closer to the center, the worse it gets. The taxi driver tells us a whole apartment building had come down in Tlatelolco Plaza, leaving the surviving residents homeless, the government deaf to their pleas, the corrupt contractors who built with cheap materials and violated codes disclaiming responsibility. A few blocks from the Zócalo we see an indelible image of futility: a lone worker atop a ruined skyscraper, swinging a pickax. How many years, at that rate, to demolish it?

The driver lets us off in front of the Hotel Guardiola, where we'd awakened the morning of the quake, and where Masako had stored her treasures. Wide cracks zigzag down the stone facade. The entrance is boarded up. Dazedly we walk around the side into the San Francisco church forecourt, stepping among piles of cement and masonry. Jagged fissures stab the crumpled window jambs of the fourth-floor room where we'd stayed, its panes blown out.

"If we hadn't left early to change our tickets . . ." Masako says somberly.

The Alameda looks like a bomb has hit it. Buildings lie slumped like sandbags, leaving views of the block behind; in others, upper floors have collapsed into lower ones as if someone had smashed a fist down on a cake. Clouds of dust rise from the fallen Hotel Regis, as rescue crews shift debris and heavy machinery cuts into the ruins. In front of the Hotel Del Prado, a work crew is bearing the damaged section of wall with Diego Rivera's lobby mural *Sunday Afternoon in Alameda Park* out into the very park it illustrates—a surreal sight the painter would have noted.

We drag our bags to the Hotel Majestic on the Zócalo, whose seventeenth-century stone structure had suffered little damage, and book an interior room for a night. We sleep uneasily in our clothes, leaving shoes, socks, passports, and wallets ready by the door.

The next morning we call Carlos and Elenita in San Miguel.

"Only the chandeliers swayed," Carlos says. "A couple of books fell from the shelves. Mexico City is fucked. Things are okay here."

Elenita gets on the line. "Come home," she says.

# Chapter 7

# Day of the Dead

LATE OCTOBER IN NORTH CENTRAL
Mexico is like a California spring: soft green
hills, bright skies, sharp air. I wear a jacket
mornings, though by eleven I've removed it.
Along San Miguel's *calles,* life feels quick-
ened, sweet: *alegre.* Abandoned by the world
since the quake, Mexico belongs again to its
people.

We've rented a casita on a street called
Quebrada, three blocks below the town center. The Ambos Mundos had become insup-
portable: a drug den, an art installation, a
madhouse. Impossible to work there, and we
work most of the time. While we were
away, a performance artist from Canada had
alighted in one of the courtyard rooms,
intent upon turning the entire hotel into an
art piece: stringing animal parts from tree
limbs, painting weird symbols on rocks and

plants, burying crosses—then photo-documenting the whole thing. Two young Mexican men and an American woman moved into the room beneath us and began dealing drugs in earnest: streams of visitors, all night parties, boom boxes around the pool in the afternoon. Crazy Jeem set fire to the shack of the cleaning woman he'd moved in with, then fled town—after passing through the Ambos Mundos and extorting money from Rafael. It was time to decamp.

*Quebrada* means gorge, or break, hence the arched bridge outside our door spanning steep Calle Canal below. The bridge offers lovely views of the town and is popular with lovers, though our doorway lies at the bottom of a dark stairwell where couples lurk and kids scrawl graffiti. Our casita is part of a large corner property owned by a shadowy American professor from St. Louis with intelligence ties, we're told. The casita, built no doubt for a live-in maid and her family, feels lavish to us after months in a hotel room. The rent is ridiculously low. The retiree who rents the big house lets us use his telephone Sundays to call our families, freeing us from the weekly vigil at the larga distancia office.

A small bedroom, living room, and kitchen lie off a tiny patio separated from the main dwelling by a high wall. Thick glass blocks called *tragaluces* let light through the bedroom ceiling, and a tall leaded-glass window looks out onto the patio. The living room sits in perpetual shade, its wood-shuttered windows facing the subterranean stairwell, more like a London basement flat than sunny San Miguel. A bright, ample kitchen with yellow walls, a big table, and glass doors to the patio redeems the downstairs. In the patio, a stone stairway leads to a roomy rooftop studio I've claimed, as Masako has kept hers at the Ambos Mundos a block away. The view from my doorway runs over the cascading rooftops west to the Guanajuato hills, and on the town side offers an illicit view into the rear garden of the cloister of La Concepción, where I can see the nuns, sleeves rolled up, tending their plants and chickens.

Our suitcases fully unpacked at last, we make trips to market and fill our plaid shopping bags with real provisions. We buy whole chickens at the shop on Calle Mesones run by the wife of the ice cream store owner who changes money. We fire up the oven, roast meat and vegetables, eat at the patio table under the stars. A Mexican red wine called Santo Tomás fills our clear green stemware, hand-blown at the glass factory at the edge of town. We talk of having people over.

Mornings we gaze up through the tragaluces as the light spreads, watching hummingbirds drink from the red trumpet blossoms that climb the patio wall out our window. Folk objects spill across the ledges in the *sala*, books thicken my studio shelves. Fruits, vegetables, and chiles overflow hand-carved wooden bowls in the kitchen. We collect boxes of wax matches called Maya, with an image of the reclining god Chac Mool on the cover, for stove lightings and power outages—and to give to my daughter, who is Maya too, and who smokes. A thin, talkative old lady presents herself at the door one morning, recommended by the maid next door, she claims. We take Felipa on to clean twice a week, wondering if she's strong enough.

Our parents will visit Thanksgiving week as planned, though we'll bring them directly here, skipping quake-blighted Mexico City. The Del Prado where they were to have stayed is slated for demolition, the Guardiola permanently shut. A memorial park will be built on the site where the old Hotel Regis collapsed that awful morning. Experts say it will take years to restore *la capital.*

This morning Masako came back from town bewildered.

Supermercado Sánchez sells a canned tuna in a spicy tomato sauce so original, so tasty that people have been telling friends about it. Quickly it sells out. Reorders have been taking longer and longer. Masako asked Señora Sánchez why it hasn't reappeared on the shelves. She stopped ordering it, she said. But why, when it's so popular? That's just it, Señora Sánchez replied. People are always asking for it. Then we run out. They complain. Too much trouble. *"No vale la pena,"* she says, throwing her hands up. Not worth it. North American dreams of instilling the profit motive here, where people proudly claim they work to live, not live to work, remain so much theory.

Mexico opens to us to the degree that our Spanish advances. I've reached the last third of *Madrigal's Magic Key to Spanish* on my own (Andrew Warhol's simple line illustration of two pipes, *las pipas;* a typewriter, *la máquina de escribir;* and baskets, *las canastas*). I can now speak of things that happened yesterday, though when I do I'm still inclined to attribute something I did to you, and vice versa. As for the Spanish future, it still lies ahead, a distant, shimmering oasis—even though I've discovered I can regularly rely upon *"voy a"* ("I'm going to"), followed by the infinitive, to skirt the problem. Reading in a Mexican newspaper of some government official named Lechuga or Paniagua no longer sends me to the dictionary; I know the first one's name means lettuce, the second bread and water—though Mexicans no more note this than we do someone whose name is Bland, or Whitehead, or Lipman.

In an attempt to step up our Spanish, we arrange for a tutor named Héctor to come and live up to his name three times a week. A chubby, gregarious ex-divinity student and trumpet player in the Sunday night band in the jardín, Héctor prefers teaching us mischievous words for bodily

functions (*pedo, mierda, apestoso*—fart, shit, stinky) and gen-
italia (*culo, pito, chicharrón*—ass, dick, dick) and double en-
tendres to shoring up the verb structure we lack. Yesterday
we spent most of our *lección* discussing the term *"huevos,"*
Mexican for eggs and slang for "balls"—which leads to endless wordplay, jokes, even bloodshed if misused. Héctor delights in pointing out that asking somebody *"Tiene huevos?"*
("Do you have eggs?") invites either derisive laughter or a
fight, while *"Hay huevos?"* ("Are there eggs?") or simply the
singular *"Hay huevo?"* will get you your eggs.

Héctor's hearty laughter is contagious. Mexicans tend to
present a serious demeanor until the least zone of safety is
established; then laughter, wit, and jokes (*chistes, bromas*)
pour forth. This beguiling blend of dignity and wit makes
them generally nice to be around. People who dance with
skeletons and skulls, have a Day of the Locos, and endure an
abysmal government with scornful laughter are de facto ab-
surdists. Yesterday at the lumberyard across from the radio
station I saw a young *carpintero* almost take his thumb off
with a saw: a horrifying, jaw-dropping event. Yet his response and everyone else's was to laugh. In Mexico, you
laugh until the tears take over.

We take our new verbs and idioms out into the town,
speak only Spanish to each other until our minds get tired or
we forget. Some days my Spanish rises to surprising heights.
Yesterday riding back from Guanajuato with Vicente Arias,
the painting teacher who has the studio in the Ambos
Mundos, a burst of lucidity possessed me like a poltergeist.
For an hour and a half I ranged richly in Spanish over Mexican and U.S. sexual habits, extraterrestrial beings, the possible existence of God, the issue of figurative painting's rele-
vance in our time. The verbs flew. When I had no word, I'd
bide time with *"como se dice..."*—"how do you say it..."—
fishing for a Latinate English equivalent that often fits, or

else letting Vicente feed me the word. This morning I woke up exhilarated, eager to speak Spanish all day with anyone on any subject. Then Felipa arrived and asked me—I later figured out—"Where's the broom?" I had no idea what she was talking about. My Spanish collapsed for the rest of the day.

After dinner, realizing we're out of coffee for the morning, I set out across the Quebrada bridge and trudge up the hill to a new local café, La Dolce Vita, whose proprietors— Alberto, a small, cheery, curly-haired man from Naples, and his equally cheery and curly-haired wife, Marisela, from Monterrey—stand proudly before their espresso machine like twin smiling angels. There is a newspaper rack, pastries, gelati, salads, and ground espresso by the kilo to take home. The town has few cafés, and the place has immediately caught on.

Mina and Paul, Elenita and Carlos, and a new friend of ours, Susana, are sitting at a table eating *dolci* and sipping coffee. I join them while I wait for Alberto to grind the Veracruz *expresso molido*. The talk is of religion, with Day of the Dead, November 2, almost upon us.

"I am atheist but I am still Catholic," Carlos says. "Do you know what I mean?"

"Not really," Susana says.

"It's a Mexican thing," Paul says softly.

Liturgy, chanting, Bible stories; ceremony and ritual, sin and salvation; baptism, confirmation, marriage, funeral. Every day of the year consecrated to some saint. You argue with an upbringing like that; you don't escape it.

Carlos seems tense lately. Sometimes I see him in the bars with Mexican friends, drunk and loud. Elenita looks sad, martyred, spends long hours with their young daughter inside the store. Things seem bad between them.

Chat drifts to secular scandals and gossip. A drug smuggler en route to Sinaloa was arrested on the landing strip above town when his Cessna ran short of fuel and had to make an emergency landing. Elenita has just come back from Chiapas in the far south and says there is unrest in the Mayan villages and in the Guatemalan refugee camps along the border. Susana says the new mayor, whom nobody trusts, is threatening to banish the outdoor market to the edge of town, as it draws vermin. He also put out an edict demanding all foreigners register at the Presidencia, then quickly rescinded it to save face when it became clear nobody was going to obey. Mina says that according to a recent UN report, the state of Guanajuato has more children under the age of fourteen than any country in the world except Bangladesh. Who will employ them all? More border crossings in search of work, more tension between the two countries.

"So is La Dolce Vita harbinger of a tourist recovery?" Mina wonders.

"Or that unmentionable horror, gentrification?" says Paul.

Susana tries to explain to Elenita and Carlos what we mean by the term "gentrification," which actually translates quite easily into Spanish.

Susana, familiar with Mexico since childhood, had been working in a museum in Los Angeles when she'd visited San Miguel and decided to stay. She's come to settle in a rented second-floor flat in a building across from La Colmena bakery. Fluent in Spanish, knowledgeable about Mexican arts, she travels Mexico on her own in a Ford van, shopping the towns and village fairs, visiting craftspeople, selling what she finds to stores in the United States.

"San Miguel has no surf, no nightlife, no airport. There are three television channels in Spanish with bad reception," Paul says. "There aren't enough phone lines or water. This is

San Miguel's one good café. How popular can a town like this become?"

He's right, for now. With the exception of the semipermanent group of hardy, silver-haired foreign retirees with their patio lunches, tennis, and amateur theatricals, and transient art students and Mexican weekend visitors, San Miguel remains quiet, recondite, out-of-the-way.

Mina and Paul rise to leave early. Paul's affliction, still undiagnosed, grows worse. Various intestinal possibilities—amoebas, worms—have been rejected. Lead poisoning from years of eating off low-fire pottery from nearby Dolores Hidalgo was the next suspect, but tests failed to turn up anything. Only fifty, Paul limps now, his hands and arms tremble sometimes, and he tires easily. Normally Mina teaches in the fall, but she has taken a semester off so they can be here.

Felipe, a chicano from New Mexico, stops by the table and tells us he's dealing real estate these days. He has some fine houses to show—old colonials, great prices. Interested? Well, if you ever are let me know. Tell Masako hello, he says, handing me his new business card.

Susana and Elenita head off to La Mama to listen to an intense German flamenco guitarist named Wolfgang, who goes by the name of Lobo. I leave them outside La Dolce Vita and head home.

Walking back down Calle Canal in the soft night air, I hold the fragrant, warm bag of espresso to my nose. A smoky round moon hangs above the roofs of the colonial buildings, casting my shadow on the cobbles ahead of me. At the outdoor taco stand on the corner of Hernández Macías, taxi drivers cluster beneath a bare bulb. The aroma of grilled beef, onions, peppers, and maize mixes with the espresso smell. On the corner of Zacateros, across from the vine-thick nunnery walls, a lone light illuminates a tableau of *objets* in an antiques store window.

Beneath the bridge, where stairs lead up to Calle Quebrada, I pass the old, bent man and woman who sell fruit and fruit drinks from a wood cart to people walking up the steep hill. It's eleven; I know for a fact they open at dawn. They look so downtrodden, so tired and tattered, eking out the barest livelihood. What keeps them going? Faith? The proximity of La Concepción? Where do they sleep those few hours in between? I help the old man lug his cart up the steep, urine-soaked stairwell to the street above and store it in a doorway. How would he have gotten it up if nobody had come along?

The lover's bridge is crowded tonight with kissing couples. Fireworks spray the sky above the jardín, announcing the beginning of Day of the Dead festivities. The moon ducks behind the nunnery bell tower, leaving only its penumbra. Stars glitter brilliantly, little nodes of electrical song. For some reason I think of the sky above L.A., which shows few stars, reflecting instead its own ambient light, narcissistically, ready for its close-up. L.A.: where passion is the name of a perfume, ecstasy a drug, adoration something reserved for film stars, and mystery a genre of fiction.

In Mexico, life isn't walled off from death. It appears more a continuum, in which forces emerge from dark and return to it. Here, another theater prevails—*lux perpetua,* an attribute of the Virgin—baffling the western urge to snatch figure from ground, light from dark, life from death; freeze it in snapshot, blurb, replay, hold it in the fixative bath. Instead, you unexpectedly come upon fleeting, exact visions of light and life—almost as if a match has been struck on a moonless night to reveal an unsuspected region, fecund and teeming, directly in your path.

Fishing with the key for the lock in the dark stairwell, I brush up against something, step back in alarm. A blind beggar I always give to is crouched against my door. Bending close, I smell that he's drunk. I grab him beneath the shoulders, haul him up. Normally he's the most dignified of men, erect and impassive, immaculately dressed in sombrero and dark glasses, with his white plastic begging cup and matching cane. He stands against buildings in the center of town, his dark, pitted, hook-nosed Toltec face never betraying expression when the coin hits the cup.

I dust him off, help him up the stairs. He grunts. How did he get to this neighborhood, so far from his usual sites, and so late? He feels his way along the wall face, then takes up a begging position beside the bridge, his back against the wall, cup extended. It's near midnight. There's nobody around but the lovers, who pay him no heed. I ask him if he'd like to be taken someplace. He says nothing. Finally I leave him standing against the wall, his cup out, catching starlight.

I enter the house, undress, crawl into bed. I can't get the blind beggar out of my mind. I climb the stairs to the roof, lean over, look down.

He's gone.

Where? How?

T he cemetery of San Miguel de Allende is seldom empty of visitors, what with the endless burials of the newly dead and those who gather daily among the headstones and crypts to visit with the departed. But today, November 2, is the Day of the Dead, and crowds throng the dusty entry road to the *panteón*, the graveyard off the Celaya road, bearing armfuls of marigolds, gladioli, carnations, and baskets of oranges and breads. They've come to picnic with their dead. Vendors of soft drinks and chicharrones line the path. Children sell geraniums in old tin food cans and draw buckets from a water truck to freshen grave plots. The attitude of somber reverence Masako and I have brought as we would to other holy sites seems out of place among these calm, smiling, outwardly serene *visitantes.*

Inside the low-walled compound, we fall in behind a procession of mourners accompanying a little *niña* in an open silver coffin. She wears a white dress, rouge, and lipstick, her arms crossed over her chest, a rosary woven in her fingers. At least fate has chosen an apt day for her departure from earth. She is one of the *niños muertos,* or *angelitos,* Mexico's countless infant dead—those who will be spared divine judgment because their souls are unstained, too young to have yet tasted sin. White gladioli, baby's breath, and images of the Virgin and Jesus adorn the open chapel where pallbearers gently set her coffin. Candles drip wax on the dirt. Roughhanded men, heads bowed, sombreros in hung hands, sing psalms in weary, cracked voices.

All week long the street and sidewalks around the Plaza Allende have been lined with tables of handmade sugar skulls, holy relics, candles, and wreaths of flowers in an open commemoration and celebration of death more pre-Hispanic than Christian. Vendors display tiny wood coffins with cheerful, grinning plaster of paris skulls (*calaveras*) inside, death's heads dangling from strings. The sugar skulls have people's names inscribed on their foreheads: Lupe, Diego, Juana. This Mexican dance with death is beyond morbidity, more like its surreal antidote. Poe would be lost here, where laughter trumps fright.

Masako, ravished by the bizarre holiday's witty, playful

brilliance, its abundance of toys and sweets and folk objects, has made her own altar in her studio composed of things bought at the street stands. This morning Irma, who is thirteen and works at the Ambos Mundos, came in with her friend. Seeing the altar of death images, they exclaimed delightedly, *"Qué bonita! Qué preciosa!"* as if it were made up not of skeletons and skulls but of furry pink puppies and Minnie Mouses. When Masako offered Irma a chocolate skull with her name on it, she smiled, took it, popped it in her mouth, and chomped it as if it were a Snickers bar.

At the cemetery, families gather at grave sites in the twilight, dust off departed relatives' headstones, install fresh flowers. (I'm reminded of southern China, where families take grandparents' bones out each year and clean them.) Some graves have the simplest of wood crosses, others carved marble headstones and inscribed crypts. Firecrackers explode, summoning the spirits of departed children. Families sit by the graves, drinking and eating and chatting. They've come to talk with the dead, tell them what has happened throughout the year, bring them up to date. Favorite foods and drink are said to entice them to return.

A tattered man stumbles by, guzzling from a half-pint bottle of tequila. An urchin I know from town thrusts a box of *chicles,* little gum packets, at us. I watch a wizened Indian woman, a rebozo over her head, place a motor oil can filled with earth and a lone pink geranium on a headstone whose inscription reads simply: *"Arturo Gómez, 1941–1985."* Her son? On another plot the headstone reads: *"Epifania Gómez 97 años y Fulgencio Gómez 99 años. Siempre unidos."* That's a long life together, here in these mountains.

Skirting a section of unmarked plots, we come upon grave diggers, unperturbed by the crowds, lowering a plain pine coffin into a fresh-dug hole. Often I pass the funerarium on

Calle Mesones where these boxes are made, displayed in the open window like in a furniture store showroom (which it is): some of simple wood, others lacquered and padded in black or purple velvet and braid—and deeper inside the shop, the melancholic sight of carpenters crafting tiny fresh pine boxes for the niños muertos. The funeral parlor also sells lumber, and the large paraffin candles people now light on the graves as night approaches.

Folk artists construct huge, diabolical *alebrijes,* imaginary papier-mâché creatures, for the Day of the Dead; Frida and Diego collected these dancing, grinning fifteen-foot-high creatures. The illustrator José Guadalupe Posada's skeletons smoked cigarettes, wore lovely Sunday hats. Abundance and joy are fleeting, all the more to be savored. The life-bringing sun will turn harsh: flowers wither, crops fail, rivers dry up, children and animals die. I think of the all-faiths pyramids the curanderas sell, with horseshoes, Buddhas, shamrocks, and crosses floating around each other in Plexiglas. Maybe that's part of Mexico's appeal to Masako and me, two hopeless eclectics: one half Presbyterian, half Jewish, with Buddhist leanings; the other a Japanese American born behind barbed wire of a Buddhist people, her grandfather a Christian minister.

At the rear of the graveyard we come to a small section of tidy, well-tended plots behind a locked wrought iron gate. This is the section the gringos have marked off for their dead. There's nobody here on this day—nobody living, at least. Who will come to welcome back their hungry ghosts?

Candles flicker in the encroaching dark. Some families will stay here all night, talking and singing with their dead. We follow a path to a wall of cement crypts, built above the oversubscribed earth to accommodate new coffins.

This isn't our first visit to the panteón. In early September, just before we left for Mexico City, a student of Vicente

Arias's, a gentle gringo doctor who used to draw outside our room at the Ambos Mundos, fell dead of a heart attack. We'd joined the small group of mourners at Ray's funeral, watched masons cement his crypt into its wall in the niche and carve his name in the wet concrete while his widow wept. Tonight we notice that a few people have placed flowers at his crypt. We add our own. Ray, refugee from another land and culture, could have ended up worse, I think: simply buried among humble people under a wide Mexican sky.

Early December. Subtropical greens fade to yellows and browns, the air cool and dry. In the fields outside of town, piles of corn husks, the smell of burning brush. Our families have come and gone, and soon we'll return to California to join them for Christmas.

We had a van pick them up at the Mexico City airport and bring them straight here. On Thanksgiving we arranged a turkey dinner at a restaurant that played swing music. Odd, to see our life in Mexico through their eyes: What are our children doing here? They're not going to stay, are they? At least it's pretty, if a bit dusty. We took pictures in front of the Parroquia, at a table at La Mama, in the museum that used to be Colonel Allende's house, at the lookout above town. While the women shopped the stores, I took the dads to a big-screen television in a bar in town to watch a '49ers game, marched them to the jardín to buy the *Mexico City News*. In the casita kitchen we cut vegetables, heated tortillas from the market, made flan. We posed for a final snapshot in front of the van waiting nearby to whisk them back to Mexico City and their planes. Bye. See you at Christmas.

From the doorway of my studio, I look down on the

flagstone patio with its tile mosaic table, wrought iron chairs, and magenta bougainvillea twining up the wall separating us from the main house. Old skinny Felipa, with her hair tightly pulled back in a bun, her bright tough eyes, her mysterious potions and teas, sweeps the stones again and again: *swoosh swoosh.* She comes to *barrer* (sweep), *arreglar* (straighten up), *asear* (clean, tidy). A few weeks ago Masako, who has a weakness for newfangled gadgetry, bought a Dustbuster from a departing Canadian lady, thinking Felipa would be delighted at this time-saver. She'd plugged the handheld plastic sweeper into its recharger the night before so it would be ready. When Felipa came, Masako flicked on the raptor-headed device to demonstrate. A roaring noise filled the *sala.* Felipa considered the object. *"Sí, Señora,"* she said, deadpan. Masako left the house to go shopping. A few minutes later from upstairs in my studio I heard *swoosh swoosh.* The Dustbuster sat in its recharger for weeks, in full view. Felipa never came near it. The object was never discussed again. Finally Masako, in retreat, unplugged it and put it back in its box on the floor of the tiny bedroom closet.

Masako's transfigurations continue. At first her studio at the Ambos Mundos filled with canvases of flowers and plants—agaves, gladioli, tuberoses—curiously monochromatic, as if Mexican color were simply too much. Delicate etchings followed: torn mesh screens, mosquitoes. Then color erupted: watercolors of the mysterious *juguetes,* folk toys she'd find at the Tuesday market: tops, lottery cards, dice, snakes. Now things fly from her fingers: drawings and paintings, jewelry made of *milagros,* sconces of tin and glass, painted ceramics fired in nearby Dolores Hidalgo. Strange wood snakes and masks, jet black Oaxacan vases, and multicolored Talavera pottery adorn her studio, the casita, her work.

Recently she began drawing an old Mexican handmade wood ladder leaning against a wall at the hotel. Next she made small colored acrylic paintings of the bumpy, irregular *escalera*. At first the ladder lay on the ground, or stood in undifferentiated space. Then it leaned upright against buildings. Now it's poised against skies, or simply floats in atmospheres. The canvases grow: six, seven feet. Released from gravity, set free from a horizon line, the ladders rise into air, drift through richly colored spaces. Ladders: the soul's ascent. She'll arrange for a gallery show this trip up to L.A.

*"Adiós, Señor,"* comes the faint croak from below. The door slams. Minutes later I hear the clanging of the garbage truck on Quebrada. How does Felipa always manage to slip out just before it comes? I close the door to my studio, descend the stone stairs. Halfway down, the hummingbird who comes to sip the blue trumpet vine flowers twice a day buzzes my face: a sudden whirring sound so intense, so urgent my heart races. In the kitchen I grab the bucket under the sink, cross the tiny bedroom where we've carved contentment. I pass through the sala, its walls oddly bare, stripped of Masako's paintings to be taken to California. Outside, I climb the stairwell to the street.

A kid walks ahead of the truck beating a metal bar to alert the block. Garbage is picked up six days a week here, keeping house and town inordinately clean of refuse: another cliché about Mexico bites the dust. My neighbors wait by their doors with their buckets. The truck pulls up, blaring Radio San Miguel. *"Hola!" "Buenas tardes!"* We gather at the back of the wood-sided pickup, hand our trash up to the skinny guy working the redolent mound. *"Gracias. Muy amable. Hasta luego."* The balm of Mexican *politesse*, softening the days.

I walk to the bridge and stand looking west into the late

sun flooding the smoky Guanajuato plain. My eyes follow steep Calle Canal down until it disappears in a grove of eucalyptus and the sun whites out everything. For an instant, I imagine I could stick, here in this mountain town.

The next morning Masako leaves for her studio early. I linger in bed reading until the sun breaks over the high wall outside the bedroom window, then dress and walk out into the patio with my coffee.

A man, a gringo, is sitting in one of the chairs. I jump back, startled.

He is thin, pale, hawklike, with oversized thick glasses, dressed in a cheap shortsleeved shirt, Bermuda shorts, old beat-up tennis shoes.

"Who are you?" he says.

"Who are *you*?" I retort.

"Ralph Towers."

The landlord I've never seen. The shadowy professor with CIA ties. Rude of him to have let himself into our patio without knocking. He offers no apology. I dislike him immediately.

Later I tell Masako of my encounter with the unsettling man, and the peculiar conversation, more of an interrogation, that had ensued—and of the man's allusions to his recent "posting in Kabul, where I taught."

"Sometimes I wish we had our own place," Masako says. "Privacy. A phone. A garden."

So our dreams draw us forward, as water whispers to the dowser's wand.

# The House on Flower Street

# Chapter 8

# Between Worlds

OUR FOURTH YEAR IN MEXICO. WE LIVE
between worlds these days, frequent flyers.
The Mexican cycles of seasons and holidays
entwine us deeper in town and country.
Friends come and go, fall in love, split up;
babies are born. Our life in San Miguel de
Allende remains the intimate sum of our
days—sensual, revelatory, engaged. Mexico,
still mired in post-earthquake recession,
muddles through somehow. New friends
emerge: Arnaud, a Haitian poet in exile who
has awakened me to Caribbean culture; a
Chilean painter and his wife; a Mexican
professor.

Our world widens southward. The
sprawling lands below the Rio Grande, a
mere blip on CNN or ABC, remain to us
norteamericanos, after all these centuries,
the New World. Often after a flight from

California we remain in Mexico City to explore, see new friends, venture out into other regions—Oaxaca, Guerrero, Yucatán, Chiapas—before returning to San Miguel, the heart's abode.

Still we feel unsettled at times, uneasily poised between cultures: losing a foothold in the old country, still on tourist visas in the new one. Masako's art bursts with imagery found here. Slowly Mexico takes root in my work, too: yet the language I hear and speak every day is not the one I write in. Gore Vidal, in an introduction to Paul Bowles's collected short stories, touches on the problem: "Great American writers are supposed not only to live in the greatest country in the world . . . but to write about that greatest of all human themes: the American Experience." A novelist friend I work with in PEN, the international writers group, says only half jokingly, "Careful you don't become a *desaparecido,* a disappeared person, yourself."

Sometimes I do fear liking Mexico too much, getting lost in it. One day I saw a scraggly, unkempt gringo on the Mexico City metro around my age with bad teeth and a bad haircut, tangled in another land, beyond return. He reminded me of Russians I'd seen in China, poor and disheveled, hunched atop bundles in train stations—the ones who'd stayed on too long.

On plane trips back to California, I gaze down at the Sea of Cortez: tidal blue stripes graduating from pale agate to turquoise to aquamarine. Salty inlets and rust basins, green algal meadows. Violet badlands etched with tiny straight-line roads, barren as Mars. We cross *la frontera,* that invisible, charged border, and belly down over L.A.'s carpet of light. From the back of a taxi running up the 405, the city spreads away before us, a bobbing, firefly-infested lake.

We stay on friends' couches, house-sit, sublet. We see people necessary to the work we do, thumbing our Rolodexes, trying to make the days count. Observing age's effects upon our parents, we make careful calibrations between desire and duty. Sometimes we talk of buying another place in L.A. just to have an anchor in the home country, but we can't summon the interest. We hurry through our tasks so we can leave all the sooner.

Old friends are busy climbing up, clinging to, falling off career ladders. The conversation is the same one we checked out on six months earlier, different only in detail, with television and movies the referent, not live experience or books. I'm losing the jargon, the codes, the names of things. In conversations I blank on celebrities' names, hip expressions. Car alarms go off like crazy toys. Helicopters throb overhead, spotlighting evil. The nightly news imbues pedestrian acts with hysterical urgency. Few people walk for pleasure. There's little time to talk, and seldom of important things. It's easier to get some tasks done, as long as you don't need another human: I spend hours deciphering new telephone message menus, wading through oceans of calling options, waiting on hold. Arnaud, my Haitian poet friend in San Miguel, refers to revisiting his beloved Haiti as *the exile of return.*

Mexico in memory can be flat, flavorless, a postcard—like trying to remember sex, or a good meal. It lives in the senses, not the mind, collapsing all abstractions into the brimming moment. Yet hearing a *corrida* on the radio, or Spanish spoken in an L.A. market, can unleash a near-overwhelming, Proustian effect, bringing tears. Now I understand better the mariachis' howling laments of memory and loss.

In California we don't talk much about Mexico. We've grown tired of the blank stares, the feigned interest, the allusions to Tijuana and the border towns, the beaches of Cabo or Cancún. Now I know why Mina and Paul used to be so reticent. In glossy, xenophobic, dollar-grubbing late-eighties U.S.A., Mexico is buzzless: a torpid blank somewhere south. Mexico, grail to generations of artists, site of primordial revelation—Mayan temples, *brujos*, muralists, hallucinatory mushrooms—has fallen off the map. This whorled, ornate neighbor civilization, secretly and essentially entwined with ours, is invisible, its people among us silent, nameless wraiths who clip lawns and clear tables.

In a West Hollywood eatery, we sit with friends, poking at endive salad, designer pizza. A plate glass window offers a view of the foothills behind the Strip. A Sade tape teases the threshold of lyric audibility. Noticing the nine-dollar taco on the menu, we glance at each other.

"Yes, but what do you *do* there?" one friend asks.

How to describe a trip to the Tuesday market? A four-hour dinner with Carlos, Elenita, Arnaud, and Colette in our patio by the Quebrada bridge? Waking up to the bells' sweet clangor? Hurrying along the cobbles in the rain, ducking under archways? How to describe Friday lunches at El Caribe, or checking out Thomas More's *Utopia* at the little bilingual library and actually reading it through? It's as if we have a secret life, in a secret place.

I used to like L.A.: the cool speed, the indifference to history, the near-monastic life of house, car, house. It freed the mind to run along some ever widening horizon line. Flatness, the absence of affect: not a bad place for a writer. There's no world out there so you invent one. I can't muster that appreciation any longer. I want taste, smell, *sabor*, *ambiente*. I want the human shape to my days.

In another sense, though, Mexico has redeemed L.A. to me. I've discovered a buried city there—a Latino L.A., warm and celebratory, where Spanish traces an invisible heart line deeper than place. In the course of my days I may encounter a man or woman hailing from Guanajuato or Jalisco or Oaxaca, and matters of truth and fullness of heart may pass between us, and much laughter: riches invisible to most of my other friends. I can trace Los Lobos riffs back to *norteño* bands that come through our part of Mexico: Los Tigres del Norte, Los Bukis. California street names and foods reveal their origins. Suddenly the century-old Anglo patina looks flimsy, conditional.

Sometimes I get energy off the displacement, the dislocation, the back-and-forth. Each country seems the antidote to the other's ills. "In Rio, dreaming of New England/In New England, dreaming of Rio," the poet Elizabeth Bishop wrote.

Sometimes it feels like the two countries, through me, dream each other.

Invariably our L.A. trips end with a visit to the storage bin in Glendale. We introduce the seven-digit code, pass through the security gates, inch down aisles of identical metal containers and cinder-block structures. We remove the lock, raise the corrugated door, and consider the lumpen detritus of our former life.

We shut the door, lock it, drive off.

Finally, our lists checked off, we head back to Mexico. At journey's end the Flecha Amarilla bus pulls into the dusty turnaround at the foot of San Miguel. We step out into darkness, as on that first night four years ago. The street dogs, the boys who want a coin to help with the baggage, the waiting taxi driver—those shades that so alarmed us then—appear to us now as town greeters, familiars. Wending up unlit streets once mysterious but intimate now from walking them, we make small talk with the taxi driver. "*Sí,*" he says.

*"Un poco frío."* A little chilly. At Calle Quebrada we drag our bags down the dark stairwell, brush past a pair of young lovers. We open the door. The dusky smell of the last mesquite fire we'd built hits us. Our luggage slumps to the stone floor, our hands unclench. We're back.

# Chapter 9

# The House on Flower Street

EARLY JUNE. WE WERE PLANNING TO
leave Friday for California. Work obliges a
visit, our families need attention. Thursday
after siesta we took a last turn through town
to pick up a few gifts. A spate of pregnancies
and births among U.S. friends has sent us
scurrying to find toys for the new kids—
pure pleasure, as Mexico is a wonderland of
toys. Masako was in search of a particular
balloon vendor who also sells a fuzzy
squawking chicken made of cut foam, feathers, and some nameless synthetic fuzz: run
your finger along the waxen string the right
way and it gives off an unsettlingly realistic
barnyard squawk. We like bringing back
handmade folk toys as a sly counter to our
American friends' bright, shiny, plastic Toys
"R" Us and Lego inventory.

As we crossed the jardín, Masako spotted

the balloon vendor over by the *portales* and headed for him. I felt a tapping on my shoulder and turned around.

"*Compadre. Cómo estás?*"

It was Felipe, our chicano friend. Felipe is a *negociante*, a small-time businessman who operates in the shadowy interstices where Mexican and gringo meet on dubious terms. He and his beauteous wife, Laura, run a small bed and breakfast north of the plaza where we've sent friends to stay. I often run into Felipe in the large distancia office waiting for a line out. A tall, lean Mexican American somewhere in his forties, he'd fallen in love with Laura one night dancing at La Mama when she was on vacation from college studies in Mexico City. They'd married and in quick succession had two kids. Now their marital woes, tumultuous and vocal, have become public spectacle. Felipe speaks mournfully of his business travails, the difficulties of satisfying Laura's emotional and material needs. Laura, who'd wanted to be a poet, feels trapped in this ill-fated liaison, her youthful spirit dying on the vine. She entreats me to visit and sit with her, listen to her poetry—which I don't mind doing because it illuminates my Spanish, and she remains lovely to gaze upon.

"So what are you up to these days?" I asked, feigning interest, one eye on Masako over by the portales talking to the balloon seller.

"Still dealing real estate," Felipe said. "Great time to buy, before next year's elections. There'll be a recovery for sure. I have a couple of listings. Want to take a look?"

"We're not in the market. And we're leaving in the morning."

"They're both nearby. My truck's right over there." He gestured down Cuña de Allende, the street running alongside the Parroquia.

Masako returned with three fluffy foam chickens: a yellow, a red, and a lurid green one the color of a Cloret. Trying to produce the clucking sound by running her finger up and down the string, she chipped a nail. "Damn," she muttered.

"You don't think kids will cut themselves on those?" Felipe said.

Masako regarded her wounded nail disconsolately. "No. Besides, people expect dangerous, beautiful, politically incorrect Mexican toys from us by now."

"Felipe has a couple of houses he wants to show us."

Felipe shrugged. "I mean, if you're up for it."

His beat-up old Chevy truck—its paint job a collage of previous owners, each dent a concealed narrative—was parked half a block away, in front of La Fragua Bar. We piled in and rattled off down the cobbles.

"Fair warning," Felipe said. "This first place is in pretty rough shape."

He turned right on Hospicio, then left down Calle Flor, a quiet lane southwest of the town's center. I often walk Calle Flor to the old waterworks, where the original town had been, and where women still wash clothes at the outdoor sinks. Its full name is Calle de la Flor, Street of the Flower, but nobody calls it that. Corto Maltese, the restaurant where we'd eaten pasta and danced to salsa music our first summer here, had been on Calle Flor until its precipitous, inexplicable closure.

Halfway down the second block, Felipe's truck lurched to a halt. We piled out in a cloud of dust. "Don't say I didn't warn you," he said, pulling a fat key ring out of his pocket.

While Felipe fished for the key to a tall, cracked mesquite door, I stepped back and looked up. The facades of Mexican houses, like their Spanish and Moorish models, often reveal little of what lies within (the analogy with the Mexican character, its riches concealed within a "labyrinth of solitude," is too keen even to indulge). Still, the crumbing whitewash surface had worn away almost entirely, revealing earlier coats of green, blue, ocher. Chunks of plaster hung loose or were missing. The molding along the roof's rim was broken off. One scarred, chipped drain spout of pink *cantera* stone dangled out over the sidewalk, another was simply a bent metal tube. Crushed beer cans, candy-bar wrappers, and plastic bags clustered in the well of a green shuttered window, its glass missing, its black iron flecked with drips of hardened paint.

A smaller door to the right bore the same street number with an "A" after it, scrawled in dripping whitewash.

"The casita," Felipe said. "It's a separate little house, part of the property."

Masako leaned close and whispered, "What are we doing here?"

"I don't know," I said.

The mesquite door shuddered open. We followed Felipe through the door into a dim entry. Two small, dark birds exploded into the sky beyond: *golondrinas,* swallows. An old iron chandelier, stuffed with nests, hung from a chain affixed to a dark wood beam twenty feet overhead. I heard chirping, then saw three chicks' raw, open mouths. At my feet, years of droppings stained the stones.

Ahead, through a tall arch, a giant, untrimmed avocado tree overhung a leaf-strewn stone patio. At the far end, above a glass-enclosed room, eroded walls exposed straw-and-mud adobe beneath. One good summer rain away from collapse, I guessed. A long white wall to our right separated the casita, dividing what must have once been a single large courtyard.

The front door slammed behind us. We stood uncertainly in the darkness.

"This place is totally abandoned," Masako said.

"It was owned by a gringa," Felipe said. "Seven years ago she was in a bar and somebody was cleaning a gun. It went off accidentally. The bullet ricocheted and hit her between the eyes. *Se murió, instantáneamente.*"

Another San Miguel story, I thought, in a town rich with them.

"Her two half-Mexican daughters inherited the house. One lives on the East Coast, the other in Oregon. They don't speak to each other."

"They never come here, obviously," Masako said.

We stepped into the patio. The weather-beaten walls of the old house to our left rose a good twenty-five feet. Felipe pointed to a door inset in the wall a meter deep. "They don't build like that anymore, *verdad?*"

"How old is this place?"

"Eighteenth century. You can look it up at the Presidencia but their records are unreliable. Bonifacio, the old shoeshine man in the jardín, knows the history of all these houses. He'll tell you for a shine."

"Nobody's watered anything in years," Masako said, looking at the patio floor of slate and dirt. Only a tenacious crawling fern survived, brittle and yellowing. A scraggly papaya tree clung to a wall, its splayed leaves frayed and dusty. Miraculously, it bore four fat green papayas along its trunk, blushing orange at their tips.

Back in the dark *entrada*, Felipe struggled with another key. A door in the side wall burst open. We could smell the room before we entered it: musty, fetid. Inside it was pitch-black. Felipe scrambled up on a countertop and pried open one of the wood shutters we'd seen from the street.

By a wide shaft of dusty light, we took in the kitchen: dead cockroaches on unglazed terra-cotta floors, mounds of

termite dust from huge pine cross beams above, rat droppings on the chipped tile countertops. Its massive walls,
streaked and stained, smelled of old cooking grease. A huge
ventilator hood, so dusty its black paint was hard to make
out, hung over a void where a stove must have been. Along
the south wall, a low door opened onto a pantry and a small
utility bathroom.

Dust, grime, dead plants, roaches. We felt lost inside this
neglected ruin, with its histories and tragedies and secrets
moaning inside the walls. It was like coming upon a great,
expiring animal. Felipe threw open another door. "The
*comedor,*" he announced.

The dining room, a long rectangle with soaring walls, was
empty but for a cobwebbed iron chandelier and an oak table.
Light from a skylight played on tile floors discolored by
leaks from the roof where years of rainwater had seeped in.
Humidity had blistered the walls, leaving damp yellow
splotches and patches of green mold. Still it wasn't hard to
imagine the high, ample room filled with candles, food, people.

We stood in the silence, taking in the space. "It's like an
old palazzo room in Ravenna or Assisi," Masako said.

"Or Frida's house," I said. We'd revisited the blue house
in Coyoacán recently, marveling at its abundant work
spaces, its rambling garden and courtyard, projecting ourselves into it with ease.

"The daughters should have sold it years ago, before it got
this bad," Felipe said. "They could never agree. Now they
need the money."

"What are they asking?"

"Eighty thousand."

"Dollars?"

He nodded.

"How long has it been on the market?"

"A couple of months."

Eighty thousand dollars. I tried to muster a frame of reference. The price of a high-end Mercedes. A year's good salary for a starting lawyer in the United States. It still sounded high. I said as much.

*"Es posible,"* Felipe said. "Anyhow, I've got another house up on the hill. *Mejor condición. Buenas vistas."*

"Let's see the rest of this one," Masako said, "since we're here."

The living room, the sala, was as large and high as the dining room. A double bed was shoved against the wall, its bedding mussed, a tarpaulin strung over it.

"Somebody's staying here," Masako said.

"I think Antonio uses it for afternoon *encuentros* with his girlfriends."

"Who's Antonio?"

"The lawyer for the daughters. He's a *macho,* an asshole. I let my lawyer deal with him."

"What's the tarp for?"

"Probably to keep termite droppings off the bed."

Masako spotted an old-fashioned black dial phone on the floor, walked over and picked up the receiver. "Dial tone."

"Something in the house works," I said.

"Worth six thousand dollars right there," Felipe said.

He was right. Even many of the town's grand houses don't have phone lines, and the only way to get one is to pay outrageous *mordida* to a fat, sloe-eyed telephone company mafioso named Efraín.

Tall windows faced onto the courtyard, where a green hummingbird sipped at a papaya blossom.

"A *colibrí,"* said Felipe, sadness creasing his face. "They're supposed to mean good luck in love."

Masako reached into her purse and pulled out a clear plastic packet about the size of a wallet. She held it up to the window light. Little good luck charms surrounded a tiny, dead hummingbird. Medicine women sell them in the market: if you want to attract your lover, wear a hummingbird close to your heart, *bruja* wisdom decrees. Masako had bought a few for friends in California. She handed this one to Felipe. "For you and Laura," she said.

*"Gracias,"* he murmured, jamming it into his shirt pocket.

Following Felipe up small stairs and through a door, we entered a towering bathroom, tiled in a yellow and green flower pattern. Beyond, through iron and glass doors, lay a rear garden.

A doorway to the right led into a narrow white room with terra-cotta floors, wood beams, and a fireplace. Tall, monastic, beautifully proportioned, it ran horizontally across the property.

"Your studio," Masako whispered.

This was the room beneath the slumping wall I'd seen when we'd first entered the house. I turned and looked through the arched windows back across the courtyard to the front of the property. A pair of swallows dropped from the sky, swooped back to their nests in the entrada. Their wings made a ghostly flitting sound inside the massive, hushed compound walls.

Ramiro Torres, a carpenter I know, told me a story once about *golondrinas*. A woman of the town had a daughter who'd been mute since birth. Doctors could offer no explanation. The girl was seven when a curandera told the mother to catch ten swallows, boil them in a soup, and have her daughter drink it on ten successive nights. The woman did as she was instructed. For nine nights nothing happened. Then on the tenth night the daughter burst into song. She is now a famous opera singer in Mexico City.

Ramiro swears by the story. It inclined me to take the golondrinas in the entrada as a good omen. What writer wouldn't welcome voice-enhancing powers? Maybe Felipe and Laura would find true love again, and I Dante's tongue. Did this mean I'd have to boil and swallow the birds? I turned around expectantly, as if to share this thought, but Felipe and Masako had disappeared out back.

The rear garden I'd glimpsed from the bath and dressing room was little more than a broken path of loose bricks through dirt and weeds. Whatever else might have once grown in the soil was long dead. Weathered walls of stone rubble and cantera boulders surrounded the garden on two sides. In the late sun they glowed, soulful and warm, re-minding me of Mediterranean walls I'd seen: places where time and age are allowed to speak.

"There's supposed to be a tunnel under this place," Felipe said, "running from the Allende house on the plaza all the way to the Instituto. During the revolution the rich families and their servants used it to escape with their wealth."

Masako pointed to a structure to our right, a separate building along the north end of the garden. Over twenty feet high, easily forty feet long, it was built of the same rock as the walls. There were two levels of windows, and a roof of some sort of corrugated sheeting, the kind Mexicans call *lámina.*

"Is this part of this property?"

"*Sí.* The guy who owned this place before the gringa was a *caballero.* That was his stable. See the old iron ring in the wall?"

Inside, the old stable was tall as a church, with mezza-nines on either end accessible by circular metal stairways called *caracoles,* snails. Had the gringa housed her two daughters up there? The tile floors were stained from years of leaks, the windows broken. Everywhere, the smell of cats.

I watched Masako taking in the room's surfaces and dimensions, its literally rock solid walls. *"Your* studio," I whispered.

Back out in the garden, we found our way to a stone bench built into a far corner of the old wall beneath two trees: a jacaranda and another large, leafy one Felipe said was a chirimoyo. We looked back at the walls of the old house, espaliered by a gigantic, near-dead bougainvillea. The stable building ran to our left, the south garden wall to our right. It was utterly silent there. The town beyond had disappeared. I reached back and clutched the iron tethering ring above my head. I wanted to sit in that ruined garden forever.

I noticed a brick stairway running along the south wall to the roof. "Can I go up?"

*"Cómo no?"*

It was thirty steep stairs up. At the top, I stepped onto a roof tangled with crossed wires, discarded glass, pop bottles, tar, broken tiles, and abandoned tool parts. I saw the propane tank that served the house, a smaller one on the casita roof, and two round water tanks.

Gingerly picking my way toward the front of the property, I stopped midway and looked up. Across the ascending rooftops, I saw the Parroquia from behind, two blocks away: a rare angle, unavailable from the street. I'd never seen it in a book or on a postcard.

It was near sunset, the town turning red, the parish church set against deepening blue sky. Jet-black grackles rushed toward the jardín, where they sleep in the trees. Snowy egrets, the underside of their wings flashing silver, cruised in formation toward their nests in the Parque Juárez, back from fishing the dam. The two flocks interpenetrated each other—a dizzying black-and-white geometry, an Escher. My heart began to race.

Turning west, I saw a clear view of Las Monjas, the nunnery, then the reservoir lake far below and the plains of Guanajuato beyond. To the south I could see San Antonio church, then east up the hillside to the Querétaro road.

Bells pealed from the Parroquia, followed by a tide of clanging from Las Monjas. I could see the nun in the bell tower, her habit whipping in the breeze, energetically yanking on the clapper. Now came San Antonio's gongs from the west. The wild baffle of bells commingled across the rooftops, like the muezzins' cries over Isfahan.

Drunkenly I picked my way back to the top of the garden stairs. Far below, Masako and Felipe sat in the corner of the old ruined garden. I saw Felipe get up and walk back toward the house.

I took the stairs down and rejoined Masako.

"So?" she said.

"It's a junkyard up there," I said, "with the best view of San Miguel I've ever seen."

She was looking at the stable, her eyes bright.

"Where'd Felipe go?"

"To the casita to ask if we can look. There's somebody renting it."

Dusk edged into the garden, settling into the old corner where we sat. A green-eyed yellow cat eyed us from the wall above. I caught the warm, dry smell of fresh *bolillos.* "There must be a bakery over the wall."

"This place is like Frida and Diego's," she said, "in the raw."

"Eighty thousand. I can't get a grip on it."

"Felipe says they turned down sixty-two. But how could we? We're leaving in the morning. And look at it."

I've always needed to know exactly where our dollars came from, who made them. I want to hook them to some merit of my own: my Puritan mother speaking through me.

Masako is more at ease with the idea that money might simply arrive by grace. In this, she's already Mexican. I'm the brakes in the relationship, the dry voice embedding spontaneous desire in the brine of relativism, reason, doubt. The difference between what we'd paid for our house in L.A. and what we sold it for was sixty-five thousand. The symmetry appeals.

Masako was looking at me strangely. "What are you thinking?"

In L.A., we often joke about "emotional Spanish"—realtors' ad parlance for some half-million-dollar Hollywood Hills lath-and-plaster job with a stucco surface and some red roof tiles. In fact real Moorish-Spanish architecture, with its soft, deep spaces, its courtyards and fountains, has always thrilled me.

"Three-foot-thick walls," I heard myself saying in the twilit garden. "Twenty-foot ceilings. Studio spaces. You should see it from the roof. And look where we're sitting. *This*," I said, "is emotional Spanish."

"The old lady who was shot. The quarreling sisters. We don't know the first thing about buying in Mexico, let alone fixing up a place like this." She stood up.

I thought of the story about the golondrinas Ramiro Torres told me. "This mute place could sing," I said.

Masako looked at me incredulously. Felipe was calling from somewhere over the walls.

We found our way back through the darkening house and across the patio. As we approached the entry, the swallows scattered again.

Outside, Felipe was waiting at the front door. I looked up the quiet, winding block and a half where Calle Flor intersects Calle Umarán. Five minutes to the bustling center, yet here all was blissfully still.

The casita had a bright white sala and fireplace, service-able tile floors, glass-blocks in the ceilings for light. It looked to have been built within the last thirty years. Two men lived there month to month. The kitchen was long, open, blue-tiled, with wide windows looking out on a tiny patio and over the roof of the main house, where in the fading light the black birds spun in the sky.

A second-floor bedroom adjoined a roof terrace and a blue-tiled bathroom with, improbably, a bidet. "You could rent this place alone for three hundred a month," Felipe was saying. This seemed a stretch; our casita on Calle Quebrada, larger if less charming, went for two-forty. Besides, I hadn't the least interest in being a landlord.

Back downstairs, Felipe lifted open a hatch in the floor to show me a large cistern, a *depósito,* with enough extra water for both houses to last out a drought, and a *bomba,* a pump, to bring it up. This is a selling point, like the phone, as water is scarce in San Miguel de Allende—a looming issue as the water table drops each year. Some say San Miguel will be a ghost town in five years; city officials get elected on the wa-ter issue.

"Let's go see the other house," Felipe said, back outside.

"No," I said, twice. Maybe I said it a third time.

W̲e sit at a candlelit table at La Mama, our attention far from food or the lilting Peruvian flutes. Are we about to join the fools, sink our money on the wrong side of the border? We have nothing in the States now; buying here might assure that we never will again. What if the wa-ter *does* run out? I talk of traveling through northern and central Italy in the 1960s, when old villas and homes could be had for nothing. Good places in good locations in good towns have a chance of working out. The intrinsic value is there: old buildings, history. Mexico will see better days. Besides, I argue, what price joy, inspiration, consonance with self?

When visiting places we like, we often talk of buying. It's a sort of pulse-taking, a measure of interest, a way of being there. Gazing up at a rickety studio hanging over the Guanajuato tunnels, we imagine owning it, living and working there. We fantasize buying an old *finca* off a square in Pátzcuaro, a shuttered town house in tropical Mérida, a grass *palapa* down a dirt road near Tulum. What if that were ours? Staring up at an old abandoned silk mill along Kyoto's Kamogawa River, a rug merchant's home in the Marrakech medina, a little art nouveau building in an *allée* off the rue de l'Ancienne Comédie. Before the fateful first trip to Mexico we'd scoured the California coast, projecting ourselves into the unlikeliest of towns: Oceano, Gonzales, Gorda (a tiny community in lower Big Sur that was actually for sale). "We could be here," one would say. "But we *are* here," the other would point out, exposing the displacement or disjuncture in the statement, as if just being there without thoughts of possession weren't quite enough. In San Miguel we've said or thought it dozens of times: visiting friends' homes for dinner, peering through some exquisite recondite doorway at a bougainvillea-clotted ruin awaiting someone's revivifying touch. What if that were ours?

In Mexico, the *fideicomiso,* the thirty-year legal instrument by which foreigners are allowed to lease through a bank but not officially own property, means we could be sent packing overnight. Mexico has expropriated foreigners' holdings before. *"Nuestro patrimonio!"* rolls off Mexican senators' lips like butter, especially where *norteamericanos* are concerned. There is unrest in the southern states, murmurs of open revolt. The peso totters, the ruling PRI is terminally corrupt. Drug money surges through the economic system like a toxin. Tourism bottomed out after the earthquake and has never recovered. "Don't put any more in Mexico than you can afford to lose," the aphorism runs.

Put all our eggs here? Risk joining those gringos forced to limp back across the border after the 1982 devaluation to a land they could no longer afford?

Some say there are too many foreigners in San Miguel anyway, driving up prices and diluting the experience— though gringos number less than 2 percent of the population. Our Spanish is workable now; we could live elsewhere in Mexico or Latin America. Still, we haven't found a better place, nor have our Mexican or foreign friends who effuse about Jalapa, Morelia, Tepoztlán, Antigua, Guatemala, the beach resorts, then either don't move there or come rushing back. It's hard to come by 450 years of history, soulful old streets and walls and houses, good weather, an international community. Even ex–foreign service types who know the world's sweet spots end up here.

The next morning I change our plane tickets to two days later. At eleven we're sitting with Felipe and Antonio Rocha, the sellers' lawyer, in the office of Señora Lucina Ramírez, Licenciada. Licenciada Ramírez, a crisp, fast-talking lawyer, peppers us with a barrage of Spanish legalese—*anticipos, saldos, permiso secretaria, valor agregado, fiduciario, registro, impuesto predial*—while we blearily thumb our dictionaries. Antonio Rocha, who smokes cigars, is the son of one of the few people I've ever disliked in San Miguel, the man who owns the hat shop on Calle Cuadrante.

We walk back to Felipe and Laura's bed and breakfast to

wait while our offer is presented. The East Coast sister thinks it's too little; the sister in Oregon is away but will call back. Antonio and Felipe are quarreling, Felipe and Laura aren't speaking. Masako and I are growing tense, wracked with misgivings.

That afternoon we visit the house on Calle Flor again. It looks even worse in full sunlight: ravaged walls, rotted floors, broken panes of glass, strands of electrical wire hanging loose like Christmas decorations. It's like coming upon the derelict hull of a once-great ship. One neighbor, Felipe tells us, is a Mexican doctor and his family, the other to the south an older Mexican couple with a daughter who isn't quite right. The bakery behind is owned by the sister of the neighbor to the south and they don't speak.

Back at the lawyer's office, we're told the daughters have turned down our offer. Felipe, suspecting Antonio Rocha of trying to hustle a fatter cut for himself, demands to speak to the sisters himself. Antonio calls Felipe a *pendejo*, a *ladrón*, a *gusano*—asshole (literally, "pubic hair"), robber, worm— then agrees. Felipe tells the daughter in Oregon that this crumbling wreck is in danger of sitting another seven years if they don't go for this offer. We make a last bid: sixty-five thousand. The West Coast sister is convinced, says she'll go for it if the East Coast sister does.

Now we begin to worry they'll accept the offer. If so, how will we pay? There are no mortgages in Mexico. Electronic transfers of funds through Mexican banks are unreliable, out of the question. Licenciada Ramírez says we'll have to make a cash deposit of five thousand to be held in escrow by her, then bring the remaining sixty thousand down from the States in cash. She explains the fideicomiso, whereby we buy the house in joint trust with a bank. Each year we'll pay the bank to administer all this; then at the end of thirty years—

*thirty years?*—it will have to be renegotiated by us or our heirs, or else pass back into the hands of the state. Will we or our heirs ever own it outright? Not under present Mexican law.

Late that afternoon, at Felipe and Laura's bed and breakfast, we learn that the daughter in Oregon has accepted.

We patch together a five-thousand-dollar deposit out of pesos we keep in a local bank, some traveler's checks, a credit card, and a personal check for the remainder—cashed on faith by the man who changes money at the ice cream store across from San Francisco church. In Sra. Ramírez's office we labor through the *escritura*, a contract that reads like something out of the Napoleonic era, which it is. Endless fees are added: *impuestos, honorarios, gastos.* Our Spanish is straining its upper limits. We need a Mexican will. What about utilities? Antonio is to pay them up to date, then transfer them into our names when we take possession. Documents are rushed back and forth to the municipal building and the banks before they close. Within fifteen days we'll have to present ourselves in Mexico with a cashier's check for sixty thousand dollars. Why not simply transfer it directly to the sisters' account in the States? Because, says Felipe, glowering, because then that *cabrón* Antonio Rocha can't get his hands on it and carve out his cut.

**M**y body is in a rented house in L.A., my thoughts somewhere on the road to San Miguel. Yesterday morning we went to our bank in Hollywood and withdrew sixty thousand dollars in the form of a cashier's check. Back out on the street, we jumped into our car, locked it, and drove anxiously away like a pair of embezzlers. Driving to the airport, we went over the plan. I'd stay here in L.A. and complete the necessary tasks. When she got to Mexico City with the cashier's check on her body, she'd take the safest-looking taxi she could find to Terminal Norte, then a first-class bus to San Miguel. She'd lock herself in the house on Calle Quebrada until morning, then get the check in Licenciada Ramírez's hands as soon as her office opened at ten. When the deal was done, she'd call.

Clearly something has gone wrong. It's eleven-thirty Mexican time and I've heard nothing. By my figuring, Masako should have been in Licenciada Ramírez's office an hour and a half ago. Adding a good hour for Mexican delay and protocol doesn't help: Dire scenarios play at the edges of my thoughts, all of them intolerable. I gulp water, pace the room. I stare at the phone like a lovelorn teen.

Further doubts had plagued me all night. Viewed from here, the idea of throwing money at that ruin on Calle Flor seems crazy. Here, keener urgencies prevail: tasks to complete, careers to kindle, money to make. The ineffable *sabor* of our Mexican life dims with the passing days to a simulacrum. Considered from a freeway at sixty-five miles an hour, an old *finca urbana* (as the deed describes it) in the middle of the Mexican mountains seems about as germane as a used lottery ticket.

In an attempt to calm myself, I grab an issue of *Artes de México,* a magazine I'd bought in the Mexico City airport. I'd been reading an article on the colorful, enduring Mexican lottery.

"To play the lottery," says the writer Gabriel Zaid, "is an attempt to tune in to divine providence, to give God a chance to intervene in my life, to deny that success is due only to my effort, to pit grace against merit." In the Mexican view, he suggests, ". . . a coin tossed into the air, the petals plucked from a daisy, or the open pages of a fallen book are not read as statistical noise but as signs, messages, a dialogue with eternity."

Waiting by the phone in California, it occurs to me that Masako and I have entered into just such a "dialogue with eternity." This idea of fate, or chance, or grace, or surrender, calms me. Surely it was by chance that I ran into Felipe in the jardín Thursday. Merit—his or mine—had nothing to do with it. And buying the house on Calle Flor is nothing but a "coin tossed in the air." As for the money, well, it's safe or it isn't.

The phone rings.

"I'm here in Licenciada Ramírez's office."

Flooding with relief, I call in to the crackling line, "So is it ours?"

"They've torn up the papers."

"What papers?" I shout.

"You won't believe this. After I gave her the sixty thousand cashier's check, she tore up the papers we'd signed right in front of me. Then she handed me an alternate set valued at a tenth the price. For the tax office, she said. Felipe says that's how they do it."

"What does it mean?"

"It means the house is ours!"

Evening. Masako calls again, furious. She'd gotten the keys and gone to the house just before sunset. As soon as the papers were signed, Antonio Rocha had gone to the house with a truck, stripped it of nearly everything that wasn't fastened down, and hauled it off to his ranch: doors, gas tanks, light fixtures, hot-water heaters, a potbellied stove. Even the toilets. Even the old dial telephone.

"Did you tell Señora Ramírez?"

"She says legally it's allowable. We're only buying the physical structure and the land." I hear the rage in Masako's voice. "We now own a big, gutted, roach-infested mausoleum of adobe and glass and cement."

# Chapter 10

# Red Refrigerator, Blue Stove

MASAKO OPENS THE DOOR ON CALLE
Flor, her hair tangled, her work shirt and
jeans flecked with white *cal*—the lime mixture used to paint walls. She's holding a tape
measure in one hand, a dictionary in the
other.

"I thought you might be the carpenter,"
she says, opening wider so I can pass.

No, it's only me, at the end of a 1,700-
mile journey. The high door slams shut. I
set my bags down in the dusty entry. Beyond in the patio there are workers and
wheelbarrows, piles of earth and cement.

"He was supposed to be here hours ago."

"Who?"

"The carpenter." Distress floods her face.
"It's been like this all week. Trapped here
waiting for guys who don't show." She puts
the tape measure in her pocket.

We hug gingerly, among dust and grime.

A workman emerges from the kitchen, talking in a rapid-fire patois. Masako asks him to slow down.

"Fester," he says. *"Impermeabilizante."*

"This is Juan."

We shake hands.

*"Mucho gusto."*

*"Mucho gusto."*

"Fester," he says again.

"It's the name of a sealant," Masako says. "Juan's fixing roof leaks."

She fishes in her pocket and hands Juan some peso bills. *"Gracias,"* he says, and hurries off to buy Fester *impermeabilizante.*

"That guy talks faster than anybody I've ever heard," I say.

"He's not from around here. The other workers don't understand him either. He's fixed maybe half the leaks. The rains started last week. Each time more *goteras* show up in different places."

*"Goteras."*

"Leaks. You won't believe how many new words I've learned. I carry my dictionary everywhere."

The swallow droppings have been cleaned off the entrada floor, I notice, though the nest is still up in the chandelier, which had clearly been out of Antonio's reach. Ahead, the place looks like an industrial site, worse than when we first saw it.

"What are those guys doing in the patio?"

"Fixing the wall of your studio. The drain was plugged with years of avocado leaves. Water had backed up and soaked into the walls."

We cross the patio. Coming closer, I see that the surface above the arched glass windows has been stripped away, revealing mud, stone, hay: adobe.

"The *maestro* says this wall is over two hundred years old. He can tell by the thickness. They're resurfacing it with cement. It's called *aplanadora.*"

Three skinny teenagers mix sand and pebbles and cement with shovels and buckets of water on the patio floor. Earlier cement mixes have hardened on the slate. I turn around and take in the casita, the soaring walls above the entrada, the doors and windows and walls of the main house. What madness led us to project our dreams into this place?

Masako walks me through a door into the sala, where we'd first come upon the bed Antonio the lawyer used for his trysts. She's bought a wooden double bed and mattress at a local furniture store and borrowed a set of sheets from Susana. A bare bulb dangles from a cord. Receipts, coins, and magazines litter a three-legged mesquite stool. A rotary phone that must date from the 1950s, a loan from Elenita, sits on the floor.

Masako points to the ceiling. "I had one of the guys get on a ladder and poison the beams to stop termites from raining down at night. It's their swarming season."

"Nice."

We walk back toward the front of the house. The tall dining room is empty but for tools on the ground and a dusty black chandelier hanging from a beam. "Almost the only thing Antonio didn't take," Masako says. "He mustn't have had a ladder high enough to cut it down."

Hilario Beltrán, the gardener from the Calle Quebrada house, passes through the courtyard carrying a tall fern in a terra-cotta pot.

"Hilario's working on the garden. He's been great. He helped me move everything over from Quebrada, found me a plumber to install the new toilets and hook up the gas tanks. The gas truck was supposed to come today but didn't, of course. Hilario thinks we'll have to chase them down in the street, slip the guys some *mordida*. They run a big hose to the roof from the truck."

"So we have no hot water."

She looks at me in frustration, as if to say: One more word and I'll have your head.

We enter the kitchen, that infested, grease-gunked grotto Felipe had revealed to us on our first visit. Two teenage girls are scrubbing it down, the glassless shutters to the street flung open for light.

"Marisa, Clarisa," Masako says. "They're sisters."

*"Hola,"* they say brightly, in unison.

"There's the new stove," Masako says, pointing.

An expensive long-distance quarrel had broken out between us on the subject of buying stoves and refrigerators. Local appliances were homely, badly made, and twice the U.S. price, she'd said. I couldn't believe the figures she'd quoted. Had she really checked around? Finally she'd driven with Susana in her van to Querétaro an hour away and bought stoves and refrigerators at a big appliance store, one each for the main house and the casita. They'd cost even more than in San Miguel. When I'd asked why, she'd said, "You'll see."

Beneath the high black ceiling vent the new stove, a bright, baked enamel blue, gleams like a Detroit auto fender:

"Blue" is all I can muster.

She points through the open doorway into the pantry. I hear it humming before I see it: a shiny, fire-engine red refrigerator.

"Well?"

"I hate them," I say.

"I figured you would. It was either this or chipped beige enamel. At least they're fun. Frida would have loved them. Think of it that way. *Muy mexicano.*"

Looking at the blue stove and red refrigerator, I realize I'd envisioned the new house as white, monumental spaces: cool, clean, spare of objects. Masako sees a big, fun new playhouse to fill with lots of colorful things.

We close the door on the last worker. Masako fishes a key from her jeans and hands it to me. "Yours," she says. "There's a set to the interior doors and the casita on a nail in the kitchen. By the way, the casita's rented, to a friend of Susana's from Quebec. Two-fifty a month. She's already moved some things in. She'll be back in a few weeks."

I hear chirping and look up. The three baby golondrinas, maws open, much bigger now, wait for food.

"Hilario wanted to kill them with a spade. He says if you don't they come back every year."

"That's what swallows do. They come back."

"I won't let him do it."

The mother golondrina is perched on the casita wall in the patio, a worm in her mouth, waiting for us to leave. I flip a switch by the door. A light goes on. The chicks stop chirping.

"Electricity."

"That's a whole story," Masako says wearily. "I'll tell you at dinner."

Twilight. I close the front door behind me and look up and down our new street. Calle Flor, two blocks long, little used by crosstown traffic, winds one way south into an unpaved lane leading to the park. Homes large and small, some well kept, some little more than shacks, line both sides of the cobbled street, their walls adjoining. There are a few parked cars on our side, none on the other; there wouldn't be room. Above the houses, dusk's deep blue eats the red of sunset. I cross to the sidewalk opposite, turn and look back at our house's peeling white facade, faded mesquite doors, bent metal drainpipe, cracked roof molding.

Masako comes out. I mime taking her picture in front of our new front door. She musters a wry smile.

"Tomorrow you stay with the workers," she says as we head for town. "I haven't been out in two days."

"Sure."

There are few commercial establishments on Calle Flor: a little *tiendita* mid-block selling Cokes and soap and toilet paper, a "unisex" hair salon, a small café on the corner that's always empty. Foreigners live in the hilly blocks above us, though all our immediate neighbors seem to be Mexicans. At Calle Umarán, where our street ends, we turn right. Half a block down from the jardín, we turn into La Mama.

La Mama, our destination at the end of every trip, had come to symbolize ecstatic arrival—reconnection to our voluptuous Mexican life. Road-weary and hungry, we'd stumble in, order from the Mexican-Italian menu, let the Andean flutes and flamenco strains release us from care. Tonight, slumping into seats at a table in the flower-filled patio, sober and preoccupied, I sense a sea change: with the purchase of the house, we've entered a more freighted, less carefree Mexico.

This afternoon, rocking along in the bus from Mexico City among cardboard boxes, campesinos, and babies in rebozos, I'd tried to form a picture of the house on Calle Flor. I could only remember the general plan, certain indelible images of decay, the breathtaking view from the roof. While I'd stayed in L.A. attending to writing and publishing work, Masako had been getting the place up and running, minimally habitable. With no phone in the house, we'd been out of touch until Elenita had loaned us one. Then the line had mysteriously died, entailing several days' fruitless effort trying to get a repairman in. Finally Felipe had tipped Masako off: go to the Telmex office early in the morning, find a repair guy getting into his truck, entice him over with a little *grasa* (grease—another Mexican euphemism for the payoff). The simplest tasks seemed to take forever. I'd tried to sound sympathetic on the phone but couldn't understand why buying an appliance, getting gas service, putting new locks on the doors were so difficult. "Just tell the water heater guy to bring the tanks over. He's only three blocks away." Steely silence on the other end. Clearly I didn't understand.

As the Mexico City bus had swung down the steep curve bordering the town, offering its first heady glimpse of San Miguel's spires and rooftops, I'd thought: We don't even own this house; a Mexican bank does. We're at the mercy of an inscrutable, Napoleonic, graft-riddled system. The whole thing rests on a perilous quicksand of trust.

Never own a house, an older novelist once told me. It sucks money and attention, the two things a writer never has enough of. We'd bought the house in L.A. after years of renting, but ownership's alleged joys—striding about the back forty, jarring up marmalade in your own kitchen, puttering in the garage—had left me cold. Why, then, own a house in Mexico, and under such perilous terms, and in this condition? Fixing up spaces together has never been our strong suit. Each of us, an older sibling, is headstrong, expects to prevail in a discussion. We're full of ideas, short on execution. Masako reads *Metropolitan Home*, keeps folders of clippings, watches the design and decorating shows; but when it's time to pull a room together she'd rather go buy more things to put in it, or get back to work in her studio. I'd spent too many young summers gardening, building, laying patios. I'd worked a year on a construction crew when I was first trying to write. I've put in my grunt hours, know a few things about houses and gardens; but those young summers left me with utter disinterest in working in them.

As the taxi had turned down Calle Flor—a street I'd savored as a kind of literary walking corridor or dreamscape connecting me to the Parque Juárez, the old waterworks, the art school—it now bore a new set of codes: money, objects, ownership, work.

Over ensalada mixta and a filete tampiqueña (thin grilled beef with enchilada and French fries), while the guitarist called Lobo furiously thrums, Masako speaks of her travails, her frustrations. Antonio hadn't paid last year's electric bill, and she and Felipe had to chase him down in a cantina and walk him to the municipio. Then it turned out the yearly water bill—there are no meters here—hadn't been paid for seven years, but by then Antonio had left town for a month.

"The first day, I figured I'd better change the door locks. The guy from the key shop on Hidalgo came and took them off. He said he'd be back right away, *ahorita*. I felt I should stay by the front door. Who would come in? What would they take? Still, I kept imagining Antonio coming back for the chandelier. The entrada floor was filthy and there wasn't a single piece of furniture in the house. I had no place to sit down. I stood by the door waiting for the locksmith to return for two and a half hours. *Ahorita.*"

"*Ahorita* doesn't mean right away, *pronto* doesn't mean

fast, *mañana* may not mean tomorrow. And if somebody says *quince días*, two weeks, you're out of luck."

Hilario Beltrán seems to have worked his way into Masako's esteem: helping with the move, staining beams, hanging new fixtures, weeding the garden. A pleasant, good-looking man of forty or so, he's clearly stumping for the job of gardener and handyman. We'll have to figure out the details: what, how often, how much. We haven't a clue. Urgent flamenco *bulerías* yield to the gentler strains of Andean pipes. Gradually the candlelit courtyard, the jasmine smell, the music, the starry sky assuage us.

We leave La Mama and walk up to the jardín. It's nearing ten by the clock tower. A few people linger about the plaza benches, chatting with friends or just contemplating the Parroquia's darkened mass, its cantilevered spires silhouettes now, erased of detail. We used to enter or leave the jardín from the other side to get to the Ambos Mundos, or to the casita on Calle Quebrada; now we live "behind" the Parroquia, with the jardín, locus of all things, in mirror image.

In the portales, one stall is still open at the far end, the proprietress and her daughter chatting beneath an electric bulb. We buy a candy bar for solace, split it walking home. By the second block of Calle Flor, there's little light and no people. The moon hides behind a cloud. The street is almost pitch-black. I've always felt safe in Mexico, after the first uneasy days when I knew nothing; Masako the same. U.S. headlines routinely trumpet Mexican roadside assaults, assassinations, and drug vendettas; Mexican dailies detail grisly horrors of their own. But trouble in this part of Mexico is uncommon, most likely to arise from negligence or passion. A few months ago, *El Sol de Bajío* reported that eighty-nine-year-old Emilio Vásquez was arrested in a nursing home in nearby Celaya for stabbing to death a ninety-two-year-old rival in love; the woman was eighty-seven. A local bus driver fell asleep while driving his Flecha Amarilla bus alone and plunged into a culvert a few miles outside of town; a week later his brother Jorge fell asleep in his car a block from the same spot and died. Each's name is now emblazoned on a roadside shrine topped by a cross. "Aren't you afraid in Mexico?" L.A. friends ask, clicking on car alarms, maintaining attack dogs, sleeping with weapons beneath their pillows, their childrens' schools patrolled by police.

A naked lightbulb shines in the broken-paned lamp over our door. Fishing in my pocket for the key, I realize I left it in my other pants inside the house.

I look up and down the street at the uninterrupted facades, each connected to the next. No side entrances, no alley. Only a key, or a tall ladder, will get us into our house. Awaken neighbors, climb over their roofs? Unthinkable. What a way to introduce ourselves. I look at Masako, chagrined.

She produces a key from her jacket pocket, glances at me. "I wouldn't have appreciated having to spend the night at the Ambos Mundos. The workers get here before eight."

I lie awake in the dark on our new *cama matrimonial con cajones* (nice Spanish wordplay: a marital bed with "drawers"—the word *cajones* dangerously, or fittingly, one letter away from *cojones*, "balls"). Masako is asleep, exhausted from the day's work. I'm still on L.A. time, two hours earlier. I feel little tiredness, only tension, uneasiness.

I sit up, fumble for a book of matches, light a small candle by the bed. The house is full of candles, *velas,* she bought at the funeral parlor on Calle Mesones for power outages, a regular feature of San Miguel life. I blow out the wax match. On the matchbox cover is Chac Mool, the Mayan god who reclines on his elbows, like me—though I don't feel very godlike right now.

We've ruined our Arcadia, I think. We'd been happy here; now we are irritable, we quarrel. Misgivings flood me. I wish we were back in our simple room at the Ambos Mundos above the empty swimming pool.

Candlelight illuminates the ceiling's recesses—the dark pine beams eighteen feet up, the unpainted bricks between them. It's a dramatic colonial room, its height allowing mind and eye to range unconstrained. Looking up into the space becalms me.

Along the north end of the room, twin sets of windows run the full height of the wall. Outside, white moonlight splashes the patio where mounds of cement harden on the slate. I can see up into the avocado tree, and the domed cupola atop the casita's second story. A night bird sings—a brief, tweeting question, repeated.

Suddenly: "Thwock!"

I sit up, startled. It sounded like a gun going off.

"Somebody's in the patio," I whisper. Mentally I inventory a defense. Knife? Candle? The interior doors are unlocked. Where to run? Who to call for help?

Masako stirs. "It's just one of those hard avocados hitting the stones," she murmurs. "They do it all night." She turns away, pulls the sheet up.

I lie back on the pillow, feeling foolish. Church bells wash over the house, soft and reverberant. New neighborhood, new church, new bells. It must be straight up on some hour. Eleven? No, there's the twelfth bell. Midnight.

I lie back on the pillow. We'll deal with problems in the morning, mañana. Forget ahorita. I blow out the candle, close my eyes.

I hear a scraping sound nearby, like rustling paper. I sit up, relight the candle. A dark brown cockroach, bigger than my thumb, freezes in the light a few feet from the bed. I stretch out my arm slowly, fishing for my sandal. The *cucaracha* skitters crazily across the tiles, nestles against the wall.

I stand up, take a single barefoot step, and flatten him with my huarache.

*"La cucaracha, la cucaracha, ya no puede caminar."*

Now you can't walk anymore. Tomorrow I'll go to Lucha's pharmacy and get that Chinese chalk she sells. Draw a white line, the roaches eat it and die.

Keeping the candle lit, I lie on my side gazing at the floor, listening to the night's sounds, on cockroach alert.

It's either them or us. I'm ready to do battle for the house.

# Chapter 11

# Casa de Misterios

A BIRD'S DESCENDING TRILL CASCADES in falling arcs, almost an octave. Mysterious, haunting. I've heard it the whole week I've been here. It begins just before dawn with the first bells, then by the time the sun hits the cupola dome of the casita it's gone. I have no idea what bird it is; hundreds migrate through the region.

Light advances down the patio walls. The tall windows, which let in indirect north light, must have been installed in the 1950s, judging by their modernist style. The original windows were undoubtedly low colonial arches, making the room very dim. The sun passes over the building but never shines in, keeping the house cool in summer.

Masako is still asleep. I get up, slip into my clothes, and step up into the dining room. Each room in the house is a few steps higher or lower than the next. We live on a hill, in a hill town. From the front door it's a descent by degrees to the garden, from the garden a climb to the front. The dining-room skylight, which leaks less now since the incomprehensible Juan gobbed its joints with Fester *impermeabilizante,* admits a wide rectangle of light onto a round, raw pine table covered with food, papers, tools. Masako bought it from a woman and her family on the road to Celaya. The unfinished wood chairs come from the Tuesday market.

Unused plastic sheeting, newspapers, spackle, and a large bucket of paint lie in the corner. Fresh paint spots the floor. Convincing a Mexican workman to spread ground cover before painting is near impossible; some machismo code dictates painting walls and ceilings without it, mixing cement on patio stones then leaving it to harden, cementing an entire wall then going back in to cut an electrical duct afterward. Cleaning up is an afterthought, if thought of at all—a task for invisible peons.

We're patch-painting the house only where it's most needed, using cal, the local lime-laced mixture that gives walls that soulful look when they peel—a process that begins distressingly soon after the paint job is done. Vinyl paint is available here now but we don't like its uniform, artificial finish; and in a country where lots of people will work for little, worrying about getting things to last, or saving on labor, seems a kind of vice. Maybe this explains why hours spent chipping paint off a floor rather than covering it first makes sense to people. More hours of work is good, not bad. Seeing a gringo do his own work when so many suffer from lack of it is not seen as democratic but penurious, ungracious.

The maestro who repaired the patio wall says that the humidity around the base of the dining room may be something we have to live with, as it seeps in from the neighbors' garden. Vague thoughts of color cross our mind, but for now we'll keep the whole place white, a victory for my spare aesthetic. To avoid unnecessary clashes, Masako and I have worked out a scheme of territoriality: the kitchen and her studio are hers to do with as she wishes, my studio mine; the dining room, bedroom, and other common spaces we negotiate.

Crossing the cool, dark kitchen by feel, I clamber up onto the counter by way of a three-legged mesquite footstool and throw open the green windowless shutters to the street. Strong white light floods in. Early workers walk by chatting. I hear a few cars in the distance, a radio from a construction site down the street.

I clamber back down and make coffee at the blue stove, which works now—though already a handle has come off in my hand, the clock has stopped, and the left burner pilot won't light. The day after I arrived I ran down the gas truck and, in the Mexican manner, enticed the driver with pesos to come fill our tanks pronto. I sip coffee at a small rectangular table, also from the Tuesday market, and tear off a piece of banana bread left over from a trip to Espino's, our new grocery two blocks away. Venturing out with our plaid bolsas, we discover, bit by bit, *poco a poco*, our new neighborhood.

Some things we don't need to leave the house for. A young girl, fresh as the roses and gladioli she brings, knocks every day. An Indian woman brings ears of corn, cactus, and tortillas daily. I've come to distinguish the various vendors' knockings from friends', and can identify the four-note whistle of the bent man who, unfolding his tiny wood box and grinder, sits at our door sharpening knives and scissors. A limping boy arrives with the daily papers under his arm, reminiscent of the kid who sold the fateful lottery ticket to Bogie in *The Treasure of the Sierra Madre*. A milk truck passes, though we buy *leche pasteurizada* in cartons from the market. Friends stop by with house gifts—a bowl from Elenita; some violets and spider lilies from Olivia, an American actress friend who lives here.

I slice a mango over thick yogurt made fresh by an Italian who has a ranch near town, and sprinkle the local granola on top. We've assembled enough ceramic bowls, plates, and cups to eat and drink from. No more sitting on stairs, plates fashioned of tinfoil on our laps. Flatware and porcelain coffee mugs I brought down from California, courtesy of Masako's parents. Susana has donated an old wooden spice rack. In the red refrigerator there's milk, cheese, tortillas. A half-drunk bottle of Santo Tomás red begun last night in the garden sits on the counter.

Slowly we take possession of this ruin. I've drawn chalk lines with Lucha's magic stick by every exterior door and between rooms, turning the house into a vast hopscotch court. The cucarachas eat the powder and keel over on their backs; yesterday morning I counted eight. The other night, climbing into bed, I spotted a dark brown, rubbery shape on the wall, its curved tail cocked.

The thing about scorpions is that they're slow. Mercifully, they tend to appear one at a time. On the other hand, if you miss your kill it scuttles into the dark surroundings. Then you've got a problem. The brown ones are less lethal than uncommon white ones, but their bite hurts; some people suffer extreme reactions, go into shock, even die. Hilario has been finding them in the woodpile out back. Each morning we shake out our clothes and shoes, careful not to walk around barefoot.

Two nights ago I whacked the scorpion with a rolled-up magazine. He fell to the ground dazed, a few inches from my bare feet. When he tried to crawl under the bed I brought

the magazine down and finished the job. Mighty hunter. As
I was about to whisk the corpse under the bed, Masako cried,
"Wait! I want to draw him." First mosquito etchings, now
scorpions. That which doesn't kill us becomes our art, to
paraphrase the expression.

Bells peal, intimate as breath. One twice; then another,
different double tone; then a single stroke. There are some
hundred bells in San Miguel's churches and chapels, eight in
the tower of the Parroquia alone. The largest, the Parroquia's velvet-toned La Luz, marks our days and nights.

I refill my coffee cup, step out into the entry. There are no
kitchen doors, as Antonio took them along with every other
removable piece of wood in the house excepting the front
doors. Standing in the entrada, I relive that moment of curiosity and dismay when Felipe first led us here a month ago.
Above me, the swallows' nest is empty: the birdlets, having
escaped Hilario's shovel, have flown until next year.

The entry is large enough to be a room. Though it's not
done around here, I recall seeing—in Majorca and in other
warm climates—entradas as sitting rooms: shady, palm-
filled, letting breezes through grillwork open to the street;
women fanning themselves, sipping ice drinks, chatting
with passersby. We think there was once a door in the entrada wall leading into what is now the casita living room.
Was it another bedroom, or the old sala of the original
house? Undoubtedly the present patio was near twice this
size before the wall was built.

In the patio, a few first plants are arrayed along the walls,
wrapped in plastic containers or clay pots: a lime sapling
Masako bought at a nursery, a magenta bougainvillea we
found at the outdoor market, some red geraniums Hilario
brought over from the Quebrada house. An asparagus fern
growing between the slate stones has turned from yellow to

deep green, doubling in size just in these weeks. Water alone seems to bring things back to life. The papaya tree has sprouted a good meter, the skin of its heavy fruits ripening to deep orange. The wall at the end of the patio, repainted now, looks solid.

Each day we decode a little more of the original house, see structure and history through the decay. Our own house as archaeological dig. Hilario and I call it *Casa de Misterios.* Surely it was a single property once, resembling other colonial homes around town: built on the old Moorish or medieval idea—patios, courtyards, fountains, niches, enclosures. The bigger ones, the haciendas, had their own chapels, livestock, tanneries. *Fincas urbanas* like ours had their own stable at least.

Our neighbors to the south seem to walk to town once a day. The mother, portly and bespectacled, leads the way, with the daughter—tall, a little hydrocephalic, it appears— walking awkwardly behind her; and the husband docilely picking up the rear. We have yet to acknowledge each other. We suspect our predecessors—the lady shot in the bar, her daughters who let the place fall into ruin, the shady lawyer Antonio with his trysts—did little to endear the place to the neighborhood, and so we expect a lengthy probation. Our neighbors on the other side are an old woman, a middle-aged one we guess is her daughter, and a grown son or younger brother we surmise is the doctor whose sign hangs over their door. The bakers' property behind our high garden wall in back opens onto the next block.

Light inches down the walls. Crossing the patio, I experience the house's voluminous solidity. Growing up in earthquake country, in houses with lath and plaster walls, I find that this sturdy earth and rock compound steadies the soul. Mexicans are good with stone, *piedra.* Pyramid makers,

builders of vast stone cities. Today's men and boys still know
that dance that stomps the earth, breaks the stone, the *tap
tap* of the *albañil*'s chisel beat heard all over Mexico every
day.

At the end of the patio I turn right and enter the dingy
storeroom, the *bodega*, leading to Masako's studio. A feather
duster atop a sixteen-foot-high bamboo stick, bought from a
man on the street, is thick with cobwebs Marisa and Clarisa
have raked from the upper corners of rooms. A "living room
set" bought off a truck—unfinished pine couch, two arm-
chairs, coffee table—made in the wood-carving village of
Cuanajo in the nearby state of Michoacán, is stacked against
the wall. We'll paint them, put them in the casita. Masako
has bought foam and fabric from La España, a store on Calle
Mesones that will make the cushions for you if you buy their
cloth. Meanwhile more shelves, tables, bed frames, mattresses, and chairs pour in. The house swallows them up.

Over the course of the week I've come to understand
Masako's frustrations better. Things happen, but slowly, and
never as planned. People don't show, or show at odd times,
and inevitably they're late. For every lapse or delay there's a
reason, by somebody's logic. A few days ago Hilario didn't
show up. Masako was furious. The next day he came and
acted as if nothing had happened. At the end of work he said
offhandedly, "Yesterday the roof of my kitchen fell in."

Getting money, even making change, is a constant battle.
*"No tiene cambio, señor?"* the shopkeeper asks when I hand
her the equivalent of two or three dollars. You don't have
change? She's not trying to be difficult; there just aren't
enough smaller bills or coins in circulation. So you wait ten
minutes while she goes next door or up the street in search
of a bit of change. Things cost relatively little, but there are
endless items to get, and we always seem to be running out

of money. At the bank off the jardín I give my credit card to the teller (the same one who, dressed in hooker drag, had danced with me in the Locos parade our first June here—an incident we've never alluded to). He has to call Mexico City to get approval, which may take an hour. In the meantime I go to Don Pedro's hardware to get a pipe fitting or electrical wire, or to Fernández the ironmonger for nails (*clavos*), thumbing my dictionary as I go. We learn the names of new things by necessity, to make our wishes known or to understand what's being said to us. Our dictionaries become dirty, bent, fingered. Nothing romantic or philosophical about *martillo* (hammer), *palo* (shovel), *escombro* (debris).

I leave the bodega and enter the arched, glassed-in room at the end of the patio, my new studio. Masako has found me a small unfinished table and a straight-backed wood chair. Hilario has stuck a lone palm plant in a red pot by the door. That's all. Narrow, white, monkish, with a fireplace. I like it. The only drawback is that it has three doorways—one into our bath and dressing area (another set of doors to replace), one to the patio, and another to the rear garden—ensuring that this will be the main route from the front of the house to the back, killing any privacy the room promises.

Back in our bedroom, I find Masako stirring. *"Hola,"* I whisper, setting a cup of coffee on the table beside her.

Undressing in the huge, dim bathroom, I think: These yellow and green tiles have to go. I stand beneath the shower, looking out through the glass doors into the rear garden, which turns green already, answering to water and attention. A mint plant spreads just outside the door where Masako has also planted basil and a rosemary cutting. Hilario has slipped in a couple of chile plants, we noticed yesterday. The chirimoyo tree's leaves show green, though the jacaranda remains yellow and spindly. We want to keep the roughness we first saw in the garden: unfinished stone walls, tangled ferns, thick palms against the stairs to the roof. A wild garden.

Drying off, I notice the spot where Hilario, patching the east bathroom wall, discovered an old gas outlet and a duct for a vent. This was the original kitchen, then, at the heart of the house, when servants were plentiful to haul groceries and supplies in and out.

A loud knocking on the front door. I climb into my clothes. Another workday begins.

S tonecutters used to live here," Hilario says, holding up a piece of burnished quartz.

"Before the gringa who got shot?"

"Sí."

"Where do the stones come from?"

"The riverbeds. The mountains. The marble quarry in Querétaro."

Midmorning in the garden. Sunlight casts bright patches through the trees. The air smells rich from the earth Hilario is turning over to plant spider lilies in front of the arched windows of Masako's studio. I sit in the corner on the stone seat beneath the ring in the wall, noting things to be done.

We've been at it six weeks. The world outside the house, let alone San Miguel or Mexico, has grown dim, except to the extent that it provides us with things we need for the house. While Masako and I work on, Hilario pursues his own thrice-weekly investigations. A willing if untalented gardener, he collages cuttings in pots in strange combinations, confuses weeds and plants. He's not much of a painter, carpenter, or plumber either, though he does a little of all of these things: *milusos*, as Mexicans say, a thousand uses, a handyman. More important, he has an appetite for taking this place on with us. He's willing to dig beneath the stones to find a sewer pipe, stand for an hour with a hose in his hand, repair a frayed electrical wire. A taxi driver on Sundays, he knows his way around town: who does what, where you get things.

Mysteries unfold. Yesterday Hilario and I found the tunnel in the backyard that purportedly served as an escape route during the 1812 revolution and again in the 1920s. It is said to run from the former Canal family home (now a bank) on the jardín to their summer home (presently the Instituto Allende art school): about a mile. An elderly neighbor across the street told Hilario that gold and silver had been buried in our garden by escapees during the Cristero wars early in this century; he suspects the lawyer Antonio Rocha of having dug it up.

We've strung a laundry line from the jacaranda tree to the washroom door by Masako's studio to hang Marisa and Clarisa's scrubbed sheets, blankets, and clothes. A new "Swiss" filter attached to our kitchen tap supposedly makes the water potable—"Clear as an Alpine Stream," the brochure claims. Two days ago we cut a drain into the channel running under my studio, routing rainwater to the sewage pipe in Masako's studio bathroom so the garden will flood less when it rains.

While Hilario digs in the gladiolus bulbs with a shovel, butterflies circle around his head—small white ones with green bodies, huge orange and black monarchs—a vision out of García Márquez. Hilario thinks we should kill the butterfly larvae that feed on the leaves. Sweet-tempered, personally benign, Hilario's view of nature and animals is unsentimental, functional, short-term. He listens politely to Masako's protests in the name of beauty, her pleas against entering lethal chemicals into the food chain. He accedes only because she is the *dueña* of the casa.

The smooth-skinned black avocados that fall like pistol shots from our tree are near-tasteless but work well as guacamole spread when chopped up in a salsa of tomato, onions, and cilantro. There are so many that Hilario takes most home to his nine children, his wife who is pregnant again (*"No habrá más errores,"* he says, a twinkle in his eye, assuring me this will be his last child), and his pig. With a growing family, he adds rooms to his house on the hill above the covered market, while his cheerful, pretty wife takes in sewing and raises her swelling brood.

From the garden corner I watch Masako moving about in her studio, making first gestures of occupancy: clearing materials from the work site out of the way, hanging a bank of lights against the west wall, stretching a few canvases. Likewise I've set up a desk in my studio, plugged in computer and printer, begun to assemble a rudimentary library of books. Our renter in the casita, Lisette, is quiet but for the welcome strains of Bach partitas and Miles's *Kind of Blue* wafting across the walls in the morning.

Each week we work on the house a little less, live in it a little more. We try to remember we have time, that time is what this is all about. We war with our gringo compulsions to "fall under the lash of completion," as one writer describes it. We bought the house not to renovate it but to live in it: a site of pleasure and revelation. "We've got to get rid of those kitchen tiles," one says. "We will," the other consoles. *Suave, suave;* gently, gently. There is nobody to make an impression upon. We have no plans to sell it, and it's paid for. Let's watch the light move, note birds that visit, discover where it's hot or cool, see where the winds run, track the seasons.

Still, decay obliges some response or we'll be entombed in dysfunction. If the three termite-eroded beams in the dining room aren't replaced soon, the ceiling will collapse. The loose wires festooning the patio walls like party streamers short out the system, become potentially lethal in storms. The fresh cracks in my studio wall that force me to move my table each time it rains will only get worse. Our water heater erupted in flames when Hilario lit the pilot, singeing his eyebrows. We still haven't a couch to sit on, a chair that isn't gathered around a table, a table that doesn't wobble. Repairs that exceed Hilario's low threshold of expertise demand *plomeros, electricistas,* and *carpinteros* who may or may not arrive. The commonest appliances aren't available in San Miguel or cost exorbitantly. So we stand over the burner with a piece of bread on the end of a fork, or fire up the entire oven, for want of a toaster or toaster oven.

There are hours in the day, though, when work ceases and we're alone in the quiet spaces. We squat against walls watching hummingbirds suck the papaya blooms, the young purple bougainvillea knit itself into the corner between the entrada and the dining room door. We stand naked in the sun-flecked garden after showers, wander barefoot through the cool, silent rooms. At dusk we experience the drama of opening the front door and emerging into the reddening town. We fall asleep in high, wide spaces that shelter long dreams. Maybe we weren't so crazy after all.

We have hot and cold water now. The new toilets have seats, the phone works most of the time.

The mint plant advances across the spice garden, the rosemary sprig is a baby bush, and Hilario is harvesting bright red chiles from his plant. We have a functioning kitchen and tables to eat from: all very spare, but with lots of candles and vases of fresh flowers bought in the covered market or from the girls who come to the door, the house shows signs of life. Yesterday we bought a half dozen woven straw mats from a grinning, gold-toothed man on a bicycle who cries *"Petates!"* when he passes by, and spread them around the floors of the house.

Ambitiously we talk of having friends who helped with the house over for a meal. Susana offers to pitch in; she has a new dessert recipe for something called mango mousse. Masako is turning a big ex-hacienda door into a dining room table with the aid of Bonifacio "Boni" Ortiz, a short, muscular carpenter whose ancient mother sells flowers door to door. Fashioning table legs of pine salvaged from the rotted ceiling beams, Boni braces them with an old ox yoke. Eight *equipal* chairs of leather and wood sit stacked in the entrada, waiting to be arrayed around the new table when Boni finishes putting a stain on it.

The telephone is a new development in our Mexican life. Suddenly we're in touch. Every time it rings I jump: shades of the life we'd left behind. Masako bought a Sony shortwave radio from a departing gringa, and Hilario rigged up an antenna out of a rusty wire attached to a nail. At night we sit hunched in her cavernous studio beneath a bare bulb, teasing out of the static Radio Havana, Radio Taiwan, the BBC World News (John Le Carré reading *Smiley's People*), or Canadian CBC specials on the maple sugar crisis, the history of the Royal Mounted Police. Masako, who gets media hungry sometimes—devouring the fashion magazines on the stands at La Golondrina, attending the weekly video movie showing at a nearby hotel on a murky little screen—is thrilled to pick up snatches of National Public Radio on Voice of America in between jazz shows aimed at the Eastern bloc in "special English," spoken v-e-r-y s-l-o-w-l-y. Then the stations fade out, leaving us with Christian revivalist radio from Texas or Top 40 from Matamoros.

In the garden, Hilario has finished planting bulbs and rakes weeds into a compost pile. Hearing a knock at the front door, I cross the patio to the entrada and open it. A burro nuzzles my crotch.

*"Tierra?"* The driver, in shaggy clothes and a sombrero, waves his switch at four burros bearing bags of earth.

"Do we need more soil?" I call to Hilario.

*"Sí."*

I buy eight bags of the rich earth he's hauled up from fields down by the lake for the peso equivalent of a buck a bag. The man, who has frizzy hair and a pink harelip, unties the bags from the burros. One by one he loads them on his back and hauls the fresh, dark soil into our garden.

# Chapter 12

# Mango Mousse

WE SHARE OUR HOUSE WITH ALL
manner of living things, divided into friend
and foe—though the list changes. All
birds—the soothing doves with their
double-note love call, the profuse brown
starlings that whir at dawn, the woodpecker
that whacks at the avocado tree late mornings, even the raucous crows—are friends.
Any manner of butterfly is welcome. The
*grillos,* crickets who turn our bedroom into a
nightly La Scala, surround us with good
fortune like Chinese potentates. Unfortu-
nately they proliferate rapidly—I found a
litter of fifteen tiny babies on the wall
behind the new armoire—and must have
called their relatives in, too, for now the
nocturnal symphony has become a throb-
bing din. Still I can't summon the same
predatory glee chasing a hopping cricket

with my shoe that I can exterminating a cockroach or a scorpion.

A sharp, intermittent night chirping in our entrada is not, our friend Pepe informs us, a big cricket but a bat's sonar. Last night in the patio it zoomed inches over my head, a spectral whoosh. Pepe, who teaches at a local secondary school (his real name is José—"Pepe" being a nickname that I just learned stands for "putative paternity," in reference to Joseph the father in the Immaculate Conception), points out that bats eat their weight in mosquitoes. This puts bats in the "friend" category, along with the thin-legged spiders, *arañas,* who patrol for mosquitoes and other microorganisms in the high corners of our rooms, sparing them a sweep with the bamboo-handled feather duster.

The cucarachas are on the run from my magic chalk stick, and thanks to Clarisa and Marisa's moppings and sweepings, traces of mice and rats have abated. One morning last week, though, we found a hole in a bag of rice and droppings by the red refrigerator. Later the same day, Hilario noticed tooth marks in a fallen avocado. He brought over a handmade wood-and-wire mesh trap big enough to bag a raccoon. Masako insisted we first try the sticky pads she'd had me bring down from the States. That night we heard a terrible squeaking but didn't care to get up to check. Morning light revealed sticky footprints but no prey. Hilario slathered his fat trap with beans and spicy salsa and set it behind the red refrigerator. The next morning we found our victim—a chubby, bucktoothed gray rat. Now we store all grains in the cabinets and swab the floors daily.

Rats and mice are on the run in San Miguel because of a recent shift in the food chain. When we first arrived in town, the fierce barking of roof dogs accompanied a walk down any street day or night. Some were left to roam their owners' rooftops, others were caged in or leashed. Though they provided a simple form of protection against intruders, most were wretched creatures, devoid of companionship. The plight of Mexican dogs in general—as the local, vocal humane society is quick to point out—is not especially happy. Yet the scruffy street curs one sees around any arcade or outdoor food area eat scraps, keep streets and floors clean, chase off other unwanted creatures: a kind of peon dog, lowly but functional, respected by Mexicans to the degree it is useful. An actress friend who visited from L.A. and stayed in the casita was so dismayed by the street dogs' plight that she bought good hamburger meat from the butcher and began distributing it, to the great amusement of San Miguelenses. Meanwhile rich Mexicans and gringos keep domesticated dogs, and even breed show dogs they occasionally march across the jardín, to the amazement of the street dogs who watch blankly, tongues lolling.

The inexplicable reduction in roof dogs makes for quieter walks in the streets; but now cats roam the rooftops unimpeded, sometimes in gangs, descending into gardens and patios. The old central blocks of town—labyrinthine, Arabic, impenetrable to humans except through doors—are porous to cats, who skirt along the tops of walls, hop spaces between buildings, pad across pipe lines. Loyal to nobody, they spray their scents on our roof and stairs and garden. They fight and fuck, fearing nobody as they can always flee across the rooftops. San Miguel de Allende threatens to become, like Venice, a town of cats.

Of course Hilario wants to poison them all. Masako argues that ill cats will pollute the ecosystem before dying—not to mention that some of these cats have owners. My argument against killing them is simpler: Have you noticed there are almost no rats these days? Thank the cats. Privately I suspect that when we leave town Hilario will put out poison anyway.

Each night before getting into bed we examine the white walls, whack the bedding, place our shoes on a high stool. We've hung gauze netting over the bed not just against mosquitoes and termites but against the possibility of a scorpion dropping on us in the night, as they seem to live in the beams. Hilario says they breed in the woodpile, then work their way into houses during the cool season or the rains. Imitating the *pica*, the bite, with two fingers, he jumps and giggles.

A few nights ago, crawling into bed, I felt a sharp sting on my temple. Jumping up, I saw the brown scorpion on the pillow. He scurried away before I could nail him. Stinging spread along the side of my face. I went to the kitchen and grabbed a *limón*, the Mexican cure-all. Slicing it open, I dribbled juice over the sting. It did nothing.

In the bathroom mirror, watching the mark turn red, I called to Masako, "If my head starts to swell, or if I hallucinate or go unconscious, get me to the hospital." Masako called a doctor friend. She said if it gets worse I should go to Lucha's pharmacy and get a shot of something called Becodon.

We beat frantically among the blankets and sheets, checked along the floor and walls, but couldn't find the scorpion. When after twenty minutes my head hadn't swelled up, and the pain and redness hadn't worsened, we started joking about it: "Well, I'm not dead yet." Still the idea of going back to bed with the scorpion still around was unnerving. But there was no other place to sleep. Finally we tucked the ends of the mosquito netting in like a blanket— which served either to banish the scorpion or entrap it in the bedding with us—and, leaving the lights on, slept fitfully. By morning the stinging and redness was gone.

So far, we survive what the house throws at us.

We must have fallen asleep early tonight, for it's only ten when we're startled awake by a mariachi troupe. They sound as if they're in our kitchen. I stumble to the front door and peer out. Ten black-clad musicians are singing at the top of their lungs in front of the doctor's house next door. *"Con corazón, amigos!"* exhorts the fat, mustachioed leader, waving his fiddle bow in the air.

In front of our neighbors' house to our right, another mariachi group, dressed in brown, starts up. The two bands overlap, some fifty feet apart: an amazing, awful cacophony.

Sleep is out of the question. We throw on clothes and climb up the back stairs to the roof. The dueling mariachis wail on, oblivious to each other—like a stereo with a different song coming out of each speaker. Above us, the moon is two days past full, the stars profuse, brilliant. Leaning over the roof's edge, I see the doctor's mother by her door, beaming, her son beside her. To our right, the lady with the retarded daughter stands contentedly with her husband.

"I know what it is," Masako says, as we retreat to the rear of the roof. "They're both named Carmen."

"What's that got to do with it?"

"Elenita told me. July sixteenth is the Day of Carmen. From the Carmelite order. Women named Carmen get serenaded."

"But both at once?"

"The mariachis are just doing their job."

Fully awake now, we sit on the roof in the moonlight, waiting out the dissonant tributes.

"You have to admit it's rather moving," Masako says.

I put my arm around her. There's no day of Masako, here or in Japan or anywhere, I guess, no yearly serenade.

Finally the first band lets up. In the relative silence, the remaining mariachis' lament—something about *"siempre mi corazón"*—sounds almost sweet. A breeze ripples across the roofs. The cross atop the Parroquia's tallest spire, its corona of electric bulbs lit for the Carmen celebration, blazes like a vaudeville marquee, or a makeup mirror.

"It's nice up here at night," Masako says.

"It's always nice up here. Come up at sunset. Or daybreak."

The second mariachi band ends off. Calle Flor subsides into its prevailing silence. We stand up and clamber gingerly among the pipes, broken tiles, and glass.

"We could get rid of this junk," I say. "Grade the roof, reinforce it. Build a stone stairway up from the front patio to make it easier to get to. And a veranda right about *here* . . ." I walk to the spot I'd picked during rooftop climbs over the last month. We stand in the dark facing the Parroquia, the hills to our right, the nunnery's domed mass ahead to our left. "We could connect all the rooftops. It would double the experience of the house."

"There are rules about changing the facades."

"Not the roofs. As long as you can't see from the street. I see people working on theirs all the time."

"One day," Masako says. *"Ojalá."*

*Ojalá*—that expression meaning "hopefully" or "God willing," with its suggestion of surrender to fate—creeps deeper into our vocabulary the more we work on the house.

"Let's have a dinner Sunday night," Masako says, "for the people who've helped with the house."

"There's no place to sit down. Boni hasn't finished staining the dining room table."

"Susana has that recipe for mango mousse."

"The kitchen barely works."

"Sunday morning we'll shop," she says resolutely.

A fierce Saturday night rain knocks fruit and blooms off trees and plants, exposing new roof leaks and taking out the phone and power lines, but Sunday morning breaks bright and clear. We gather up fallen avocados and a papaya, spread a few towels on the floors to soak up leaks, and head off to market with empty bolsas to shop for the big dinner.

Passing the horse-drawn ice cream cart in front of the Parroquia, we cross the jardín diagonally and head down Calle Reloj. A new food specialty shop—harbinger of that ominous "gentrification" Mina and Paul had darkly prophesied that night at La Dolce Vita?—stocks goat cheese, Black Forest ham, Spanish-style sausage, and pâtés smoked with dusky chipotle sauce. Many of the delicacies come not from the global marketplace but from nearby ranches run by French Mexicans who arrived during Maximilian's era, or Italian, German, or Swiss farmers who settled here generations ago. I buy a bottle of Chilean red from the pipe-smoking proprietor, but Masako finds little of interest: for hors d'oeuvres, she has in mind a simple ball of string-type cheese from Oaxaca served with *tostaditas,* tortilla chips.

A few doors down at La Colmena we pluck a hot loaf of sesame bread and a dozen flat sugar cookies to go with Susana's mango mousse, then head up Calle Mesones to buy candles. Travelers used to bed down horses and mules in the *mesones,* the big courtyard inns that lined this street and gave it its name: much like the *caravanserai* of North Africa. Hilario remembers coming as a child by burro from his rancho with his father, checking in their saddles, sleeping on a horse or mule blanket, and paying in the morning on the way out. One *mesón* remains a hotel; the others are either closed or have become restaurants or furniture stores. And horses are rarely seen on the street these days.

At Inhumación Gonzales, the funeral parlor, we buy a dozen long paraffin candles. It's likely the power will remain out, as it's Sunday and the repair crews are off. A half block up, nestled in the stone walls of San Francisco church, La Nueva Lucha sells candles, bags of grain, and brooms. Across the street, behind San Miguel's first gas pump—Pemex #1, a rusted metal artifact out of a 1940s Walker Evans photo—La Balanza stocks dry goods, rope, mops, and the stubby candles in yellow and red wax paper that say *"Lux Perpetua"* beneath a stamped image of a young, grieving Mary. Masako buys a few dozen for tonight: in the absence of electricity, furniture or decor, candles and flowers will serve as our smoke and mirrors.

In Martín's dimly lit vegetable store, the proprietor's hulking, taciturn son heaps lettuce, tomatoes, carrots, avocados, chiles, and asparagus into my bolsa. I grab a tub of mesquite honey fresh from a nearby ranch while Masako buys *caldo de pollo*, chicken broth, for the squash blossom soup she decided to make only this morning, when a willowy Indian girl in a green sweater showed up at the door with buckets of bright orange-yellow calabaza flowers and blue corn tortillas.

The main course we've planned lies within our kitchen's rude capabilities: blue corn chicken enchiladas with *mole*, rice, black beans, and a side dish of *rajas*—green chile strips—and onions. The chicken lady down the street also sells Guanajuato-style mole, dark and sweeter than its Oaxacan cousin. She ladles it from a tub into a plastic bag, ties it at the top, and places the jiggling black concoction atop my food-swollen bolsa.

A block away, the outdoor market is in full Sunday swing, indifferent to rumors that the mayor plans to relocate the stalls down by the river and turn this area into a paved civic plaza with an equestrian statue of Allende. Beneath a canvas awning we pick ripe yellow mangoes and magenta cactus berries called *garambullos* for Susana's mousse, four fat green chiles, and a sprig of *epazote,* an indigenous plant called wormseed in English, to spice the squash blossom soup. Masako buys diced cactus for salad and dried red hibiscus leaves for an iced tea drink to go with the fresh grape juice we bought Friday at a stand on the road to Dolores Hidalgo. In a small grocery store by the covered market, I load Tehuacán mineral water, Dos Equis beer, tequila for Carlos, and rum for Arnaud into my second bolsa, which strains at its seams. Inside the market, we take a couple of stools at a *licuado* stand to get off our feet.

"Do you notice how clean meat is here?" Masako says. "When you walk past the *carnicería* it never smells."

"San Miguel used to be a livestock center. A community of Mulatto tanners had their own church right down the street until a Spanish family bought them out in the early 1800s and turned it into the Oratorio church."

We sip orange and banana *licuados,* eggs blended in.

"What happened to the Mulattos?" Masako asks.

"They intermarried, blended into the population. Like the eggs in this licuado."

"Let's get a taxi home. Those bottles are heavy."

"It's mostly downhill."

On the way out of the market, Masako stops at the flower seller's and picks red and yellow roses, lilies, and margaritas. The vendor snips the longest stalks, binds the flowers in old newspapers.

Lugging our cargo home, we pass the Hotel Ambos Mundos. Rafael is standing out front smoking. He considers our bulging bolsas. *"Compraron mucho,"* he says. *"Compramos una casa,"* we tell him proudly. *"Felicidades,"* he says, and invites us in to take a look at the new hotel paint job.

We step through the tall entry and set our bags down in

the hotel office—as we'd done that first evening four years ago. Pedro the courtyard parrot greets us with his rote *"Hola!"* Rafael's daughter Verónica, back from architecture studies at the university in Guanajuato, has begun an orange and blue color scheme on the courtyard walls to questionable effect.

It seems a long time ago, our months at the Ambos Mundos. Crazy Jeem, the quarreling Gabriela and Gustavo, the Canadian performance artist, the drug dealers who finally drove us out. Who lives in old Emil's studio now, the one Masako had coveted and finally gotten? A hundred-and-two-year-old lady painter, Rafael tells us. *"Qué milagro!"* María the cook calls, waving from the kitchen, smiling through new gold teeth.

Wandering the old hacienda grounds, we come upon Ramiro's once-beautiful vegetable garden, sadly fallow. Rafael tells us he'd fallen dead there one day of a heart attack.

The clientele appears a little more sedate these days, the price of a room nearing a semi-respectable nine dollars a night. New cleaning girls bear bundles of fresh sheets in their arms. Out back, the weedy field by the ice factory has been cleared for some new project of Rafael's. Vicente Arias's art studio is still there, next to the washing area— he'll be coming for dinner tonight—and the empty swimming pool collects new waste. Our old room against the barracks wall appears to be occupied by a sculptor, judging by the twisted cast-iron forms in the window.

Odd, to revisit the old hotel. Ambos Mundos: Both worlds. Was our life in Mexico, this town, the house on Calle Flor prefigured in that moment we first stumbled into the lobby, bearing weary, fractured selves?

On the way out, we find Rafael talking to a chubby, pregnant woman with a little boy at her side.

"Isn't that Conchita?" Masako whispers.

The woman turns, bats flirtatious brown eyes at us. Yes, it's Ramiro's eroticized daughter, heavy with second child now. Seeing her, something heavy settles on me too and I don't want to carry the bolsas the remaining blocks home. We wave down a passing cab, which turns out to be driven by Hilario, doing his Sunday turn as a taxista.

Clarisa and Marisa never stop talking. What do they say in their idiomatic teen slang? Is it all about boys? Tirelessly they jabber, scrubbing glasses and dishes, grinding foods and spices on the heavy stone pre-Columbian *molcajete,* while Masako cooks the squash blossoms in chicken broth, purees tomatoes and onions. With the electricity still out, the ice trays have melted and we can't call anyone to bring ice because the phone is down.

The air is thick with sweet, bitter *mole* aroma and the charred smell of rajas cooking on the comal, the flat cast-iron griddle built into the blue stove between the burners. I'm sent out into the garden to pick rosemary, red chiles from Hilario's plant, and little *jitomates* off the vine for salad. I array forests of candles in the interior rooms, entrada, patio, and garden: the tall ones in ceramic holders, the short Lux Perpetua candles grouped on metal Corona trays. Let there be *Lux.*

In the dining room, Boni Ortiz's stain is dry to the touch, and the ox-yoke brace supports the water-filled flower vases I place on the table. I arrange new leather and wood chairs between metal ones, put out extra stools, and spread a beautiful piece of *manta,* muslin from the Aurora factory outside of town—that pure white cloth the campesinos used to wear, a threatened industry now—as a tablecloth. Blue and white plates, saucers, and bowls from Dolores Hidalgo will serve tonight. Fresh flowers explode out of dark blue glass vases.

"Today when we were shopping," Masako says, setting the table, "I thought of Paul and Mina. That first time we saw them on the street and followed them home to their kitchen."

"I wish they were here."

Paul's illness has been diagnosed at last: ALS, amyotrophic lateral sclerosis, a degenerative muscular disease of unknown origin—the condition the physicist Stephen Hawking has, though Paul's form is even more deadly. Apparently Mexico had nothing to do with its onset. Already Paul is unable to paint and, confined to bed, has taken up writing on a word processor. Mina tends to him at their home in California. The outlook is poor: a year at most.

Susana drops by midafternoon to take her mangoes and garambullos over to her apartment on Calle Reloj, where there is electricity and a blender to prepare the mysterious mousse. She promises to bring ice tonight.

By late afternoon the house is quiet, the garrulous girls have left. Still no electricity or phone. Rain clouds rumble out the window. Nice if they'd discharge and pass by dinner hour; we'd hoped to use the patio and garden, as the kitchen and dining room still leak.

"We may be in for a wet dinner," I say, as the first fat raindrops hit the patio stones.

B y eight, winds have joined the summer squall, which shows no signs of abating. The dark entrada—

all the outdoor candles have blown out—fills with umbrellas and slickers as friends arrive. Inside, we mill around the candlelit kitchen and among the table settings, interrupting preparations. There is no other place to gather, as our sala is where we sleep. Felipe and the beauteous Laura, their growing estrangement on hold, have come together for tonight; maybe the magic hummingbird packet Masako gave Felipe has taken effect. Susana arrives with her mousse makings and a bag of ice, which means I can make *agua mineral,* and Bacardi *añejo* for Arnaud, who takes it with great ceremony as Haitians will: the lime, the ice, the precise jigger from the cap. Vicente Arias is content with Dos Equis, while Elenita and Arnaud's wife, Colette, share a bottle of Santo Tomás red with me. Masako sips chaste mineral water with *limón* as she cooks.

Crack of thunder, strobe of lightning off the high walls. Water pools beneath the entrada door. Damp patches sprout on the dining room ceiling; the corners drip. Juan's roof job never did address the erosion between layers, so the leaks simply migrate.

We cluster around the table, ten of us, glasses raised.

"To the new house. *Felicitaciones.*"

"*Viva.*"

"And to Paul," I say. "*Viva.*"

"Yes. And Mina."

"And to Felipe for bringing us here. To all who helped."

More toasts: To Arnaud, who will soon return to post-Duvalier Haiti. To Antonio Rocha, the scoundrel, for *not* being here. To little, big-eared Carlos Salinas de Gortari, the Mexican president who took office by fraud in everyone's view but seems to be pulling a few programs together and jailing big-time crooks in a show of political machismo. To Susana's mango mousse, already famous without anyone having tasted it. And to the weather, which inconveniences us but blesses the farmers as long as it doesn't flood.

"We used to set our clocks by the rain," Vicente says. "Four o'clock every day, clear skies by sunset. No more."

"Global warming," Elenita says, frowning.

Masako and I serve the squash blossom soup from a tureen. *"Riquísimo,"* Carlos says, sipping his. All agree. The dense yellow is like pigment, or a glaze, the *epazote* giving it a kick.

Colette, a writer who lives in Arnaud's considerable literary shadow, has a taste for good gossip. "Did you hear about the *narcotraficante* found in the La Siesta Motel in a bathtub, encased in cement?"

Laura, her olive skin aglow in the candlelight—how long will she remain single if she and Felipe really split up?— quietly announces that the man who was killed was her cousin.

In the silence, I wish for the music I'd hoped to play tonight, but there is no power.

Chicken enchiladas with mole, rice, beans. Sliced, grilled rajas with onions. Rainwater drips in the corner like a clock. Flicker of candlelight, smell of tallow and paraffin. Vicente's beer tips over, to laughter; the table we've made of a door is full of ditches, bevels, hillocks.

In the storm's enforced intimacy, we talk about gringos and Mexicans. Is Masako a gringa? Colette wonders. No, the Mexicans at the table insist, she's a *japonesa.* Colette points out yes, but with all due respect, Masako thinks and acts like a gringa. Felipe, Mexican-born, U.S.–raised, confesses to feeling neither fish nor fowl. A travel book has come out by a New York woman whose absurd, paranoid descriptions of walks through San Miguel's ominous night streets reduce us to gales of laughter.

Stories fly. A Canadian woman most of us know, unhappily married to a philandering Mexican husband, has fled north with her daughter because her husband was about to have her committed—a device used to deprive a woman of all rights in a divorce proceeding. Susana tells a story I've heard in a dozen variations, about an old American woman who died here. Her grandkids, wanting her cremated and not buried—which is the law in Mexico—drove down from Texas, wrapped her in a rug, tied it to the top of the car, and headed north for the border. They stopped to eat at a restaurant along the way and came back out to find the car stolen, Granny, rug, and all.

"Do you remember the old Corto Maltese?" Arnaud asks.

Sure, we all do. It was up the street on Calle Flor, our first summer here. The restaurant with the great music, fresh-made fettucine, and espresso. Then suddenly it closed one day and nobody ever knew why.

"I'll tell you why," Arnaud says. "Do you remember Paolo, the guy who ran it?"

Paolo, the handsome, quiet young proprietor in his black T-shirt and chinos, hovering about the pasta kitchen, sipping espresso, reading books. How did he manage to get those great salsa bands up from Mexico City every weekend?

"First of all," Arnaud says, "Paolo wasn't his real name. He'd been in the radical Italian underground, the Red Brigades—the guys involved in the Aldo Moro killings, the ones who sliced off Jean Getty's ear. The Italian government was after him for murder and wanted to put him away for life. So Paolo was on the run, hiding out in Mexico, running the Corto Maltese to get by. Then some arrangement was made for him to return to France and serve a long jail term there instead of in Italy. So he went back. That's why the Corto Maltese closed."

"But for a few years afterward," Masako says, "you could buy Corto Maltese pasta in boxes in the stores."

Collete says, "A Mexican friend of his kept making the fettucine and sending Paolo the money in jail."

"He may have been an anarchist or a murderer," Felipe says, "but he was a good businessman. He ran a good restaurant, and the music was the best."

"*Paolo* ..." His name resonates down the corridors of memory. Masako and I rise and begin clearing the table, still moving to those salsa bands that mysteriously materialized each weekend at the Corto Maltese.

Only now, in the silence following Arnaud's story, do we notice that the rain has let up. "Look," Laura says, pointing outside at a spreading stain of white moonlight on the patio wall.

We take candles and wander out into the fresh night among jasmine smell, the sounds of dripping on the stones.

"*Luna llena,*" Vicente says. "Full moon."

Holding our candles, we walk back across the patio, drawn irresistibly toward the garden. Clouds cover the moon, then reveal it, its light uncommonly bright, the house still pitch-black.

"This is like *La Dolce Vita,*" Carlos says.

"Or Buñuel, his Mexico period," says Colette.

"Susana and I will bring dessert," Masako calls.

We find our way to the far corner of the garden and dry off the old stone seats. Setting our candles on ledges, we sit in the moonlight.

Susana and Masako arrive with trays. We see the dark red shadow of the pureed garambullos, the cactus berry sauce, atop the yellow-orange mousse in clear glass dessert dishes. Spoons are passed around. The sauce is dusty, sour-sweet. The custard, blended with thick cream, gelatin, and lime, dissolves on the tongue. The manila mangoes we bought this morning, combined with the cactus berries, fuse into something unspeakably ambrosial. The wild flavors of Susana's mousse seem to hold all the stories we told at the table in the rainy Mexican night.

Slowly the electricity seeps on—a yellow-orange color not unlike the mangoes. As if the house were laboring to give birth to light. From the dark garden we watch Masako's studio come to life, a theater set. Then my studio and the main house light up.

Now we can see Susana's dessert clearly in its green glass-stemmed dishes: the concentrated magenta of the cactus berries, the spun gold of the mangoes.

"Mango mousse in moonlight garden," Arnaud says.

"Tonight, Susana," Felipe says, "you have created a legend."

# Chapter 13

# V oyages

MEXICAN SUMMERS TURN IMPERCEPTI-
bly into fall, marked less by weather or
landscape than the arrival of the September
fiestas—though the rains do ease, the earth
at its fullest green. After months of work,
the house on Calle Flor is up and running.
We talk of taking a break, getting out into
Mexico. Lock the doors, there'll be something here when we get back. San Miguel,
once voyage's end, becomes a point of departure.

O n a quiet Monday
morning I run into Carlos at Supermercado
Sánchez. "Let's drive to Pozos for the day,"
he says. Masako has gone to a workshop in

Dolores Hidalgo to make pottery for the house. It's been months since I've left town. We round up *tortas* and Coronas for a picnic lunch and take off in Carlos's Nissan van.

We rumble east along a two-lane road, past mesquite and madrona trees, cultivated croplands awaiting harvest. Carlos seems glad for the companionship. Elenita is in Oaxaca on a shopping trip for the store—a pretext, he suspects, for a visit to a Zapotec rug weaver she's taken an interest in. Things worsen with them.

The town of Pozos, hardly larger than the cemetery we pass on the way in, has a small plaza, a few grand old houses set by a stream, an old miners' church. Sparse ancients perch like lizards on benches in the flat sun. A deeply rutted road winds up a dusty mountainside dotted with elaborate ruins. Hard to believe Pozos was home to 80,000 people when the silver sluiced rich here. Today there is only the hum of insects, the wind's whisper, the bleat of sheep on sun-baked plateaus. Pozos, like Sutter's Mill or Fitzcarraldo's rubber-boom Iquitos, is a litter of abandoned dreams. Its name, which means "pits" or "wells" or "mine shafts," has accrued a more ominous meaning in our time: those prisons below-ground where Latin American generals sent their political opponents, the *desaparecidos*, the well of time that drowns memory.

From the hilltop, the sky runs past the eye's grasp. Clouds rain on a far golden plain, as in a medieval biblical illustration. Slumped doorjambs frame hard blue sky, the buildings that once surrounded them mere ghostly, platonic suggestions. Faded frescoes of melting adobe walls bear faint lettering: yardage store, tool shop, mining enterprise.

"It's like a Sergio Leone Western up here," I say.

"*Sí.* You wouldn't believe how rich this place once was."

Avoiding the open wells, we roam past mounds of dark

tailings, slag from the three-hundred-odd mines where silver, mercury, copper, and gold were extracted. Skirting dead reservoirs clotted with green algae, we descend a mine shaft, our voices echoing in damp darkness.

Back out in the sun, I carefully slide upon my stomach to the edge of a well and lean over. The intense mountain light eerily reflects the blue of the sky perfectly in undisturbed well water hundreds of feet below. I see my face in detail, as if in a mirror held at arm's length. I drop a shard of slate, wait fifteen seconds to hear the sound of the splash dissolving my image. Dizzily I stand up, having imagined my fall: the tumbling, the scream, echo, impact, oblivion.

We spread a blanket beneath a pepper tree. Carlos cracks out the beers and *tortas cubanas*. Hungrily we munch among stubby cactus and gray-green agave plants, grazing cows and wild horses. A few yards away, a dense swarm of black ants dismantles the remains of a mole.

For two hundred years, Carlos says, Pozos was a vast mining enterprise. Engineers and miners from Germany, Italy, and the United States settled here with their families, accumulating tremendous wealth: grand homes, the best imported European and American goods. Traveling theaters and circuses came from all over the world to perform.

"What brought Pozos down?"

"The workers flooded the mines during the 1910 revolution to spite the owners. That's what some say. Others think it was the owners who flooded them to punish the workers."

"I've read that the mines closed because the banks froze the credit."

"Nobody agrees on what happened. An old man I know says it was simply because the price of silver fell on the world market. Maybe if the price rises again, Pozos will come back."

The last time I looked, silver slumbered at four dollars an ounce on the world market.

"By 1940 Pozos was a corpse," Carlos says, slugging back another Corona. "See that cross at the top of the hill? Every year the descendants come and climb the hill, offer prayers to the *Santo Patrono de los Mineros, Señor de los Trabajadores.*" Jesus, in his guise of friend to workers. "There are stories from the revolution of mine owners' bodies being brought here in the dead of night and tossed down the wells."

"It *is* a spot for the perfect crime," I say, recalling my vertiginous look down the well shaft.

"It almost was." Carlos laughs. "Do you know the story about the man who was killed twice?"

I've heard different versions of the tale ever since coming to San Miguel—a local leitmotiv that seems less a concatenation of facts than a way a town talks to itself. In Carlos's spin on the story, several years ago René, who runs a bookshop in San Miguel, became involved in a dispute with an older Englishman who lived there. In the course of the disagreement, René beat the man senseless—to death, he thought. Panicked, he piled the body in the trunk of his car and headed for Pozos, intending to dump it down a well. Somewhere en route he heard a banging from the trunk of his car. The man was still alive. René pulled over, took a tire iron, and finished off the job. Then instead of driving to Pozos, René, in a fit of remorse, turned around and drove back to San Miguel, turned himself in at the police station, and confessed. He was convicted and sentenced to life in prison.

Carlos's version differs from ones I've heard around San Miguel, which all differ from each other. No, it took place in a bar on Calle Insurgentes, not in the man's house. No, the reason René got caught was not remorse; he simply ran out of gas on the road—that's why he never made it to Pozos—and that's where a policeman found him at dawn, sobbing uncontrollably. No, the second killing was by suffocation, not a tire iron. Besides, the man he killed was an awful man, deserving of it. Not at all, others say: he was the sweetest of men. Portrayals of René vary equally: a golf pro, an astrologist, a gentle scholar of pre-Hispanic Náhuatl, merely a man defending his honor. The story's dizzying variations make me wonder if there was ever a murder at all, let alone a René in the town jail.

"You see," Carlos says, "the double intent to kill is what the judges held against him. Killing a man once is one thing, but *twice?* We have a legal term in Mexico: *rematar.* To re-kill. That's why René got a life sentence. He re-killed the man. It goes back to the Catholic idea of remorse, penitence, embedded in the law. Otherwise it was a crime of passion, forgivable in Mexico. And with his background . . ." Carlos waggles his hand, palm down, in that Mexican gesture indicating the essential relativity of all things. ". . . a deal could have been made."

"Where is René now?"

"In jail in the Presidencia. You can go visit him any Wednesday. Ask him yourself what happened."

Carlos is getting drunk. I begin to scheme on seducing his keys away from him. He is miserable. Will idealistic Elenita, her political and spiritual frustrations fixated now upon a brooding Oaxacan shaman and rug maker, leave him? The midday heat scorches the plateau, the air fills with insects. We stand up, gather up our scraps, and head back to the van.

"We speak of murder," Carlos says, waving his arms around. "But isn't Pozos itself the victim of a murder whose perpetrator cannot be found?"

Walking back to the car, we come upon a French-Mexican movie crew filming a western among the ruins. They've filled empty arches with fresh adobe, painted old walls red and ocher and azure, turned the abandoned hillside into a simulation of a U.S. frontier town. By the tall, pyramidal ovens that once amalgamated mercury and silver in the extraction process, a director in Nikes and a backward baseball cap squints through a viewfinder, shouting Gallic instructions. Illusion laid upon illusion: Is it possible to ruin a ruin?

"Nothing lasts," Carlos says sadly as we reach the van. "Elenita and me. Graduate degrees in history, *veteranos* of *sesenta y ocho*, sixty-eight, the killings in Tlatelolco Plaza. Now we run an *artesanía* store. Elenita says we have become petty bourgeois. She is hungry for new meaning. Me? I've settled. I admit it."

Gently I remove the keys from Carlos's hand and slip behind the wheel of the van. He doesn't resist. At the foot of the mountain we stop to visit a commune of musicians, their hair long and dyed red like the fierce Guachichil Indians who once lived on this mountain. They craft pre-Hispanic instruments: rattles and gourds, flutes, cowhide drums. I hold a *palo de lluvia,* a bamboo rain stick, to my ear, listening to pebbles fall like rain showers on forest leaves. I buy it, and a stone flute and a hand drum, for our new house.

By the time we pass the miners' cemetery on the outskirts, Carlos is snoring in the seat beside me.

Driving west, I think about all those gringos who came to Pozos with their families, dreams blown away in the dust of time. And René, who killed the man twice but never did get the body down the well. And Carlos and Elenita, torn apart by changing times. What of Masako and me, *sesenta y ochos* ourselves? We've assumed this landscape in some new way now: with the buying of the house, our axis has shifted.

We begin to inhabit these narratives we're told, adding our stories to theirs. We've planted our wanderers' flag here in Mexico, linking ourselves to generations swallowed by history's tumult. *Residentes* or *visitantes?* Pioneers or escapists?

I come in sight of San Miguel from the caracol above. Twilight bathes the town in flame. My eyes trace a path from the Parroquia's spire down the line of blocks to Calle Flor. My daughter's name is on the deed of that house we don't really own. Will she come one day to the cemetery on Day of the Dead to commune with us, try to explain to her children the faint music of lives lived here? Or will we have left long before, driven out by some unseen exigency, wobbly ghosts on aluminum walkers, plastic identity tags around our wrists, doddering somewhere in the labyrinth of the U.S. health-care system?

Back at the house, I find Masako's new hand-painted ceramic cups and dishes piled on the kitchen table: geometric whorls, circles, dots. I lay the rain stick, the stone flute, and the hand drum beside them. Here we will eat and drink off our own pottery—lead content be damned—and make our own music, and we will be content.

The road west from San Miguel winds through towns—Celaya, Yuriria (with its brooding old convent), Cuitzeo, Moroleón—where Indians famously resisted Spanish troops, priests spread the alien balm of gospel, and revolutionary battles were fought. The two-lane road is mostly level, as we are still on the *altiplano,* the mile-high Mexican plain. A speeding Flecha Amarilla bus passes us in the other direction, shuddering our rented VW van. My hands tighten on the wheel.

Driving on Mexican roads requires an attitude of fateful surrender. Trouble could come from anywhere: a stray animal or human, a truck veering inches across the sliver-thin divide between whizzing lanes. Mexicans cross themselves to pray for a good journey, erect crosses by the roadside to mourn failed ones. Running this narrow strip between hope and sorrow, I know that the weathered Chevy Nova in front of me, visibly listing on its wheelbase, could easily exfoliate a hubcap, a tire, or the entire wheel itself, dooming us both. Out here on the Mexican road, I have veered into the realm of casual anarchy, where the instruments of recourse may be worse than the problem that occasioned them. I could become a double victim at the hands of a cop who has pulled me over and, ignoring my "How may I be of assistance?" (the ritual opener to a payoff), decides instead to take me to the station for further extortion, or to a motel to molest my wife. This is why Mexicans often run away from the scenes of accidents: bad can quickly turn to worse. Still, good people have unaccountably come to my aid at roadside at no profit to themselves, and seen me to the end of my trouble as if I were family.

Mexican buses are reliable, cheap, and safe—from fume-belching local buckets-of-bolts to sleek, speedy Mercedes carriers with *música estereofónica* and rest rooms. Luis Buñuel's film *Mexican Bus Ride* famously builds an epic journey around one such trip. But our voyage to the state of Michoacán would have entailed six different buses coming and going, and we want to meander at our own pace, look for things for our house. Hence this pre-dented white VW van with its rear seats removed.

Along the roadside, women in rebozos trundle loads of

firewood on their backs. Running walls advertise soft drinks, rock bands, politicians. Signs futilely appeal to Mexicans not to use their land as a garbage dump: *No Tire Basura.* In each town, *topes,* or *vibradores*—axle-cracking concrete bumps in the road—slow traffic long enough for vendors to lean in at our window and hawk peanuts, fruit, crucifixes, iguanas, *chicles.* At one tope, a peso gets me a Cruz Roja windshield sticker, inuring me from the next swarm of volunteers in Yuriria; it's Red Cross Day all over Mexico. In towns with stoplights, kids attack our windows with soapy water and newspapers before we can protest.

We creep for miles behind a truck full of fluffy, white, red-wattled chickens in stacked cages, feathers swirling about us. At last it pulls off the road by an outdoor market, leaving us on the bumper of a pickup carrying a pair of huge, hairy pigs soon to become Sunday *carnitas* in Moroleón. Masako hangs halfway out the window with her camera, shooting a pilgrimage of dusty, singing campesinos bearing banners with images of a local *Virgen.* Since she bought a Pentax K1000 a few years ago from a departing French photography student at the Instituto Allende, she's been shooting street scenes, landscapes, architectural details—for herself mostly, as an art sketchbook; but now a publisher has commissioned her to do photographs for a book on Mexico.

A boy rides a burro through a field of burning corn husks. A man in a brown serape walks a dusty path to an empty horizon. A woman with an infant wrapped in a blue rebozo crosses a mudflat. I think of Orozco's paintings, Harriet Doerr's description of her first drive into Ibarra: the Lone Figure on the Landscape, emerging and disappearing, in imperceptible increments of time. A standing lake ripples as clusters of white egrets take flight. Suddenly after a stretch

of scrub earth, a Moorish church dome, glittering with varie-
gated tiles, rises over a little mud and brick town. Oases of
moments: the nondescript flaring into the brilliant, the poly-
chrome, the surreal. Every step was leading you to this Mexican moment.

BIENVENIDOS A MICHOACÁN, says the sign. We've left
our state of Guanajuato. As the land rises, we see the first
pines, feel the slight cooling of the air. The names get richer:
Uriangato, Salvatierra, Pátzcuaro, Tzintzuntzán, Uruapan. I
pull into a green and white PEMEX station.

"*Lleno?*" the attendant asks.

"*Sí.*"

Masako heads off to the rest room. I sip a *refresco* and
watch the uniformed attendant fill the tank. There is only
one brand of gas in Mexico: PEMEX, the national oil franchise, wrested from American companies who tried to colo-
nize the Gulf of Mexico oil fields in the 1930s. When the
world oil shortage hit in the late 1970s, Mexico became rich
on paper, setting off a borrowing frenzy. Cultural and social
programs were begun, roads built—extravagant swaths of
superhighway, desolate now, their tolls so high only the rich
use them—until oil prices collapsed, leaving the country flat
again, mired in debt.

Masako emerges from the *baño*. The gas jockey brings me
my change. An Indian woman appears by the side of the car
brandishing a hibachi made of Michoacán license plates. Delighted, Masako buys it for what she asks, takes the woman's
picture.

Mexico fills Masako with such pleasure. In this vast bazaar of a country, she plumbs the roots of her joy. Her visual
raptures infect me, dweller in language and concept, awak-
ening me to the material, the sensory, the seen and touched.
Mexico insists I live more through my eyes.

We come in sight of the city of Morelia, the state capital, wrapped around its mountaintop like an old Castilian fortress town.

A brass band plays lunchtime waltzes in the sunlit plaza opposite Morelia's busy downtown arcade. We sit eating *corundas,* a regional dish of small tamales wrapped in the leaf of the corn plant. Masako pans her Pentax from the plaza to me.

"Another great Mexican city," I say. Click.

"We could live here," she says.

"We could." Click.

As if we hadn't just bought a house. As if we were still at liberty to alight anywhere we wished. Still, it eases us to play our old game.

After lunch we buy *morelianas,* flat disks of burnt milk and sugar, and walk the well-heeled provincial city, where soldiers and priests once conquered the Purépecha people whose empire had stretched beyond Michoacán. The local priest-hero Morelos, like our state's Father Hidalgo, studied and taught here before leading the revolt against Spain. We gaze up at gilt-encrusted, angel-headed facades of churches, browse extravagant baroque mansions now housing government offices and shops, stand outside the doors of a music conservatory listening to a boys' choir sing *St. Matthew's Passion.* When Masako steers me into a rambling, two-story ex-convent, now a museum and bazaar of Michoacán folk arts—La Casa de Las Artesanías—I realize she'd been heading us here all along.

As we pass through room after room of exhibits, I understand why we brought the van. The museum both displays and sells the brilliant handicrafts made in villages or towns lying around Lake Pátzcuaro an hour away, each devoted solely to a single art: copperware from Santa Clara del Cobre, guitars from Paracho, green pottery from Patambán and San José de la Gracia, bizarre ceramic narrative figures from Ocumichu, delicate brown figures on off-white pottery from Tzintzuntzán (a delicious Purépechan onomatopoeic word meaning "hummingbird").

Standing before a cluster of head-high terra-cotta storage jars with blackened burn marks from a wood-fire kiln, we envision a pair in our entrada. An intricate, green-glazed Patambán punch bowl shaped like a pineapple and hung with cups will inhabit our new dining room. Masako sets aside carved wooden bowls with painted floral designs, a fish-and-dot-patterned casserole dish from Capula, thick cotton *cambaya* cloth for bedspreads, tablecloths, napkins.

I walk back to the parking lot to retrieve the van. By the time I pull up to the *museo,* Masako has added wooden chairs from Cuanajo, small, thin-woven *petates* for the terracotta tiled floors of our bathroom and bedroom, place mats of the same weave to sit beneath dinner plates. We climb into our booty-crammed van for the hour's drive to Pátzcuaro. It's already twilight.

"What if we stayed here overnight instead?" Armies of starlings swarm the laurels in Morelia's plazas.

"I was thinking the same thing."

We find a room a block off the main plaza in an old hotel, a former coach station for Augustinian monks. After dinner we sit cross-legged on the *cama matrimonial* staring at a color television screen—it's been months since we've seen a tube—watching an overdubbed American flick called *Cherry Dos Mil,* featuring Melanie Griffith hired to infiltrate a twenty-first-century robot warehouse operated by psychos. A Mexican version of *CHiPs* follows, with the original Erik Estrada now policing Mexican highways. Somewhere we fall asleep, wake up at dawn to bright light pouring through the curtains, choruses of birds.

Approaching Pátzcuaro, steep Chinese peaks rise above loamy black and red earth, pine forests. Wood burns in crisp air. Around a bend, we see a silvery broad lake with green glimmering islands, where lone men in dugout canoes cast spidery nets. I glide the VW van through moody, low-slung cobblestone streets, past houses painted red below, white above, with orange tile roofs. At La Basílica, an old inn above the town, we drop our bags on the tile floor of a white room with a fireplace and windows overlooking the town and the lake.

It's market day in Pátzcuaro, and in minutes I've lost Masako among piles of wool serapes, hand-woven basketry, and golden-faced, black-braided Purépecha vendors in embroidered blouses and pleated skirts. I wade out of the mercado into the oxygen of the Plaza Chica, where old men shine shoes, boys hawk dailies, and radio strains of ranchera music slide into Mexican reggae. Sipping an orange and banana licuado from a plastic bag, I hike up wide, sloped streets through interlocking plazas, past rambling fincas of faded colonial munificence. Soulful, shuttered Pátzcuaro, where every November thousands come from all over Mexico to witness the dead come alive.

In a barrel-vaulted library, once a church, uniformed schoolgirls sit at pitted wood desks beneath half-empty bookshelves. On the far wall, a narrative mural depicts primordial Janitzio Island, with a volcano behind it, descending into a Purépechan dreamworld of tigers and bare-breasted women on horeseback; then armored conquistadores facing down starving Indians, while a benign Bishop Quiroga offers "Utopia," portrayed as a church with a fountain. Finally Zapata's troops become bra-less women with hammers and sickles. Inscribed at the bottom: *"Silencio,"* by Juan O'Gorman, 1942.

You labor to untangle the pre-Hispanic from the Catholic Spanish from the contemporary. This occupies you for a long time in Mexico. Finally you realize it's like trying to separate the different parts of a plant (a "burning flower," the desert Huichol people call life's origins). Apostate from the cult of tomorrow, you begin to see that the future has already passed, many times, and around you lie the ruins of old futures dreamed. You arrive, with a bump, back in the layered, resonant Mexican present, your eyes open, your reality wider.

After lunch Masako and I drive to Santa Clara del Cobre, a village a few miles west, where the streets echo with the tapping of copper artisans. In a workshop we buy a set of copper pots and pans Masako has always dreamed of owning, and two rust-toned vases we'll fill with cool water and lilies and set on our dining room table. The van full to overflowing, we set the copperware on the floor around Masako's feet.

That night, eating whitefish in a restaurant near the lake, I say, "This is a place we really *could* live."

"Lots of Purépecha, few gringos. It reminds me more of the Mexico I first saw when I was a girl."

She tells me about a friend in grammar school in San Francisco whose family had a place south of Puerto Vallarta, when you still had to take mules in and you could go naked on the beach.

"My friend's mother always wore beautiful Mexican jewelry and handmade clothes. I used to think, 'I have to go to Mexico one day.' Finally when I was fifteen my mother put me on a tour. Mexico City was much smaller then—no pollution, little traffic. More like Morélia today. We stayed at the old Hotel Cortés on Alameda Park, rode colorful boats through the floating gardens of Xochimilco. We drove south to Oaxaca by way of Taxco. It was magical. Hills and cobblestones and donkeys—like San Miguel. In Oaxaca I loved the bright hand-woven textiles and indigenous clothes the women wore. No jeans, no sneakers—just muslin clothing and *huipiles*. I'd seen rural Japan, but never anything like Oaxaca. I met Doña Rosa, the originator of the burnished black Oaxacan pottery. I fell in love with flan there."

We order it, here in Pátzcuaro, to commemorate.

"I wore all black—you know, young artist from San Francisco—and Mexicans would say to the people on our tour, 'It's so sad about that girl, widowed at such a young age.' "

The flan arrives: spongy, orange-flavored.

"Was it like this in Oaxaca?" I ask.

"No. Creamier, with a dark caramel sauce. This is good, though."

The flan, pale yellow like the Corona beer I'm drinking, dissolves on my tongue.

My first Mexico memories are vague, unconnected to the country I know now. "I was nine, ten maybe. Tijuana, for a day of sight-seeing and shopping."

"There's a picture in your parents' album of you and your sister and your parents gathered around a little burro in front of a fake desert backdrop. You have a big sombrero on, a serape slung over your shoulder. You look miserable."

"I got an Aztec skull ring that trip. It turned my finger green but I wouldn't remove it even to bathe. After a couple of years I'd grown so much they had to cut the ring off."

I tell her of another trip to Baja with two college friends after finals one year. High on Dexamil, we drove all night from Palo Alto and crossed the border at dawn. We kept going past Rosarito Beach and Ensenada, talking the entire time, riffing on some mad vision of reality. Halfway down the Baja peninsula at dawn, the paved road ended but we didn't notice; the car bogged in a muddy ditch and some friendly farmers in a pickup helped us pull it out. We drove back up to Tijuana, still talking, then headed east to Mexicali and south along the Gulf of Mexico to a tiny fishing village called San Felipe, where we rented an outboard and sped around the bay. That night we crossed the border, still not having eaten or slept, and drove all the way back to Palo Alto, the conversation intact.

"Do you remember what you talked about?" Masako asks.

"Not a word." I call for the check.

Outside, we walk down to the lake. Fishermen's lanterns bob offshore; water slaps against the pilings. "Did you ever imagine you'd end up living here?"

"Europe maybe, Asia. Never Mexico."

We drive slowly back through Pátzcuaro's Plaza Grande. A few shadowy strollers, dogs, and kids cluster around a guitar player on a bench. Back at the hotel, a caretaker swings open the parking lot gate. As we step out of the van, firecrackers explode and a band starts up somewhere below.

*"En la Plaza Chica,"* the *mozo* says. *"Una fiesta."*

We hurry down the hill, where a crowd has gathered in the dark square. Purépecha girls in floral blouses and loose embroidered skirts, blue and black rebozos pinned to their heads, dance and sway in columns, holding lacquered plates.

A fifteen-piece band plays a march with a ranchera cross-stitch in the second beat. In their dance, the girls dip rose-colored napkins into confetti on their plates, then wave them in the air, showering the heads of children in the audience. Bewitchingly beautiful in their costumes and slow, serious gestures, the girls range in age from fifteen or so down to six or seven. Young mothers in the crowd, surely once dancers themselves, intently watch the dance. The old woman directing tonight's dancers frowns with censure at missed steps, nods when it's right.

The tight circle of watchers parts to let the dancers file out into the street. Waving their lacquer plates above their heads, they snake up a moonlit lane, the racketing band following behind—hooting saxes, yowling clarinets, tin-can cymbals, flabby bass drum, spitting tuba. Mesmerized, we drift along behind until a cloud swallows moon and dancers, band and crowd, breaking the embroidered link with the primeval chain, leaving us alone on a dark corner in Pátzcuaro, back in ordinary time.

Walking to the hotel, I say, "I wonder what the occasion is."

"Womanhood, beauty, tribe, harvest," Masako says. "The dance *is* the occasion."

The next morning we sit on a jetty at the foot of the village of Tzintzuntzán where forty thousand Purépechans once lived. Sipping Uruapan coffee in Styrofoam cups, we watch the sun burn mist off Janitzio Island, then climb into the van for the drive back.

# The Embrace

# Chapter 14

# The Pink Comb

THE DAY AFTER NEW YEAR'S, 1991.
I walk up Calle Flor, drawing my jacket
collar tight against the morning chill. Lit
fires sting the air with mesquite. This cold
snap, which swept down from the Rockies
through Texas and Sonora, will last through
Three Kings Day on January 6, according to
reports. Last night in La Mama's open
courtyard, braziers were lit against the cold,
and even the Peruvian musicians wore
sweaters. Gardeners fret over lost blooms
when it cools like this; but on February 2,
Candelaria Day, the Parque Juárez will fill
with flowers and plants and seedlings
brought in from the *campo,* and we'll all
carry them off to renew gardens and homes.

"*Feliz año.*" "*Felicidades.*" The greetings
ring out along Calle Flor, supplanting last
week's "*Feliz Navidad.*" In the jardín,

sweepers and street dogs dismantle revelry's remains: bottles, cans, papers and food scraps, charred firecrackers and flares. Drunks' acrid urine fumes curl up from the base of walls and dispel on the keen air. After a day of sleeping it off, stores reopen haltingly. Hungover tourists line up at the Presidencia to get their license plates out of hock from police, who strip them off wrongly parked cars. The annual nativity crèche at the jardín bandstand—a live lamb, a calf, two goats, and a donkey in a hay-strewn, fenced manger, beneath the tender gaze of a life-sized plaster Mary with swaddled baby—will stay up until after Three Kings, the Mexican day of gift giving. Reaching over the heads of wide-eyed kids, I pet a hard-headed little brown goat.

Away for the holidays this year, I missed the *posadas* that run the nine nights before Christmas, when children go from house to house asking for room at the inn only to be turned away by everyone except the prearranged family—in our neighborhood, the doctor's family next door. There are *luces de bengal* (sparklers), piñatas, and the little bags of candy and fruits called *colación*—peanuts, cane sugar, oranges, and tangerines. I missed the *pastorelas* at the Bellas Artes, too, when hundreds of kids and adults dress up to stage those miracle plays that still go on all night in the ranchos.

Crossing the jardín beneath a canopy of bells, I set off upon a round of errands. Some I could have done in California but find so much more pleasurable here. Crazy, I suppose, to buy a watchband from the pitiable selection at Emilio's tiny *relojería* on Insurgentes: but the walk to get there, Emilio's warm *"Feliz Año"* as he pushes back his eyepiece and smiles, and the cartoon jokes in Spanish pinned on the walls, beat a featureless trip to some gold-soaked California watch emporium. I could have re-heeled my shoes at a high-tech L.A. shoe boutique, but Jaime's dim, aromatic shoe shop behind the covered market lies at the end of a sensual adventure. Subjecting my boots to the unlabeled pastes and waxes, glops and creams the shoeshine boys in the jardín use may not do the leather any good, but I get the best seat in town and great gossip. At Eréndira's Unisex Salon, I squeeze in among Mexican matrons reading scandal magazines beneath bubble-headed hair dryers and let Eréndira shear me before a cracked mirror for the peso equivalent of three dollars. And no matter how I look when she's done, Eréndira always stands back and coos, *"Ay, muy guapo,"* as if she really means I look that good.

I pass the Teatro Aldama, the town's only movie theater, which occupies an eighteenth-century building on Calle San Francisco, a few doors down from the sombrero shop, next to a restaurant called El Jardín that nobody goes to. I like to stop and scan the lurid lobby posters pitching upcoming films: Charles Bronson and Bruce Lee staples popular with the cowboys and campesinos, goofball domestic comedies, true-crime dramas. It's rumored they run soft-core flicks late Saturday nights (they have to end before Sunday, by church edict), though I never see lights on inside when I pass. A long-running favorite, *Vaselina Dos*, remained mysterious to me until I spotted the preening, ducktailed star on the lobby poster: *Grease II*.

The Teatro Aldama has been closed since October, its doors plastered with tax-lien notices. Carlos says it has to do with a drug baron who owns a rancho outside of town and payback for certain unnamed favors not granted. Maybe the Aldama's eventual closing is inevitable: the town's first video store has opened only two doors up, and a new shopping mall above town will house a four-theater cineplex. A cable television company is installing a transmitter and big silver dishes down on Calle Zacateros, visible from our roof. Nowadays in the *puestos*, the stalls, sellers watch the irresistible Mexican soaps called *telenovelas* on little color screens and chat less with customers. Gossip has been farmed out.

Yes, things are changing in Mexico. There's a tremulous recovery going on. Money repatriates, Wall Street turns bullish, tourists return, prices rise. Mexico has a credit line with the world again. Rumors fly of a free trade agreement with the United States and Canada. Last week the food market next to La Golondrina bookstore was evicted, its goods simply stacked on the ground in the portales; the landlord plans to rent the space out to a Fuji film franchise at triple the price. Down Calle Canal, a new store called Europa stocks Chilean and French wines. At Lucha Contreras's pharmacy, Retin A is the big item these days. The local weekly *Atención* says hotel occupancy has risen and restaurants are doing better.

Coming in on the bus last week at night, I noticed the town lit up like a tree, electrical decorations lacing the *colonias*, the neighborhoods that during the years following the earthquake and the peso crisis were shrouded as if in mourning. We have a new bus station—a clean, lit cement structure a mile down Calle Canal, obliging a taxi ride up into town, to the taxistas' delight—though I miss the old dusty turnaround with its scruffy dogs and kid greeters. From our roof on Calle Flor I watch new brick-and-cement communities mushroom overnight on the outskirts. Flashy chilangos in new cars arrive in San Miguel for loud weekends.

Yet the myriad poor remain. The government's social programs line the usual pockets, while campesinos flood across the northern border in search of work. The bellwether price of a kilo of tortillas inches up. Staples like corn and milk must be imported. Elenita, back from southernmost Chiapas, tells of hunger in the villages. Clerics' and social critics' warnings of social unrest fall on deaf ears. Everyone suspects drug money is subsidizing the boom, but nobody wants to spoil the party.

These changes in town and country occupy our conversation at the weekly lunches at El Caribe. We commiserate, cling to each other a little. Maruja mourns the loss of grace, patrimony, the old customs. Billie growls at the crass tourism and the duplicity of Mexican politicians. Yet the book racks of La Golondrina swell with new titles, an espresso café has opened in the Bellas Artes, and we all prefer the new cash machine in the wall of the old colonial Canal mansion off the plaza to waiting in line for hours at Banamex. In some deep, uneasy sense, we understand that we are conspirators in the very trends we bemoan.

Friday lunches aren't the same without Paul and Mina. Paul has spent the last couple of years in Los Angeles, no longer able to paint. Now even writing on a word processor is impossible. Mina has to feed him with a spoon, and he has difficulty swallowing. Often we allude to Paul and Mina elegiacally over *cocteles de camarón,* or while walking back up Calle Canal after our lunches.

Hazy sun disperses the chill in the steep shadows along Calle Reloj. Passing the Blue Door bakery, I catch a whiff of the new year's first fresh batch of bolillos. Heading for the *biblioteca* to return overdue books, I cross Calle Insurgentes where the outdoor market used to be. Now it's a cement plaza with iron benches and a towering statue of Ignacio Allende astride a horse. With time, people may find a way to reinvest this swath of concrete and bronze with life and color, but for now people simply walk through or around it.

The bilingual library, gathered around a courtyard usually filled with students and readers, is empty today in the cold. Hard to begrudge the fines on books I kept over Christmas, as they help pay for literacy programs in the countryside and the purchase of more books. In the reading room I nod to Gloria, the spry Canadian librarian arranging her ancient wood card files. I wish my father, similarly elderly, could find such good uses for his time.

We'd visited my widowed dad at Christmas in the house on L.A.'s west side where he's lived since the 1950s, his life endlessly repeating itself. At a family gathering, laughter, pleasantries, endless questions about Mexico. We'd seen movies and art we'd missed, attended to our books and articles and exhibits. Mexico's back on the U.S. radar screen—folk art, Fridamania—and friends are interested in coming for stays in the casita. After a visit to Masako's family in San Francisco, we'd taken a midday flight out. Touchdown in Mexico City, and that familiar, deep, pleasurable exhalation. Back to long stretches of work, five-hour dinners, books read cover to cover, the endless round of fiestas, processions, weddings and funerals, and that humanizing ambience we now equate with life itself, in this town I can walk end to end, carrying a single key in my pocket: the key to the high mesquite door on Calle Flor.

Outside the library on Calle Insurgentes, sun burns through the morning mist, heating the air instantly. Light divides into high color and sharp shadow as I watch, warming the street with life and motion as if a movie has just begun. A keening ranchera ballad drifts from a radio. An old yellow flatbed bearing rows of young green palms passes in front of a wall painted *azul añil*, a deep saturate blue. The sudden explosion of colors stops me in my tracks.

Went to Espino's and El Tomate. Be back soon. Need to talk to you."

The note on the kitchen table sounds faintly ominous; Masako doesn't send up casual alarms. Putting uneasy thoughts aside, I pour a mineral water and squeeze in a lime from a tree on our patio.

The countertops groan with fresh food: dark green broccoli, chubby white onions, shiny peppers and chiles, delicate orange squash blossoms, blue corn tortillas, a ball of smooth ranchero cheese. What more could Masako possibly need to shop for? There's also a *rosca de reyes*, that ring-shaped cake served on Three Kings Day that hides a little pink plastic doll inside: by custom, the celebrant who gets the slice with the *muñeca de plástico* will give a party for the others on Candelaria Day, serve tamales and atole drink—one fiesta twining into the next.

I open the green wood shutters, letting sound, light, and a little dust from the street in. Odd, how the things we were most intent upon doing when we first moved in, such as putting glass in this window, remain undone. The pale floral kitchen counter tiles are still here, a backdrop now for the copper pans we bought in Santa Clara del Cobre, standing wood racks filled with dishes and cups, wooden spoons in terra-cotta pots—and the dozens of little votive paintings on tin Masako has hung above the kitchen sink.

Go slowly, we'd decided. The place has stood hundreds of years without us. For Americans, change is easy, letting something alone hard. So we sit unhurried at this kitchen table, sipping tea or coffee while pots bubble, talking or reading. We ponder the merits of installing glass blocks to let in more light, replacing the rotting beam in the entrada ceiling, repainting the patio walls a warm Mexican red. Then we drift back into our studios and take up the work that is the locus of our days. With the arrival of "the gigantic red evening," as the novelist Malcolm Lowry called it, contentment overwhelms all desire to alter things. This house on Calle Flor, site of solace and surprise, answers only to the bells.

In the still of this compound, we log the motion of days by the shift of shadow and light on walls, the temperature of the stones on our feet, the migration of birds, butterflies, and cats through the garden. The sky turns against the rooftops' hard edges. *Sisus, moneda,* and bougainvillea vines enlace the walls. Papaya, limón, and avocado ripen and drop into our baskets. What seeds fall to the ground grow: iris, violet, agapantha, palm. Chile, arugula, mint, and rosemary migrate from the spice garden to the kitchen chopping board. Violent summer rains course down walls and flood the garden floor. Jacaranda, chirimoyo, and avocado leaves blanket the patio and garden each fall until Hilario climbs up with his machete to lop off the long branches, which become our firewood. Sometimes the midday silence of the house is so large it's like a thought. We come upon each other padding between dining room and kitchen, or on the stone bench in the corner of the garden, or in the entrada—one arriving back with food or news, the other leaving for a walk to the old waterworks—and the silent looks or touchs we exchange are like affirmations. Sometimes lying in bed watching the moon pass behind the casita, one of us whispers: "This house is the best thing we ever did."

One day last May I found Hilario and Masako staring pensively at the corner between the entrada and the dining room door. A freak hailstorm had battered the foliage, tearing holes in the leaves and killing a young bougainvillea that had begun twining up the patio wall promisingly.

*"Se murió,"* Hilario said matter-of-factly.

Masako didn't take the loss so lightly. The next day in the open market we stopped at a *vivero,* a nursery with a cluster of bougainvillea plants. We couldn't seem to find one with the same colored bloom—deeper than rose, paler than purple.

"How about this one?" I said, pointing to a reddish-pink one.

She looked at me in alarm. "No, it has to be right. We're going to be looking at it for the rest of our life."

We walked back through town in silence. It was the first time either of us had said it aloud.

At the kitchen table, sipping *agua mineral,* I try to imagine former owners, generations of them, stretching back to eighteenth-century men on horseback and women in Spanish dresses. Horses tethered to the garden wall, iron bathing tubs, wood-burning stoves. Once I tried to find the old shoeshine man Felipe said knew the histories of the houses but he'd retired. Maruja thinks our entire block was a single hacienda once, a dizzying thought, for there must be twenty separate properties on it now. Who lived here when Allende and Hidalgo rebelled against Spain, or when the 1910 revolution broke out? Did this house lie empty when San Miguel became a virtual ghost town, stirring back to life only after World War II? The old man across the street, once a colonel in the Mexican army—he still dyes his hair and mustache jet-black at eighty—claims every house on this block hides buried treasures left behind by fleeing landowners in 1912. *Pura plata,* he claims. Pure silver, not coins. *"Efectivo no vale nada,"* he mutters in disgust, flopping his hand at the end of his wrist—by which he means cash, the peso, isn't worth a damn.

One day I answered a knock on the door and a handsome Indian woman with gray hair stood there. Excuse me, señor, she said, but I used to live and work in this house. It was a long time ago, I was passing by and my heart began to beat. I have such warm memories, and *discúlpame,* señor, if I mo-

lest you, but I was curious to know who was living here now.
No, no, come in, I said. We stood in this kitchen. Thirty-five
years ago, she said, a Cuban woman and her English husband lived here. They drank a lot but they were good people,
she said. I was just a girl then, and I had my two daughters
in that tiny room where the red refrigerator now stands.

We walked out into the entrada. No, she said, the casita
wasn't there, only an arched door in this wall that led into
the sala, which had a fireplace. There was not that wall in
the middle of the patio either, but a lovely *pila,* a fountain.
And where the casita kitchen is, those were arches and a veranda where *la familia* would sit in the evenings. What
about our bedroom, I asked. It was the same then, she said.
The kitchen, the dining room, the bathroom, all the same.
Except that room there—she pointed to my studio—was
where the señora slept. And the señor slept in the bedroom
where you are. Our eyes met and she nodded, intimating
that maybe things were not perfect between them. But they
were good people, she repeated. Out back in the garden, she
gestured toward Masako's studio. The *cubana* used to do her
work there, she said, while the husband—she turned and
pointed up the back stairs to the roof—had a studio up there.
I was incredulous. *De veras?* I said. *Sí, señor,* there was a
room up there, where the Inglés would paint. The señor also
had a horse that grazed in this garden and also next door, because there was no wall here, just a humble shack and a poor
family who lived there then, and a field. Oh, señor, those
were happy days. . . .

The dominating fragrance of dark-roast Veracruz coffee
arouses me. I stuff the plastic kilo bag, bought at the back
door of Alberto and Marisela's restaurant, in the small
freezer of the red *refri.* Marisela and Alberto have moved on
since their Dolce Vita days—helping to start the café in the

Bellas Artes, then cofounding an Italian restaurant in the old dining room of the Ambos Mundos, and finally establishing their own trattoria a few blocks south of us. The new restaurant—it has a name, but everyone calls it simply Alberto's—was an immediate success; it turned out Alberto is a brilliant cook. But then one night a dozen diners fell inexplicably ill and all ended up at the Hospital de la Fe with acute food poisoning. The culprit was a crate of mushrooms Alberto had bought from a passing seller. Racked with remorse, facing ruin as word quickly spread, Alberto and Marisela brought fresh flowers and deep apologies to the hospital. For months diners stayed away; but now Alberto's is crowded again, the mushroom tale entwined in local lore. Even Alberto, jiggling his little daughter on his knee, laughs when reminded of it.

I hear the faint scrape of a chair next door in the casita. An American translator staying there receives weekend visits from her Mexico City boyfriend, whose dog howls inconsolably when the two go out at night. As various friends, family, and renters have come to use the casita, we've learned we're indifferent landlords, impatient hosts; one visiting couple we thought we knew well we now no longer speak to. We imagine knocking down the wall one day and restoring the old courtyard and sala. Meanwhile real estate prices are reaching the point where Felipe's wife, Laura, a realty agent herself now, says we could sell the casita for what we paid for the entire place. We trust none of it, and take it as a first axiom that come the revolution (a code name for any number of dire eventualities), we could lose it all in a day.

Outside the kitchen door, a shaft of white light bleaches the entrada stones, glimmers in a puddle. Hilario has been here and watered, leaving his blue bucket by the spigot. A straw broom leans on the wall beside it. Our lives enmesh with Hilario's around the project of the house, whose very first stones we moved together. He gets estimates on repairs, screens workers who come, looks after the place when we're gone. He gleans lore from neighbors, fixes things that break. He fills me in on local political scandal and who isn't to be trusted. Enterprising, crafty in his way, Hilario's gentle, insistent opportunism is forced upon him by circumstance. He continually trades up his old cars, adds rooms to his house. He always asks us to bring things back on trips to the States, usually a device or tool unavailable here: a Makita drill bit, a hammer, a mosquito bug light. Like so many Mexican men, Hilario can fix almost anything—a house, a car, an animal—or bring a discarded thing back into use. I've never been to his house in Colonia Azteca on the hillside above the covered market, but imagine it to be full of gimcrackery: timers, buzzers, plugs. His oldest son, Diego, gifted in mathematics, wants to become an engineer.

Clarisa and Marisa, both married and with jobs around town, stop by separately to show us their latest babies. Inseparable as teens, they no longer speak to each other, the origins of their alienation having something to do with the husbands, who don't get along. An erratic succession of helpers succeeded them—part of the problem being that neither of us knows exactly how to tell a housekeeper what to do. Now Lucrecia, who is young and has big eyes and a child out in the campo, arrives three days a week to stab at the stones with her broom, run water over the dishes, change the beds, and gaze at herself in the armoire mirrors.

The clunk of the front door closing announces Masako's return. She drops her plaid bolsa on the kitchen table. I spot the outline of a chicken, some mangoes, embroidery cloth, a book.

"I got your note."

She looks around. "Is Hilario gone?"

I nod toward the bucket and broom in the entrada. "He must have left to get something. Lucrecia isn't around either."

"That's because I told her to leave."

I look at her, startled.

She beckons to me to follow. In the bedroom, she strides to the nightstand and holds up a large, pink comb. "I found it in the bed this morning. It must have been left there when we were away."

"Who do you think . . ."

"On my tape player in the studio there's a cassette—*Música Romántica*. Upstairs in the loft," she says with rising heat, "there's a red lightbulb screwed into the socket."

"Hilario and Lucrecia," I mutter.

"In our house. *In our beds,*" Masako says angrily.

Do we cry? Laugh? How even to think about this?

"It's not that he's doing it with her," Masako says. "It's that he's doing it in our house. And what about his wife and ten kids?"

"Does Hilario know you let Lucrecia go?"

"I haven't said anything. I was afraid I'd scream at him."

Recent events begin to fall into place: The days Hilario showed up smelling of drink, leaving hoses and buckets about. The night we arrived home unannounced from California to find him stumbling out of Masako's studio, hair rumpled, stuffing in his shirt. The suspicious depletion of two bottles of tequila I hadn't noticed until friends came over for dinner. The morning we saw him driving through town with Lucrecia beside him. The time Lucrecia had all the ice trays out, and when I asked why, said, "Don Hilario likes his Coca with lots of ice." *Don* Hilario? We'd laughed. Now Masako is telling me that the woman staying in the casita heard a banging on the door one night and opened it to find Lucrecia's little girl standing there looking for her mommy, who turned out to be inside our house with Hilario.

"We're conspirators in this," I say. "He's a handsome, middle-aged guy with a wife and ten kids. She's a pretty young girl whose husband is in Texas working for months at a time. They're alone here for days on end when we're away. And there are beds from one end of the house to the other." Last fall Masako had bought five antique wrought-iron beds from a local dealer with a consignment of them and arrayed them in the studios, the entrada, the garden. "It's a sexy place, a pleasure palace. When the cat's away . . ."

"It bothers me that I fired her and not him," Masako says. "What sort of macho privilege does Hilario claim? Who's the seducer here? He's the older one, in charge."

"He's worked with us since the beginning, helped us put this place together. Lucrecia was here maybe three months. You said you were going to let her go anyway, as she never cleans anything. It's not as if Hilario stole something."

"You're defending him."

"No. I don't know how to think about it either."

Hilario and I have carried mattresses up and down streets, hauled trash barrels, lifted heavy beds together. Our Mexican neighbors, even the poorest, would never do this. We North Americans presume to treat those who work with us as equals, an obvious fiction. I don't answer to Don Antonio, and reluctantly accept "señor" and the formal *usted* from workers only because it's customary. Mexican middle- and upper-class people, who have terrible prejudices against people with Indian blood—which means most Mexicans—find our democratic leveling presumptions ridiculous, hypocritical, when it is obvious that we are different by education, money, and privilege.

"Hilario's been trustworthy," Masako concedes, "even if he is a terrible gardener."

"Here's your chance to find a better one."

"When something like this happens, it suddenly reminds me we're foreigners. I feel so helpless."

"I'll talk to Hilario."

"What will you say?"

"I don't know yet."

When Hilario returns, I follow him out into the garden. Masako remains in the kitchen.

"We need to talk," I say peremptorily.

"Sí, señor." He follows me into Masako's studio. We sit on chairs across from each other.

"You and Lucrecia have been using the house."

He looks perplexed, confused.

"We're only going to talk about this once. *No me interesa lo que haces con mujeres.* It's not my business what you do with women. But there's a line you can't cross." I divide my jeaned thigh with the edge of my hand. "And you know where that line is. You can't use our place for *cosas personales o sociales.*"

"I don't know what you mean, señor."

When I tell him what I mean, he says, "We're just friends." The tequila bottles low? Impossible. I tell him how angry the señora is, and that if he wants to stay, *no más incidentes.* I feel like a bad actor in a cheap British class drama. Sí, señor, he says, as if he agrees but doesn't know what I'm talking about. We shake hands awkwardly. He walks back out into the garden shaking his head as if the señor is *totalmente loco.*

A little while later we are sitting in the kitchen when Hilario skulks through the entrada and slams the front door loudly behind him.

Days pass. Hilario arrives, does his work, and leaves. We barely exchange a word. Normally pleasant and unflappable, he is sullen, angry, the wrongly accused victim. On Candelaria, usually a joyful day when the three of us pick plants from among the thousands in Juárez Park and carry them back to the house, Hilario accompanies us but doesn't say a word. The next week he arrives with a piece of paper listing what he's willing and not willing to do around the place. We agree to it. We don't know if he'll stay or leave, or what we want to happen.

"It's like walking on eggshells around here," Masako says.

More weeks pass. Spring arrives, the jacarandas bloom purple. Still Hilario comes, and still we barely speak. A new housekeeper signs on: middle-aged, bespectacled, portly. She'll work alternate days to Hilario.

Gradually, as the days grow longer and the warm weather sets in, a wary semblance of normalcy, short of our old relaxed demeanors, takes hold. We fall back into the old routines.

"Maybe we're bound to Hilario for life," I say to Masako one summer night in wonderment and resignation.

"Like family," she says.

# Chapter 15

# The Man Who Was Killed Twice

THE STORY CARLOS HAD TOLD ME THAT afternoon in Pozos about René, who had killed a man twice, mightn't have stuck with me if I hadn't kept hearing it in different forms around town. Each version seemed to reveal more about the teller than the perpetrator, while what actually happened remained masked behind speculation.

One warm spring afternoon I was standing in La Golondrina bookstore, talking to Maruja and Billie, when Amalia, a successful painter of local street scenes, came in, swathed in colorful indigenous garb in the manner of Frida Kahlo. She had a rapturous look on her face, as if she'd just seen an angel. "Get a load of her," Billie said under her breath, fanning herself with a copy of *México desconocido,* the monthly travel magazine.

Amalia, her eyes shining, said she'd just visited René in jail across the street at the Presidencia, and he'd read her horoscope in Náhuatl, the pre-Hispanic tongue. René is a living saint, Amalia said, who sees to the very core of people's beings. I waited for Billie to make some sort of crack, but she only rolled her eyes. Amalia, who visits the jail every Wednesday, is apparently but one of René's legion of admirers. "Náhuatl horoscopes my foot," Billie said after she'd left, attributing Amalia's adulation of René to some menopausal possession.

A few nights later Masako and I attend a dinner at our English friends Martin and Blake's grand house up on the hill—always a piece of theater—when the conversation turns to René.

"If you'd known that insufferable Texan he murdered," Martin says with acid drollery, "you'd forgive René much worse."

"Uncalled for, Martin," clucks Blake, Martin's foil. The others around the table laugh uncomfortably.

I'd met Martin our second year here when we knew few people in town, Mexican or gringo—soon after we'd left the Hotel Ambos Mundos for the rental on Calle Quebrada. One day in La Dolce Vita an older Englishman asked if he could sit at my table, as the café was full. When he introduced himself I recognized his name from films. Martin had retired from directing stage and screen and lived in San Miguel part of the year. He invited me to his house for dinner the following Saturday. Delicately, for he was evidently gay, I asked if I might bring along my wife. "You'll like her," I added, certain he would. Indeed it turned out that Martin and Blake adore Masako, whom they call "the darling Japanese."

That Saturday we'd arrived at seven-thirty before a large

door on a narrow street high above town. We heard the barking of a dog, then a servant appeared. We followed him up long stairs past stately rows of trees and an old stone house. At the top, a lone white duck floated on a small fountain set against an ivy-covered wall. Passing under a stone arch, we found ourselves in a second garden with a long, tiled swimming pool, sprays of water tossing off rainbows. Far above, at the top of winding stairs, two men stood in jackets and ties in a large gazebo, drinks in hand.

Martin introduced us to Blake. Soon others arrived: the director of a local art institute, a Lebanese man with a ranch outside of town who seemed to be involved in munitions, a prominent Mexican artist whose surreal work I've seen in Mexico City museums—and a tall, silver-haired woman in black, chain-smoking cheap Mexican Faros, huge rings on her fingers. She introduced herself as Bridget, her sepulchral voice emerging from a hollowed face with a thousand lines. Conversation in English, Spanish, and French filled the gazebo until dinner was announced.

We descended the stairs in procession, drinks in hand. It was as though we'd entered another Luis Buñuel movie, or an Agatha Christie drama—unlike any Mexico we'd encountered. Entering the stone house, we passed through a sala full of books, hundreds of them, on shelves and tables. Martin, noticing me eye them, told me his lawyer flies them down weekly from New York. We were led downstairs to a dining room with a stenciled wallpaper motif borrowed from the walls of a chapel at the shrine of Atotonilco.

At dinner that first night, Martin had held forth wittily, autocratically, while Blake, his companion of many years, fed him his cues. Over a three-course meal, the conversation veered from local gossip to political punditry. An English postcolonial evening in the far provinces—yet everything was a little off, mixed up: the croutons in the potato soup reeked faintly of *jalapeño,* the quiche tasted Mexican somehow, the paraffin candles dripped all over the centerpiece flowers. Afterward Masako and I stepped dazedly back out into the Mexican night, half-charmed, half-appalled by the improbable dinner.

Tonight at Martin and Blake's, Bridget has no sooner mentioned René than someone makes an allusion to the murder. From then on the subject sweeps aside all other conversation.

Martin insists it wasn't a crime of passion at all but simply personal animosity.

Jules, René's victim, had lived for years in a large house behind the covered market. Martin describes Jules as difficult, unpleasant even, a drinker and sometimes a cruel man, while Blake recollects him as rather generous. Each reshading of the victim's character inevitably alters my impression of René. I've passed Jules's house, a hulking yellow edifice on a lively corner a block up from the market, its massive second-story arched balconies just visible from the market side—the walls peeling, the windows shuttered, desolate and melancholy, a monument (in my mind, at least) to some misbegotten hedonism.

During dinner, I hear fireworks crackling over the town below. Somewhere a fiesta is going on, in some Mexico impossibly distant from this house, this dining room, these people.

Theories proliferate about René. René has a terrible temper and is subject to sudden, irrational outbursts. Jules knew an awful secret about René, and René was duty bound to destroy him. Drugs were involved, and drink.

Dessert arrives, a chocolate soufflé, slumping a little on its silver serving plate like a hat somebody sat on. "Still, you have to be loco, over the edge," Juan Carlos says, "to *rematar* somebody, kill them twice." He shakes his head. "You are offered your redemption, then you refuse it."

"What I don't understand," says Blake, "is why, after René had killed Jules the second time, he didn't just go ahead and dump the body down the well at Pozos. He never would have been found out."

"Remorse?" Masako ventures.

"No, he was seen by somebody," says Juan Carlos. "Or else he would have disposed of the body, finished off the job."

"I think he just came to his senses at that point," Blake says. "The way I heard it, he drove back to the San Miguel police station and turned himself in."

Nobody seems to know or care much what really happened. The story has far outgrown the event, burnished into myth, become a town heirloom.

Bridget, who has been silent, lights another Faro from the old one. "Let's be honest, darlings," she croaks. "Who among us has not wanted to do away with someone?"

"Of course," Martin says. "It stirs our own ghosts. It's Shakespearean. This is why René's story still interests us. After all, he's been in jail seven years now."

"The sentence was for twenty and some," says Blake. "But they give you an automatic seven or eight off if you behave."

When I mention Amalia's visits to René in jail, and the Náhuatl horoscopes, hilarity breaks out.

"René is a bright man with scholarly inclinations," Martin says. "But Náhuatl prophecy? There's a sign right there of something odd. And Amalia is a bit impressionable, to say the least."

"It's so Catholic," Juan Carlos says. "The idea of going to a murderer for confession."

"I hear in jail they call René Mother Teresa."

After coffee in the sala, we gather at the bottom of the stairs to say our good nights. Bridget offers us a ride home, a dubious invitation as she's drunk. Martin discreetly suggests I take the wheel. Masako and Bridget and I cram into her decrepit VW bug, which doesn't start until the others give it a shove. I pop it into gear and we lurch off down the near-vertical street on brakes that barely grip the cobblestones. A warm breeze ruffles the *pirules* in the Parque Juárez as we rattle past.

"I heard a rumor," Bridget rasps, "that René may be released soon. His mother told me a deal may be struck."

"Why didn't you mention it at dinner?" Masako asks.

She cackles gaily. "What would Martin and the others have had to talk about?"

Bridget, whom we'd liked immediately, is the daughter of an Italian noblewoman and an English military man. She'd arrived in New York during the war as a teenager with Ernst and Duchamp, studied at the Art Students' League, become a high fashion model, then fled to Mexico City during the high-flying 1950s. She'd been friends with Frida and Diego, Barragán, Huxley, Stravinsky, and Edward James, the wealthy English surrealist who spent millions building an extravagant, outrageous "art park" in the jungle a half day from here. At some point Bridget had run off to the state of Michoacán with a Mexican taxi driver and lived there for years until campesinos chased her off her ranch. Now, aged and suffering from emphysema, she's come to San Miguel. Elegant, irreverent, original, Bridget strikes us as a last connection to a disappearing Mexican bohemia.

We pull up in front of our house. I guide Bridget around to the driver's seat. Her long, veined, ring-bedecked hands quaver like butterflies over the steering wheel, ashes dripping on her black clothes. "Come and visit me, adorable darlings," she says. "Soon." We trade kisses, long-lost *amis*. She weaves off down the cobbles in her VW bug.

Often when I walk past the Presidencia I think of René. It has to be uncomfortable in the jail in the summer heat and winter cold. In Mexico, prisoners are provided with little more than a cell, and must rely upon family, friends, and their own handiwork to subsist. Many make sweaters or other crafts to sell. On a trip into the Sierra Gorda to see Edward James's mad jungle folly, Masako had visited a jail with a friend and acquired an extraordinarily detailed ship in a bottle made by a prisoner.

Regularly too I pass René's mother's dress shop. I see her alone in the dim interior, fussing about her racks or sitting bent over her desk. Masako, who sometimes shops there, describes her merchandise as tasteful, the woman pleasant.

One night Anna, a photographer friend, calls and invites us over for dinner Sunday. She says René's mother will be coming—with René.

"You mean he's out?" I ask.

"His sentence was reduced for good behavior or something. I didn't know how to say no to his mother. Do you think we should be frightened?"

Anna lives in a small, restored dwelling down the street from the Bellas Artes and the Angela Peralta Theater—an area we jokingly call the "theater district." Walking there Sunday evening, Masako says, "What do you think René looks like?"

I suppose I imagine him as dark, good-looking—a well-built guy the doomed Jules had become fatally smitten with (and by). Still, René's interest in Náhuatl gives the picture a twist. We're going to dine with a killer. I think again of Buñuel, whose memoir I've just read, and his two decades living and working in Mexico. He'd have appreciated this surreal moment.

Soon after we enter Anna's tapestried, candlelit living room, René's mother appears, trailing a pleasant-looking man in his late thirties with a mustache, dressed in khaki slacks, a tennis sweater draped over his shoulders. We're introduced. His voice is warm, mellifluous, polite, his manner soft, unprepossessing. I feel ashamed of my wariness.

After René has turned away to speak to someone else, I hear someone say, "Do you play golf?"

I turn around. René's mother is looking at me.

"Actually no, I don't," I say, which happens to be true.

"Too bad. My son is looking for a partner."

Over dinner, the talk is determinedly small, about a piece for a French magazine Anna and I are doing on the shrine of Atotonilco. There's no mention of René's situation or of his release. Surely he must know that everyone at the table knows about the murder and wonders how he got out of prison so soon. But does he realize how much speculation and debate he's incited in San Miguel?

In the weeks following, people seem divided on the subject of René. Carlos describes a dinner he attended with René where one man stood up, threw down his napkin, and said, "I'll be damned if I'll sit at a table with the man who murdered a friend of mine," and stalked out. Bridget defends René, pointing out that he's paid his debt to society by Mexican law and has been forgiven, and should be allowed to get on with his life. Where is Catholic absolution? she asks.

Rene has resumed golf. He looks ruddy and tanned. He has a girlfriend. He has set up a small antiquarian bookstore a block up from us on Calle Flor, where he sits at a rolltop desk reading the Mexican newspapers or studying pre-Hispanic texts. He counsels his acolytes, talks pleasantly to the few customers that enter. Around town, the intense interest in the murder seems to have abated, as if the real killer wandering freely among us is an affront to the titillating fiction he'd engendered, an anticlimax, impoverishing the extravagant lore that had built up in his convenient absence. The only remaining drama is whether he will kill again, a prospect that incites fear but not much dinner conversation.

Back from a short trip, I'm walking across the jardín when I notice a huge, gaping hole in the facade of the Presidencia. Piles of slumped masonry and cement block the sidewalk. It turns out that a gang of rogue policemen from nearby Querétaro, caught robbing local houses and jailed, had tried to blow their way out. One died, another lost a hand, a third was apprehended. Meanwhile the explosion destroyed the records in the city offices next door, so there'll be no water bills this year—a development nobody mourns.

The next morning, passing René's store, I hear him hailing me. He holds up the front page of the local paper, *El Sol de Bajío,* filled with pictures of our damaged prison and city hall. Shaking his head sadly, René says in his arch, honeyed voice, "That *never* would have happened in *my* day."

I've never openly discussed the murder with him, though I've thought of it. He must assume everyone knows: for one day, with no prompting, he suddenly referred to Jules his victim as "that man I so lamentably bumped off."

*That man I so lamentably bumped off!* His rich locution

clings, with its mixture of regret and braggadocio. René has remorse for the act, I think, but not for the man he killed. How *do* you explain yourself to yourself after killing someone? Reason unravels in Mexico; extravagant behavior erupts. I think of Crazy Jeem the speed freak and the other twisted souls back at the Ambos Mundos; Ambrose Bierce, who disappeared into Mexico never to be heard from; William Burroughs, who shot his wife to death here; Howard Hughes's descent into madness and decrepitude in Acapulco.

One day my curiosity gets the best of me. I find René in his shop, busying over a woman's horoscope. When she leaves, I come right out and ask him about the murder.

He's quite willing to talk about it. They were both very drunk that night, and stoned, René says. They'd been playing Trivial Pursuit with some other people, and afterward Jules kept on him about something in René's past he was acutely sensitive about. René decided he'd had enough. He clubbed Jules into unconsciousness. Panicked and thinking him dead, he stuffed the body in the trunk of his car. He drove wildly around for hours, ending up on the desolate plateaus of Pozos at dawn with the intention of throwing the body down one of the wells. Instead he drove into a ditch, opening a gash on his head and stranding the car.

He heard banging in the trunk. Opening it, he saw that Jules was still alive.

"What did you think then?" I ask him.

"Jules was pretty far gone. He wasn't a young man. Even if he'd survived he'd never have been right again. So I killed him a second time."

*Rematar:* to re-kill. That was the moment when René could have saved himself, at least before the law.

René holds up his thumb and forefinger. "If you *squeeze* the glottis like *this,* and *hold . . .*"Raising his chin, he demonstrates on himself. I think: He takes a certain melancholy pleasure in doing this. "After about two minutes he convulsed, had a heart attack. I smelled the feces. I knew he was dead."

Somebody came along and saw René's car in the ditch. René put up no resistance. Back in San Miguel, he confessed readily—a tactical mistake, he claims: his lawyer defended him indifferently, then took $40,000 and went off to Acapulco. René was given twenty-three years, with a portion to be taken off for good behavior.

His early release, he tells me, came about by sheer good luck. One of his visitors in jail told him of a cache of books dating back to the revolution that a woman had found in the walls of an old San Miguel house she'd bought. She'd sold the books to a New York rare-book dealer for a lot of money. Knowing how possessive Mexicans are about their patrimony, René offered to provide the details of this transaction to the Mexican government, as long as the friend would be spared prosecution and he would be let out of jail early. An emissary was sent from Mexico City, a deal arranged. The books were found in good shape, in Tokyo, and René was released as promised.

Rene regrets the murder and will always bear its stigma. He prays daily, he says, for "that unfortunate man," as he refers to Jules. At the same time the killing, and the years in jail, whose details he recounts with an undeniable savor and immediacy, have formed part of his identity, providing him with a kind of local currency. He has become a confessor figure to others who admit to having had the same impulses—even some who did murder, he says, but unlike him weren't caught. Still he finds absolution in the eyes of others hard to come by. Mexicans, he says, are more forgiving than most Americans and Europeans, in whose eyes he is forever condemned.

René walks through San Miguel in a straw hat and shoulder bag. He married, I'd heard, though someone else wasn't so sure if it lasted. René is a survivor. He works afternoons in his little bookstore, where, if you wish, he'll do a Náhuatl reading for you.

# Chapter 16

# Faith and Fiestas: The Magic Waters of Tlacote

*The poor are not poor*
*The rich are not rich*
*Only those who suffer pain are poor*

SIGN OVER THE PATIO GATE

OF THE NIÑO FIDENCIO

HOLY WEEK LOOMS, THE YEAR'S biggest holiday. The dry, dusty air befits the season of crucifixion. Two hotter months lie ahead before summer rains turn the parched yellow hardpan earth lush again. On Candelaria Day in early February, townspeople bought plants and flowers in the Parque Juárez and carried them through the town to their homes. On Ash Wednesday the faithful were marked with black crosses of cinder from last year's Palm Sunday fronds. Tonight, two weeks before Easter Sunday, Our Lord of the Column, that flayed and weary Jesus who leans on his brown wood stanchion in Atotonilco shrine all year, will be borne through the night by pilgrims to San Juan de Dios church a few blocks below the center of town. Thousands will witness or join the dawn procession.

During these holiest of weeks, the gardener nuns of Las Monjas, the ones I used to watch from my studio window on Calle Quebrada, will forsake trowels and hoes for formal habits and duties: faith and fiestas. On Wednesday, the entire town will become an outdoor church, as marchers, beginning at the Oratorio, will visit the fourteen stations of the cross—symbolized by carved stone niches in worn building walls—ending at the stone chapel at the top of Calle San Francisco.

Meanwhile, thousands of supplicants line a dusty road in a tiny Querétaro suburb called Tlacote, less than an hour from here. They've been coming from all over Mexico, and as far away as Russia and Japan, since last May, bringing empty bottles and cans and jugs to a well whose miraculous waters are said to cure cancer, obesity, high cholesterol—nearly every human affliction. Since a farm dog lapped up some of it, and was allegedly cured, Sr. Silva, the well's owner, has been giving the water away to up to ten thousand visitors a day. The state health director says the water's chemistry is like any other, though Sr. Silva claims it weighs less than normal water. A gift from God, he says.

A few weeks ago Vicente Arias and I drove to Tlacote. Unable to get any closer than a mile away, we parked in a dusty turnaround. We walked down the line of crippled ancients, children with festering skin eruptions, squawling babies ill with incurable diseases, women with huge tumors, and hymn-singing delegations from distant towns and provinces and countries. A running ditch beside the path served as both latrine and sleeping quarters on one side; on the other, a spontaneous community of vendors sold *refrescos,* tamales, chicles, tissues, plastic water bottles, and newspapers. Finally we arrived at the head of the line. An arched entry led into a courtyard where attendants were filling pilgrims' containers from a fountain. The recipients hurried out lugging their bottles and jars, faces shining, full of hope and belief.

Sr. Silva, perhaps thinking we were reporters, came toward us. He seemed eager to talk. The water has been studied microbiologically in Belgium, he said, and it's been confirmed that it brings genetic changes on a cellular level. Flipping through his guest register, he showed us names from all over the world—pausing for my benefit on Magic Johnson, the HIV-afflicted basketball star—then had us sign it. Vicente and I had brought no known afflictions to cure, but Sr. Silva insisted we each take a bottle of Tlacote water. On the way home we drank it, to no apparent effect one way or the other: it just tasted like water.

A few days later I ran into Vicente in the jardín. He said there'd been a report on television of thousands flocking to another well on the Guerrero coast—situated on a property owned, coincidentally, by Sr. Silva's brother. Simply further evidence of God's work, the brothers Silva responded when questioned by journalists. No surprise when last week bottles of Tlacote water began appearing at Espino's market alongside the other bottled waters, though at a slightly higher price. The brothers Silva, perhaps obeying God's further instructions, have gone into business marketing the magic waters.

But devotion has its own power apart from fact; and Mexican daily life is steeped in the miraculous. Here there are no ordinary days: each belongs to some saint at the least, and the Virgin appears continually in myriad guises—in a tree, in a subway station, by a river. A few days ago I came across a singing procession bearing a new statue of a Virgin glimpsed last year by a campesino outside our town. The image had been rendered by, for some reason, a sculptor in Yugoslavia. They were carrying her to San Francisco Church to reside there for Holy Week. Working my way closer, I looked up into a pert, pink-faced Virgin face with aquiline nose, tiny chin, and thin lips—looking more like Barbie or Bo Derek than anyone from around here. Did the campesino really see a *Virgen* who looked like that in a tree, or was some instruction lost between here and Yugoslavia?

This town and region are rife with stories of faith healing and miracles. Las Monjas, our nunnery, was founded by a local girl known as María Josefa of the Most Holy Trinity, whose life, according to her biographer, consisted exclusively of "fearing, desiring, admiring, and loving Christ." Three days before her death in 1770, she exhaled worms from her nose that turned into butterflies. Even now, a local priest at the nunnery, Padre Tonio, dispenses magical ministrations to visitors from all over the region.

Recently Carlos gave me a book about a faith healer known as El Niño Fidencio, born in our state of Guanajuato at the turn of the century, one of twenty-five children. In youth he read his classmates' minds and told them their futures. He liked to help the midwives wash the clothes of women who had just given birth. By the age of twenty-nine he was famous—extracting tumors, caring for mothers who had just given birth, attending lepers. He was a good singer with a high soprano voice, and two women would hold him while he sang, giving him beer to drink and lighting his cigarettes. The Niño Fidencio's healings began each day at dawn, and he'd often work days without food; he claimed he

even attended the sick when asleep. Combining pre-Hispanic nostrums, Christianity, and spiritualism, his work was
tolerated by the Church, though he was regarded by local
people as a virtual Christ and had his own "nuns" and
"priests." In 1928 the president of Mexico, beset by a painful
illness, visited the Niño Fidencio and came away relieved.
Two years later a Harvard-educated health official in the
state attacked the healer as a charlatan. Soon thereafter the
Niño Fidencio died, though he remains as popular as ever today—a symbol of native religiosity, the subject of documen-
tary films, his image adorning soapboxes, matchbooks,
charms.

Not only the spiritual world gets celebrated these days.
This year, 1992, marks the controversial quincentenary of
Christopher Columbus's arrival to these shores. A few mornings ago, walking past the stone statue across from the Café
Colón, I noticed the explorer's head lying at his feet, chiseled
off during the night by anticolonialist protesters. Spanish-
descended local ranchers quickly laid a wreath at the base of
the statue and a sign decrying the desecration.

This year also marks the 450th anniversary of the town's
founding by Fray Juan de San Miguel. Commemorative
posters and speeches are being prepared in earnest. San Miguel Day at the end of September will probably exceed its
usual mania this year, though the benign statue of the ton-
sured Franciscan, photogenically situated just outside the
Parroquia's forecourt and across from Allende's statue—
head bent, hand lying paternalistically on an Otomí's
head—is probably too much an object of local affection to
warrant beheading by anticlericals.

In the midst of all this ceremony and ritual, we mark
changes in our own lives. Bridget has smoked her last Faro,
her pinhole-sized alveoli refusing to admit another gulp of

air, and at a small ceremony at the little church on Insurgentes we honored her and the extravagant, eccentric
Mexico that passed with her. Maruja and Billie decided to
move their bookstore off the jardín when rents went up, and
Vicente gave up his painting studio at the Ambos Mundos
for the same reason. Elenita is working for the leftist PRD
and continues her "shamanistic spiritual work" with the rug
weaver from Oaxaca, to Carlos's great distress. Letters from
Arnaud bringing news of literary life in post-Duvalier Port-
au-Prince are passed around; he promises to come visit. New
friends arrive to replace old, and guests move rhythmically
in and out of the casita.

The shifts in our town mirror those in the world beyond.
Articles in travel magazines bring more tourists, and a new
airport an hour and a half away accommodates international
flights. In the Hotel Taboada's new *"centro de comunica-
ciones"* you can send or receive a "telefax" for a few dollars a
page. We have an answering machine now, and a few weeks
ago Masako brought home a color television and VCR she'd
bought from a departing Englishwoman. It sits in her studio,
glassy-eyed and ominous, awaiting cable hookup, threatening to admit inside these walls that other life—cool, electronic, agitating—that we'd left in L.A. January seven years
ago for this intimate, voluptuous, sense-driven one.

In other ways, we watch gringo and Mexican cultures
blend, collapse, begin to resemble each other: free trade
agreements, computers, drugs. Still it often takes two weeks
for a letter to arrive here, and people hand-carry each other's
outgoing mail to the States. The power goes out regularly,
returning us to candlelight's mysteries. The burros and knife
sharpeners and petate sellers still ply the streets, and festi-
vals seem actually to increase in fervor: this year's Day of the
Locos was twice as big and bizarre as the last. Calle Flor remains a lightly used one-way leading away from town into

an inconvenient dogleg, though a dry cleaners has moved in where the old Corto Maltese restaurant used to be; and on the next block there are two new cafés, an art gallery, and a hair salon. Still, early mornings or late evenings, when the Texas twangs, Bronx brogues, and German gutturals abate, and the new Benetton store and the Century 21 realty branch close, the town relapses into the hands of its Mexican residents, 95 percent strong. Climbing up to our roof by way of the rear stairs, I see new houses creeping up the hillsides like the *moneda* vine along our garden wall—and still I dream of building a veranda up here.

No alarm clock is needed to rouse me this morning. Fireworks and church bells begin well before sunup, stirring faithful and faithless alike. I clamber into clothes and hurry off through the cool dawn to San Juan de Dios church, hoping I haven't missed the arrival of *El Señor de la Columna* at the end of its all-night pilgrimage from Atotonilco.

The church where Jesus of the Column will spend the next twelve days—before being carted onto the Parroquia on Good Friday, then eventually home—lies a few blocks below the center of town on a break in the hillside's descent. Already the wide forecourt is filled with people, though salvos of fireworks in the sky to the north place the all-night marchers still a good mile away. Impromptu food stands line the blocks around the church, selling tamales in corn husks and hot atole drink. Crowds assemble along the approach road: most are smaller, darker, Indian-descended, the bulwark of the faith here.

I take up a position along a wall across from the *campo-*

*santo,* the former graveyard, now a tangle of headstones and weeds. The approach road is carpeted with green laurel branches and yellow and purple confetti. A brazier threads the air with copal incense. The crowd, in spite of the morbidity of the occasion, is cheerful.

The procession has entered town on the north road; we hear their singing as they approach. Bursts of fireworks scatter the starlings in the treetops as a smiling girl pours purple confetti into my cupped hands. Three tired, ragged lute players appear first, strumming and singing praises to Jesus, followed by a man holding a two-foot-high replica of Jesus of the Column in a glass box. A phalanx of girls passes, bearing bouquets of *lágrimas* (baby's tears), marigolds (their foul odor associated with death), and wilting sprays of chamomile. Tiny crones plod past on wooden walking crooks, shawls over their heads, singing hymns.

Then Jesus of the Column appears, aloft on a float covered in white trumpet vines. Ivory-white, he leans bare-chested on his wood stanchion, a purple loincloth hanging to his knees, his back flayed and bloody. It's a deeply tragic image, expressing an extraordinary attitude of burden. I have no idea who carved the statute; a visiting friend of mine, a painter and draftsman steeped in Italian medieval and Renaissance depiction, couldn't get over this figure and collected images of it to study. I've read that the column represents, in medieval theology, the *axis mundi* the gods used to travel between the three realms of the universe—in modern Christianity, the link between heaven and earth. The statue's perplexed, exhausted expression, and the blood, remind me of the stuck bull in the ring near the end. At the bullfight the audience plays the pagan Romans; here, the identification is with the crucified.

We want so much to be moved. In Catholic Mexico—and

Mexico is overwhelmingly Catholic—it's hard not to feel the power of adoration, the urge to surrender to some ideal of purity, redemption. I've felt this before, in the Arab world. Still we know the price our century has paid for such absolutist yearnings, and so we curb them, pretend they don't exist, burrow back into a secular world whose blanket never quite covers us.

"The first thing you need to understand about us Mexicans," my friend Ofelia said to me, "is that we are Catholic. We may be communist. We may be atheist. We may be Sufis. But first we are Catholic."

As Jesus moves slowly past, I toss my purple confetti with everyone else. Behind him, as far as the eye can see, stretch thousands of the devout, carrying white lilies, oranges, roses, and candles, walking as they have since 1741. I see Yolanda from the paper store, Abel the checkout clerk at Espino's grocery, Salvador the garbage truck driver. The last to pass are those who joined the procession at the edge of town: fresh-dressed latecomers, Mexican tourists, oversized gringos in shorts and sunglasses looking through cameras or camcorders.

The procession pauses in the crowded forecourt of San Juan de Dios, where by custom Jesus must wait for entry. After more singing, firecrackers, a brief sermon, and the blessing of statues, the church doors open at last to admit the bloody, bowed figure—freeing the rest of us to wander off into the widening day and find a warm breakfast.

Eleven at night, the Friday before Palm Sunday, Night of Sorrows. Anxiously I stand in the doorway of Lucha Contreras's pharmacy, three rows back from the counter. The fireworks erupting in the skies over the Parroquia bring me no pleasure tonight. My daughter, Maya, who is visiting, has fallen suddenly, inexplicably ill.

Lucha briskly ministers to customers from her post by the cash register: Indian women from the country with coughing infants wrapped in rebozos; old men with the shakes, their hats in their hands; gringas demanding facial creams or diuretics. Evidently I'm not the only one in need tonight.

Maya, who arrived Monday and quickly made herself at home in the casita, will stay for Holy Week; then we'll fly up to L.A. to join Masako for the opening of a solo exhibit of her Mexican ladder paintings. We've spent the days exploring, eating, talking, catching up. At La Gruta, the hot baths outside of town, we soaked ourselves into oblivion. I've watched the glow return to her cheeks as she untangled from her L.A. multimedia producing job, the recent breakup with her long-term boyfriend. She's flexed her Spanish, already good, and roamed the town taking photos of walls, burros, children. She bought a woven bag from Chiapas, a Guerrero mask for her apartment, Mexican wrestling posters, and a mouse pad with the Virgin of Guadalupe on it.

On Tuesday, the night when the town's churches throw open their inner precincts to visitors, we'd joined the crowds wandering the half-lit town bearing candles, greeting priests and nuns, kissing holy relics. We'd explored the sacristies and sanctums closed the rest of the year. We'd seen Maruja and Billie that night, Vicente, and Elenita and her daughter *sans* Carlos. Hilario had been there with his fecund family, his wife amazingly fresh-looking. We even ran into ageless Felipa who used to clean our house on Calle Quebrada.

Tonight, after an early supper with friends, we'd visited the altars to Mary that people build in their homes each year, and the public fountains decorated with wreaths and flowers. Soon after we got home, Maya fell violently ill with vomiting, sweats, and diarrhea that wouldn't stop.

Lucha's pharmacy is part proxy doctor's office and part secular shrine. Alongside standard medicines and basic vanity items—shampoos, perfumes, creams—she sells homeopathic remedies and folk curatives straight from the stalls of the Tuesday market: bee pollen, snake venom, herbal concoctions. Oft-married, rumored to own much real estate around town, Lucha is an object of veneration and suspicion—a contemporary *bruja*, a saint of chemistry.

A gringa is prattling on to Lucha about her poodle's skin rash. Unable to wait any longer, I edge in. "Excuse me," I say. "My daughter is very ill."

When I describe the symptoms, Lucha sells me a bottle of Lomotil and chewable Pepto-Bismol tablets. I hurry off through the dark.

Back at the casita, Maya is on her knees, dry heaving, in a cold sweat. She can't keep anything down, even water. A fierce case of the turistas, I want to think; but she's getting frightened and who can blame her? It's after midnight. I haven't a clue what to do. I've had no dealings with doctors in San Miguel. Finally I call a friend, who advises me to call the American consul in town.

He answers sleepily.

"My daughter is very sick."

"Be right over," he says.

Fifteen minutes later he's standing in the doorway, his car

idling on the street above. I bundle Maya in a blanket and get her up the stairs and into the car.

I'd seen this man around town, the consul: dressed in khakis, cropped hair, chomping on a cigar. An operative if I've ever seen one. Here to keep tabs on Central American insurgencies, drug-dealing gringos? Right now I don't care. He's gotten out of bed in the middle of the night and is taking us to a hospital.

"I can't thank you enough," I say.

"S'okay," he barks. "Comes with the territory."

At a tiny hospital on Calle Hidalgo, two uniformed nurses appear at the car and help me get Maya inside. A doctor has been called, the consul says. Maya is shivering, ghost-pale, near-unconscious. Waiting with her, I think of stories I've heard about Mexican doctors and hospitals: anesthesiologists shooting up patients with stale drugs, doctors operating with rusty scalpels or removing the wrong organ. It consoles me little to recall that I've heard the same tales about North American hospitals.

A bearded man in a raincoat arrives. The consul explains the situation in Spanish. Dr. Baeza quickly introduces himself, then orders Maya be taken to a hospital room and bed upstairs. Immediately he puts her on an IV, injects her with an antibiotic. The immaculate nurses flit about.

"It's good you didn't wait until morning," Dr. Baeza says.

"Why?"

"Typhus."

The word rings out into the room, dire and terrifying, something out of the tropical medicine cabinet. "How did she get it?"

*"Quién sabe?* Something she ate, or touched, or breathed in."

"Will she be all right?"

"I hope so."

He nods toward the second bed in the room. At first I
don't understand what he means. Then I realize he's inviting me to stay overnight. Of course. Why don't North Americans do that?

"I'll be back in the morning," Dr. Baeza says.

Maya lies on her back, eyes closed, a tube running into
her arm. I crawl into the other bed. Her vomiting has
abated; now as fluids fill her, she stumbles up and heads for
the bathroom, dragging the IV trolley behind.

"Hi," she whispers, crawling back into bed.

"Hi." It's the most intimate thing we've done together
since she was a kid.

I lie awake, anguished. Kind and beautiful and smart
Maya. The thought that something bad would befall her
turns my world dark. On this Night of Sorrows we'd drifted
through the *calles* with the crowds, entering the opened
homes and admiring the sincere, touching altars—some
with hand-painted statues and sand paintings, all with purple flowers, bitter oranges, fresh yellow-green wheat plants
and gold flags: symbols of the event and the season, com-
memorating Mary's sorrows. I'd admired it, as I do so many
things here, as religious and aesthetic vernacular expression,
never for a second identifying with any of it. In Mexico I've
known no sorrow until now.

**D**ad. You awake?"

We must have both fallen asleep. Daylight fills the room.
Dr. Baeza is standing over Maya taking her pulse. The perfect ladies arrive with trays of juice, eggs, toasted *bolillos*.

"I think she'll be okay," Dr. Baeza says. "Tomorrow maybe she goes home."

Dazedly I get up, throw water on my face. After breakfast I walk outside. It's Saturday morning and traffic is stalled as visitors pour in from all over Mexico for *Semana Santa,* Holy Week. The air is sweltering. In the puestos, the stalls, people fan themselves and watch the Mexican soaps on their little TVs. Passing the fountains filled with wilting flowers from the Night of Sorrows, I head down Calle Flor to pick up fresh clothes for Maya. Inside, the house feels somber, desolate, drained of cheer and color—like the first day we saw it.

On the way back to the hospital I pass the Church of La Salud, Our Lady of Health, with its ornate, whimsical Byzantine tower and great carved shell over its entry with a god's eye in a Masonic triangle. I slip inside, past the altar dedicated to Santa Cecilia, patroness of music, who every November 22 receives a serenade from the town musicians. Drawn forward into the silence, I find my way to the chapel area to left of the main altar, where a small, pale doll stands in a glass case, his white garment affixed with hundreds of *milagros,* junk silver charms: Piled at the feet of *Santo Niño de la Salud,* the Holy Child of Health, are toy cars and footballs, babies' dresses, rattles, and hair ribbons. Discarded splints and casts are stacked high outside the case, with hundreds of snapshots of children inscribed with written words of entreaty, thanks, or praise pinned to the altar.

I sit down on a bench in front of the little effigy. I have no reason to thank this inanimate piece of painted wood for restoring my daughter's health; still I suppose I feel no differently than thousands of parents who've come there before me. If I had a photo of Maya in my wallet, or one of Masako's milagros, I think I'd add it to the others. Instead, I fish in my wallet and dig out an old Chinese fortune-cookie paper from an L.A. restaurant. It's enigmatic, Zen-like message had delighted me enough to save it. It says simply: YOU MAY BE CERTAIN OF IT.

I stand up and affix it to the cluster of charms.

Turning to leave, I think I see Maya standing at the entrance, backlit in silhouette, waiting for me; but it's only another pretty young gringa with a Nikon, here for the Easter celebrations.

Back at the hospital, the consul has stopped by to see how Maya is. She's talkative, cheery, color has returned to her face.

I stay with her that night. Lying in the dark, she asks me about Semana Santa, as if taking inventory of what more she may have to endure on this trip.

"On Friday, no bells," I say. "Eerie, as if the world is holding its breath. Jesus of the Column will be borne to the Parroquia. Then at noon the Seven Last Words of Christ are delivered in a three-hour sermon."

"About twenty-six minutes a word," Maya quickly calculates, her brain none the worse for the typhus.

"Then a procession bearing holy images guarded by Roman soldiers wends its way through town. I usually skip that. On Saturday, though, it gets pretty raucous in the jardín. They blow up giant papier-mâché Judas dolls."

"What about Easter Sunday?"

"An anticlimax. Just cars streaming out of town as visitors leave."

"We'll be among them."

"Right."

The next morning, as we're packing to leave the hospital, I say, "I'd wanted you to enjoy Mexico."

"Oh, I have," she says bravely.

We bid good-bye to Dr. Baeza, the saintly nurses. How to

thank them and the consul? If I'm ever sick, please bring me to this little hospital on Calle Hidalgo. The charge for the two days comes to the equivalent of sixty dollars.

Outside, it's Palm Sunday. Maya and I walk home by way of the jardín, pausing in front of the Parroquia, where vendors are selling fresh-woven yellow and green palm fronds, symbols of spring renewal. Maya buys one to take home. I buy two, one for the house and one to bring to Masako for the opening of her show.

A sleek L.A. gallery. Glass, steel, white walls. Milling crowds in black, white wine in plastic cups. Outside, a sweltering 100-degree heat wave. Wildfires have broken out in the foothills. On one wall, a cluster of small paintings of wooden Mexican ladders, *escaleras:* lying against the ground, standing up, ascending into space, floating through air. On higher, wider walls, large paintings of ladders rise into diaphanous air, cross fiery Rothko skies, mirror themselves below. Their Spanish titles speak: *Alzamiento* (Rising Up), *Levantamiento* (Ascent), *Viajero* (Voyager). Utterances of light, and time. Ladders that float: a wordless distillation of Masako's Mexican revelations.

As friends and collectors gather to leave for a celebratory dinner, the director ushers a man over to introduce to Masako. Haltingly the man says he just lost his hillside home in the fire. All he had left was his car, with an invitation to the show on the front seat.

*"Escaleras,"* he said. "I figured what the hell, it must be a sign. I drove here. Look. That ladder rising over fire. That's it. Hope. You go on. Right?"

# Chapter 17

# O*bra Suspendida*

LA LUZ IS THE NAME OF THE BELL THAT
marks our hours and days, parting the misty
dawn, laying midnight to rest. Sometimes
from the roof of the house I watch the
skinny bell ringer on tiptoe drawing down
the Parroquia's rope like a runaway kite in a
windstorm; and when it clangs, scattering
the belfry pigeons, I swear I can see sound
waves rippling toward me like breakers on a
beach. Of the hundreds of bells that hang
from campanarios around San Miguel—
eight in the tower of La Parroquia alone—
La Luz, cast in 1732 of gold melted in with
the bronze to heighten and clarify the
sound, is the largest. In the 1960s somebody
recorded the bells for a Nonesuch album
called *The Sounds of San Miguel;* I came
across a copy once in an old Mexican hip-
pie's moldering LP collection. Back from a

trip away, La Luz's musky rumble rings me home, smoothing me back into place. One visiting writer friend, though, considered the bell a curse and fled the casita clutching her head.

La Luz tolls the turning seasons inside the kitchen walls, where Masako adds to her collection of tin ex-votos. Pots and pans dangle from iron hooks above the blue stove. Spoons and spatulas and whisks cram terra-cotta bowls. A paint-spattered radio punches out ranchera music when cooking's going on. In the dining room, an old wood *trastero* dish rack is stacked with bright ceramic cups and plates, mirrored in an antique armoire full of glasses and liquor bottles. Books and magazines in both languages litter our bed and the floor around it, sit in piles on carved chests called *baúls* and the glassed-in bookshelves Boni Ortiz has built to hold them. Masako has embroidered *Mi Corazón Es Tuyo* (My Heart Is Yours) on bed and chair pillows. Outside, a new purple bougainvillea climbs the entry arch, and in the garden the jacaranda has tripled in size, combining with the chirimoyo tree to provide a double canopy for the violets, the butterflies, and us.

Summers we linger in the cool, ample southern rooms, and when it gets cold we migrate to sunny garden patches to warm ourselves on the patio stones, or stay by fires I build in my studio of wood cut from our trees. Sometimes we sleep upstairs in the *tapanco*, as Masako's studio mezzanine is called, where morning sun beams straight in. It's nice to linger among her paintings of ladders, *artesanías* collected from the markets, new watercolors on pre-Columbian bark paper called *amate*, and a growing collection of photographs. At my studio table, my back to the patio, words become stories and books, essays and articles, and lyrics and liner notes for albums, something I also do. The house, little changed but for patched leaks, paint, furnishings, and plants, is refuge and work space, monastery and site of the sensual: food, sex, garden. After five years, we feel we know the place a little.

Still, small events surprise us. One day while taking a shower I noticed that the sisus vine along the back garden wall, green a day earlier, looked denuded. I went outside and found hundreds of leaf-cutter ants snipping and transporting the fresh green leaves to their underground nest, as in some Amazon nature film. Another time a mysterious shuddering sound beneath the floor of the casita bedeviled us for days until Hilario learned from our neighbor to the south that the pump in the large subterranean water deposit—proof against the droughts that beset the town—had gone into its death throes. Last Sunday morning Masako found a clucking, red-wattled chicken in the patio. It had flown in over the wall. After overcoming her shock, she began feeding it grain, and by noon it was part of the family. Then a knocking came at the door. It was our neighbor two doors up, Señora Martínez, looking for her chicken. She chased it around the patio and grabbed it by its neck in a flurry of feathers and squawking. At the door she thanked us. *"Comida,"* she said, smiling. Lunch. For the rest of the day Masako was inconsolable.

House connects to street and town, to plaza and park, to spires and skies above and glimmering lake and plains below: a geography rippling out into the greater world. In the spring of 1993, the Canada–U.S.–Mexico free trade agreement called NAFTA is slated to go into effect at year's end. *Narcotráfico* mirrors insatiable U.S. appetites for dope. Colombian courier networks fly Cessnas into remote lawless jungles of Veracruz State and Guerrero, and in the desolate north, far off the maps of Sinaloa and Chihuahua, Uzi-toting *banditos* guard hidden landing strips and refineries. Little of it touches us here, though a dealer who used to live at the Ambos Mundos now resides in the Guanajuato jail. International money pours in ahead of NAFTA, but does little to diminish border crossings, the unofficial economy, the payoffs. The monolithic PRI shakes as President Carlos Salinas de Gortari, soon to end his six-year reign this year, legitimizes the Catholic Church (officially outlawed since the revolution), greases the way for his cronies to remain in power, and changes Mexican property laws to permit foreigners like us to shed that tortuous document called the *fideicomiso*, linking us forever to a bank, and instead own property outright. Once we're certain the law is for real, we visit a lawyer on Calle Hidalgo, pay hefty fees to a half dozen officials on the food chain, and take possession of the house on Calle Flor in perpetuity.

Soon after New Year's, word comes that Paul has died in California. He was just over fifty. His ashes reside in a mirrored box he and Mina had built for them. Now Mina, who lived and made films in Mexico for twenty years, talks of coming back. We wonder.

A fter five years of climbing the back stairs to this scrambled roof whose view so enthralled me when we first saw the house—*qué buena vista*—my desire to spend more time up here remains. I'm convinced the shaded compound below needs to be liberated up into this aerie of birds, light, and church spires. The unused half of our house, I keep telling Masako, lies up here.

The way the buildings knit up the hill and stack around the church has always reminded me of medieval Italy or

Spain, or of Moorish Tangier. Most Mexicans don't particularly value such views, their rooftops the province of watchdogs and refuse—their Spanish natures hewing to the medieval enclosure, their pre-Hispanic selves to earth and tribe. I lived in Kyoto for two years, teaching and studying, and it was like that: mountain trails coming to sudden ends far short of the peaks where only crazy monks lived; views contained in sand gardens, *koi* ponds, the moon's reflection instead of the moon itself. But if my neighbors along Calle Flor tend to stay within their walls, it doesn't mean Mexicans don't love to build: consider the great stone edifices of Palenque and Teotihuacán, Puebla's churches, the sprawling haciendas. Mexicans have no fear of stone. The country is in endless construction and reconstruction, every roadside piled with bricks awaiting the mason's trowel, swarms of teen youths pouring into the trades, the tapping of chisels and hammers throughout the town as pervasive as the bells. Loose building codes and accommodating officials make Mexico a builder's paradise, province of endless invention.

Squatting up here among the old pipes and tar, birdshit and glass shards, I fill a notebook with sketches and diagrams. I imagine a leveled, reinforced rooftop running over the old kitchen, dining room, bedroom, and bathroom, with possibly some glass-block traigaluces to admit light below. Standing with my back to our southerly neighbors' roofs, I envision a veranda with a tiled roof held up by narrow stone columns, allowing for the unimpeded sweep up across the roofs to the Parroquia. From this point, the hillside on which the town rises lies to my right, and to my left the tumbling slopes to the lake and beyond. Included in this siting is a view, to the left of the avocado tree, of the nunnery's great dome and bell tower. Built-in banquettes on which to sit, table and chairs, a hammock even. Mornings with sky and birds and bells as the sun splits the peak above the lookout on the Querétaro road. Red dusk among swirling black grackles and platooning white egrets. Summer nights of fireworks and distant bands, oceanic stars and moonrise over the church tower.

*Veranda:* a place from which to *ver,* to see.

The only way to get up here is by way of the rear garden stairs, which are steep, treacherous, inconvenient. The front patio is the obvious spot for a stairway; on a descending lot like ours, the closer to the entrance, the shorter the ascent— a twenty-foot climb in front, thirty in back. How to build a stairway that big in the patio without ruining it? Mexicans favor the circular caracol, or snail, which saves space at the expense of banged elbows and spilled drinks during the mount. Or we could build a stairway inside the house somewhere. Masako and I stalk the town, studying stair treatments, balustrades, roofs, verandas. We become voyeurs of solutions, design burglars. Masako makes sketches to scale of a built-in planter, seats, walls to hide the water and gas tanks. At the same time we build a veranda we'll attack those kitchen and bathroom tiles, the dangling electrical wires, the missing glass in the front window. We'll patch, we'll paint. All the things we never got around to.

Our house ideas tend to collapse of their own weight at just this point, subverted by the languid allure of the place as it is, or the claims of our own work. Our roof plan is undoubtedly headed for the same fate when Roberto, an architect friend, arrives one day trailing a stubby, bullish-looking contractor named Epifanio.

"You'll love him," says Roberto, beating a quick retreat, leaving us alone in the patio with *Maestro* Epifanio.

Epifanio stands on the roof squinting in the sun, making tape measurements, scribbling with an old ballpoint pen in the palm of his hand. Permits? No need, he says gruffly. I know everybody at city hall. With his pitted basalt face, flared lips and nose, he looks like one of the Olmec statues at El Tajín.

Back down in the patio we tackle the big question: where to put the stairs. Squatting, we draw lines on the ground with sticks, gesture with our hands. *Pos, aquí. Así. No, no sirve. Eso es.* Epifanio prefaces each sentence with *"pos,"* workers' slang for *"pues,"* meaning "then" or "well." We decide on the corner just inside the entrada by the dining room entry: a cantera stone stairway arching over the door. This is the way to build, I think: architecture without architects.

Epifanio's estimate is reasonable but we scowl, dicker, let numbers hang in the air. He throws new terms at us: *maya,* a kind of gridded rebar roof material; *tesontle,* a lightweight volcanic stone; *escombro,* which means rubble, waste, trash. We need to work fast before the rains start in late June, Epifanio says, because then we can't get stones and gravel from the riverbeds, the cement won't dry, the workers can't work. We hammer out an estimate, a rough weekly figure, a timetable: two months. When do we start? Epifanio shrugs. *"Pos, mañana?"* No, Monday. Okay, let's go. *Andale.*

"A maestro named Epiphany," Masako says bemusedly that night over dinner at El Campanario, a new restaurant across from the nunnery. We've heard stories about Mexican builders: how they construct entire walls, then go back in and chip out electrical ducts instead of doing it as they go; how masons mysteriously measure by eye the vaulted ceilings called *bóveda* to come out exactly right when the last brick is placed. Remodeling is not our strong suit: the one time we tried it in California we almost split up. Walking home down Calle Flor after dinner, I feel a weight settle on my shoulders reminiscent of when we'd first bought the house.

The next day we buy flowers to take to each of our

neighbors. Hilario and Masako make the visits, explaining what we're about to do. When they come back I ask how it went and get a noncommital "fine" from both.

Monday morning, April 26. A loud banging on the door at 7:40. Epifanio is leaning against a car, arms folded, glowering at fifteen scrawny urchin kids and a couple of guys a little older. They shuffle in, heads down, muttering *"Buenos días."*

Nervously we hover over coffee in the kitchen. Unimaginable that these straggler youths off the ranchos are going to accomplish our stairs and roof. We begin a daily log sheet in a cheap Mexican schoolbook with lined paper. At the top we list Epifanio the maestro, then the two albañiles, and down to the kids, the *peones,* by name: José, Juan, Guadalupe, Feliciano, Zapatero, Delfino, Sustínez, Paulo, Luis, Ramón, Benito. Below that we list materials: *cemento, arena* (sand), *piedra* (stone), *grava* (gravel).

The morning progresses. Planks of wood and four-by-four beams arrive, rise in the air to become a steep, wobbly ramp leading from the patio to the roof. A truck brings bags, *bultos,* of cement, which we count and pay for; another brings metal rebar, another volcanic pumice, tesontle. In no time we're out of pesos. Masako heads for the bank to get more. Our entrada fills with *materiales,* the kitchen table with receipts. In the patio, workers mix gravel and water for cement, shovel it into an encrusted wheelbarrow, dispatch a kid up the ramp to the roof.

By noon Epifanio has left for another work site. Strangers crawl over our precious walls and gardens. Hammers and chisels begin demolishing the house as we've known it. A peón amputates the papaya tree we've seen out our window every morning, the one the hummingbirds come to; it's in the way of the new stairway. A short, fat, sweet-faced mason named León, whose pants keep falling off his hips, revealing his butt crack, slowly chips away at the patio floor where our stairway will be, breathing heavily, asthmatically. At this rate surely he'll finish in a couple of years.

Hilario arrives midafternoon and takes in the proceedings. He's made no secret of his disapproval of Epifanio, whom he considers a scoundrel. Too late now, I think, as chisels ring off walls and dust settles over everything. Besides, Hilario doesn't approve of anyone who comes over since we broke up his *amor* with Lucrecia.

A layer of cement dust coats every surface inside and out. The ramp to the roof, Masako discovers while undressing, looks directly down into our bedroom. We drape curtains over windows, throw sheets over shelves and counters. The half-hour lunch break is the only respite from the pounding, chipping, and scraping of shovels. Around four I visit the casita to talk to the sullen, busty Canadian teenager who is staying there while allegedly studying Spanish at the Instituto. She answers in her nightgown. Earlier we'd offered her the chance to move out but she'd refused; surely after today she'll change her mind. No, she wants to stay. The workers will love getting glimpses of her, and I imagine the little siren courting their attention.

Just before six, Epifanio's workers drop their tools. When the door slams behind the last one, we stand there drained, as if we, not them, had done the day's work. Wiping grime off her face, Masako says ruefully, "Only two months to go."

The next morning, awakened by knocking at 6:30, I stumble into jeans and stagger to the door. A man who looks to be from the lower depths with grimy, blackened clothes and face and mustache, is standing in front of the oldest running truck I've ever seen, piled with huge pink boulders from a riverbed. He and a boy unload them into the patio until there's barely room to pass, then start shoveling the previous day's rubble into the empty truck just as Epifanio and his workers file in. Another day begins.

Each morning we admit a dozen strangers, fork out pesos to Epifanio for obscure services and add-ons, desperately flick through our dictionaries for building terms. The ringing of the albañiles' chisels bores into our brains, our cells. Even on weekends when they're gone we hear it, like a song you can't throw off. Dust settles permanently into our hair, our ears, our clothing. Each night, exhausted and jangled, we stumble out into the town to get away from the house.

Still, things progress. León, having filled a deep hole on the stairway site with cement, begins chipping boulders and adhering them to smaller stones, stopping every few minutes to pull his pants up over his exposed ass. Salvador and Juan Rico, the young masons, are good with their trowels, and I like to watch them scoop, slather, and edge off the new roof flooring and walls. Even the scrawny peones who looked so fragile, so inept at first, bear heavy cement sacks on their shoulders, run concrete-filled wheelbarrows up the ramp, all for a few bucks a day. From time to time one of the boys slips out to the little market up the street and brings Cokes back to the others. They live on Cokes. They joke, they laugh, they get a day's work done.

The roof is level now, and it has a new foundation of gridded rebar and tesontle. A webbing of string marks plumb lines. Mexican builders don't use carpenters' levels to establish a horizontal. They fill a hose line with water, hold one end at the height they seek, then watch where water bubbles from the other end to determine a level: fascinating, and accurate.

By early May, the dry heat clamps down. Work slows.

Epifanio comes less and less, and we have to wait to get questions answered. León's cantera stairway ascends a third of the way up. Chip chip, tap tap: like water dripping. I have to go to California for the publication of a book, leaving Masako to run the project. We buy a fax machine to stay in touch.

For the next several weeks, in a cottage in Venice, I receive faxed sketches and news: "A few days ago Epifanio said that some fiesta was coming up and there would be no work yesterday. There would be a party and I was invited with whomever and told it was customary to contribute money for the expenses. We've become good at contributing expenses. I invited Clarisa, who was helping me clean house, and Hilario, who would drive us in his car. Yesterday a lone worker came early in the morning and built an altar with a blue cross on the roof of your studio for Albañiles' Day. It was beautiful, especially since it was such a private act. We put flowers there.

"The party was all men, all masons. They barbecued steak and sausage they call *barcelonesa*. Lots of tortillas and beer. A little band played norteño music. I said 'norteño music!' to which Epifanio said 'Of course norteño music. We are albañiles!' As if that explained anything. At some point an architect and an engineer who work with Epifanio on various jobs arrived, and another client. The barbecue was *delicious!* Clarisa was thrilled to be there. Hilario was amused. We ate and left. Apparently these fiestas were occurring all over town, as they do each year. I liked everybody better after that.

"The altar's gone already. If I'd known it would be over so quickly I would have taken pictures, or asked to keep it."

The following faxes are less cheery. Masako is trapped in the house all day except when Hilario comes. The water

tank had to be moved to shift a wall. The workers have spotted the sexpot in the casita and throw bottle caps and coins at
her window. Hilario claims tools are missing and suspects
the peones. "You don't have any *seguro social* for the workers?" a Mexican woman we know asks Masako incredulously. "You know, if one of them gets hurt the wife and
children can demand money for generations." I can sense
Masako's strain, her weariness. "I'll tell you one thing," she
says, ending off one fax. "It was a big mistake to live in the
house while this is going on."

At last I arrive back in San Miguel. Walking toward the
house, I notice our water tank is visible from the street. By
law, no structure can be placed within five meters of the
roof's edge, to visually protect the old historical center. I arrive at the door, furious. How did this happen? We could get
in trouble with the city. Masako says the tank needed to be
moved and Epifanio decided to put it there. The next morning, early, I climb around the place. The new roof floor is
finished and the surrounding walls are half-done. Other al-
terations have sprung from nowhere, including enough new
light and telephone outlets on the roof to hold a global conference, when all I'd wanted was a place to sit and see the
sky. When Epifanio arrives I tell him to move the water
tank back from the edge of the roof or we'll get busted by
Obras Públicas, the public works office. Okay, he says
gloomily. Afterward, Masako and I quarrel.

Each morning new kids log in, as workers disappear back
onto the ranchos, leave for the border, or simply don't show.
Only León remains from before, huffing and wheezing over
the cantera arch that rises above the dining room door, and
the stairs we can now mount halfway up. The stairway looks
beautiful, actually, as if it had been there for centuries. Will
it land flush at roof ledge and wall when the last stones go

in? How can León possibly know? I've never seen him take a measure.

Masako leaves for California to see her family and arrange an exhibition, leaving me among the pounding and dust to pay bills, monitor the ingress and egress of materials, stare balefully at the roof crew whose efforts have slowed to a crawl. The weather turns dry, blistering. Still Epifanio hasn't pulled the water tank back from the street. Hilario comes by, though he can do little but irrigate the rear garden and look at me as if to say: I told you so. Kids lean on shovels and wheelbarrows, chat, guzzle endless Cokes, harass the girl next door when I'm out of sight. Epifanio checks the workers in each morning, then disappears. A couple of the new workers are so hapless, so sullen, so suspect, that I tell Epifanio. "*Un flojón?*" he says with fake incredulity—a slacker?—and fires them on the spot.

I fax Masako: "Ran into the neighbor lady to the south, never friendly as it is. I sent the crew over to repaint her side wall and clean up but she's still cranky. 'The noise is terrible, señor. When are you going to be done?' 'Soon, señora, I hope. It's bad for us too. I'm sorry.' Rain clouds the last few days, sprinkles at night. No way we'll beat the rains. We'll never finish, ever. Even the bells sound sour this morning. At least the Social Security came through."

May 21. I'm on the roof with the workers when León calls up from below: "Señor!" I look down and see two men I don't know, one tall and one short, standing in the patio looking coldly up at me.

"What do you want?" I call down sharply.

"Obras Públicas," they say, flashing badges. "We're closing you down."

"Why?"

"You've violated codes."

"What codes? We're just doing some interior remodeling."

The shorter one points to the water tank that Epifanio has failed, after many urgings, to move back in from the roof's edge. The official calls out for everyone to stop work immediately. Shovels and chisels and hammers fall silent. León, huffing and sniffling, wipes his shirtsleeve across his forehead, hikes up his britches.

"So what do I have to do?" I ask.

"Get permits from Obras Públicas. Then petition INAH, the National Institute of Anthropology and History."

They can't be serious. "How long will that take?"

"*Depende.*"

*Depende.* An ominous word. "But this is ridiculous," I say. "We were about to move the water tank back out of sight. It was just an error."

Impassive silence. A gringo offering *mordida*, I sense, could exacerbate things; these are town officials after all, and the workers are looking on. I experience a sinking, hopeless feeling. The taller of the Obras Públicas minions hands me a sheaf of signed and stamped documents. The other unfurls from his briefcase a meter-long banner, walks out to the street, peels off its sticky back, and burnishes it onto the facade above the front door. Then he marches up the workers' ramp from the patio to the roof, leans over the edge, and affixes another banner so that the entire neighborhood, the town, all of Mexico can read the big black letters on white: OBRA SUSPENDIDA.

After the officials leave, the workers file out. "Go find Epifanio and tell him," I call after León.

For the first time in months, excepting weekends, I'm alone in the house. I stand incredulous on the roof in the blazing afternoon heat among piles of hardening cement, abandoned tools, beams, and boulders. I've been moved onto a Mexican time I don't like, one with no foreseeable end.

*"Alarming developments . . ."* my fax to Masako begins.

At day's end Epifanio shows up. *"Pos, no hay problema,"* he says, shrugging, maddeningly indifferent to his own culpability in having placed the tank there in the first place, then failing to move it. "Tomorrow morning I'll see my amigo Engineer Gonzales at the Presidencia."

Who turned us in? Hilario suspects the neighbor lady to the south. So do I. Walking up Calle Flor into town that evening, I feel like Hester Prynne. A ban has been posted on my house, a stain laid upon my character: *Obra Suspendida.* I feel the vague, disreputable workings of Mexican law close around me. I've never felt more a foreigner. Mexico, site of revelation and grace, has turned upon me.

The next morning passes with no word from Epifanio. My gloom deepens. Finally around two he shows up, shaking his head. "Obras Públicas isn't like it was when Engineer Gonzales was there. *Pos,* they sent me to a new guy, Architect Almeida. He'll fix it."

"How?"

"He'll come over, draw a plan, send it to the INAH office in Guanajuato for approval."

"How long will that take?"

*"Pos,* maybe a week, two. *Quince días.* Don't worry."

I look at him, rub my fingers together. He knows what I mean.

*"Vamos a ver,"* he says. "Let's see. Maybe it won't cost too much."

"I want to talk to Architect Almeida."

*"Cómo no?* He's at Obras Públicas, upstairs."

That afternoon I cross the jardín and enter the Presidencia for the first time. Inside the soaring colonial entry, I can't help but think that somewhere in here is the jail where René spent his penitent years after the murder, doing his Náhuatl horoscopes. In a tiny upstairs office I find Architect Almeida, a young, birdlike man. *"Cálmate,"* he says, telling me to relax, though it is he, fingers fluttering, who seems nervous. He'll render a plan of the building site with the new water tank five meters back from the street, get it approved here and in Guanajuato. No problem. I'll stop by your house later, he says.

Days pass. No sign of Architect Almeida. Epifanio has disappeared and has no phone. I try to take advantage of the silence and work on a book I have to complete, but I can't quiet my agitation. I feel exposed, vulnerable, at the mercy of forces I can't see. Friends kid me about the stickers on the house. I avoid the woman next door, whom I actively dislike now. The house will remain like this forever, I think: cement-encrusted, unfinished, doomed.

At last one morning Architect Almeida shows up. I follow him up to the roof, where he takes a few measurements, makes a couple of rudimentary sketches. Who reported us? I ask him. The man who lives in the big house across the street, son of an old San Miguel family and influential local preservation hawk. I feel ashamed of suspecting the neighbor woman, and hasten to tell Hilario that afternoon who really reported us.

June. Masako is back. The first rains hit, washing loose dirt and cement dust down the drains, clogging them and covering our green garden in a gray soup of concrete solution. Architect Almeida's plan sits on some desk in Guanajuato. OBRA SUSPENDIDA blares from our facade. The exterior of the house is a dump site of abandoned materials. León's incomplete stone stairway looms dank and lonely in the storms, like a Dalí or De Chirico.

"That upended wheelbarrow frozen in the cement," Masako says one rainy day in the kitchen, huddled over tea. "We could open our house as an art installation."

"What will we call it?"

" 'Deconstruction.' "

A few days later Architect Almeida shows up with an unsmiling, mustachioed inspector from Guanajuato. They pace the property, confer. The inspector leaves. He wants us to change the slant of the veranda roof we've planned.

"But why? Is there some code?"

*"Cálmate, señor,"* Architect Almeida says, nervously.

I ask him about the position of the water tank. The inspector didn't even mention it, he says. But that's the whole reason we got shut down, I remind him. He shrugs.

The next morning Architect Almeida arrives with our approvals to continue. The fees are nominal, about a hundred fifty dollars in pesos. My fears of extortion had been baseless. Still, some sort of assistance seems in order for Architect Almeida. Unsure what to do, I offer him the equivalent of a hundred dollars in pesos as a token of our gratitude, which he accepts with such reluctance and embarrassment that I wonder if I should have done it at all. Was it wrong, or simply too little?

My faith in Mexico restored, I hurry home, get a ladder, tear down the OBRA SUSPENDIDA stickers and replace them with new ones: OBRA AUTORIZADA. Then I set off to track down Epifanio.

The next morning, a sunny day. The work site lurches to life, like a movie projector starting up after a power failure. Tools are scraped clean, hardened cement chipped away and stacked by the door to be hauled off by the grimy escombro man the next morning. The music of building resumes. We've lost three weeks. Of the earlier crew, only maestro

Epifanio and León remain. If León's edifice has cost us our papaya tree and some space, this tubby little man's arching stairway, with its gentle weave of river boulders and stones and cement, is truly beautiful, the work of an artisan. Before long we can stand on the highest step and look, if not yet step, onto the roof. For the first time, we taste completion.

J uly. The new roof is done and dry. Walls are up, and in the Mexican fashion, Epifanio's workers go back in to hack out the ducts for the *conducto*, the tubing that will encase the electrical wiring. The boys throw bottle caps at the window of the exhibitionist teenager in the casita until finally I go over and forcibly close her curtain. Meanwhile the veranda columns, mirroring those in the old patio below, rise to receive their roof, and built-in banquettes are sculpted in concrete from Masako's sketches.

The electrician arrives to lay in the wiring, the plumber to hook up new water and gas tanks and taps. We can now hop from León's stairs to the roof. Trucks arrive with huge beams from Michoacán, bricks, and curved terra-cotta roof tiles. Amazed, we watch Epifanio and his mason spread grass mat petates and newspapers across beams balanced on the columns, then lay bricks and wet concrete upon them. Later they whisk away the petates and newspapers, leaving a brick roof perfectly in place. Then they lay the roof tiles on top, loose. It remains to paint the house, tile the roof floor, finalize the stairway, attend to a host of details.

As we draw closer to completion, work mysteriously slows to a crawl. The few peones who show up labor as if drugged. We lose hours to the daily afternoon rains: tarps thrown over cement, workers huddled in the bodega, fresh paint running down the walls. Epifanio and his workers will be here forever. We will not finish this job in our lifetime.

Hostage to our house, we've seen little of friends since April. Susana stops by on occasion to watch the progress, Carlos tries unsuccessfully to drag me out for a drink. On the few occasions when we do get out with people, we are boring monomaniacs who talk only of our troubles with the house and the crew. Maruja at La Golondrina counsels that this always happens near the end. You pay by the week, the workers want to stretch it out. Why shouldn't they?

Walking home from the market, we pass a crew painting a wall in the next block of Calle Flor. "That's it!" Masako cries out. She rips a page out of her sketch notebook, dips it in the painter's bucket, and bears it home. Mexican walls are painted an infinity of colors, but in San Miguel shades of red rule, from pinkish *rosa mexicano* to deep magenta. The color she's chosen is neither florid nor dusky but the warm glow of a San Miguel sunset. The next day Epifanio mixes up some cal—slaked lime whitewash with a binder of cactus juice—and powdered pigment. He brushes a sample on the entrada wall and leaves it overnight to dry. The following day Masako checks it against her swatch. This goes on for days until she's convinced it's right. Taking a deep breath, we unleash Epifanio's workers to paint the entire white exterior a deep rose.

More weeks drag on. The painters inch across the high walls on precarious ladders. Quarantined in the house, we are close to going mad. Epifanio, a good builder but impatient with detail, presides over a series of small daily disasters. The other jobs we'd planned to address—tiling the kitchen and bathrooms, fixing doors and windows—are long forgotten. We just want everyone out of here. In early August we sit Epifanio down at the kitchen table and tell him next Friday is it, finished or not. He agrees to put on extra workers for a final push.

Friday, August 6. We paint the neighbor's wall a second time, earning a faint nod of thanks from the husband and more scowls from the wife. A delicate black iron railing Masako designed goes in on León's stairs. When I mention to Epifanio that my studio roof remains unpainted, he all but snarls at me. I snarl back. We're dead sick of each other. He tells his workers to slosh on a coat from a can lying about which turns out to be indoor paint, guaranteed to last all of a few months. He doesn't care anymore, and neither do I.

Saturday brings merciful silence, broken only by Vicente, who stops by late afternoon with a bottle of Santo Tomás red to celebrate the project's end. We mount the new stairs to the new roof, scatter cushions along the veranda seats. We sit gazing up at the Parroquia.

*"Qué vista,"* Vicente says. *"Vale la pena."* Worth the hassle.

Masako looks at me, then at Vicente.

"Easy for you to say," she says.

# Chapter 18

# A ño *Loco*

THE LOCOS PARADE WENDS ITS WAY
down the hill into the shadows of the buildings on Calle San Francisco, a sea of bobbing
masks and twisting tubas. The annual June
exercise in street theater, seen through my
video camera viewfinder, seems especially
demonic this year: the prancing dervishes
twisting in torment, the trumpets harsh and
mordant. Floating among the rubbery, por-
cine Clintons and Kissinger masks, hairy
Fidels and Ches, florid priests and hookers,
are some new entrants: President Salinas
with devil horns, poignant effigies of the
recently slain presidential nominee Colosio,
and the black knit ski mask and pipe of
Mexico's new hero, Subcomandante Marcos
of the Zapatista Army of National Libera-
tion.

Not yet half over, 1994 traces an ominous

arc across Mexican time. It was on the first of January—the day the free trade agreement between Mexico, the U.S., and Canada went into effect—that the Zapatistas rose out of the Chiapan forests with wooden rifles, bearing messages of an unresolved past and a suffering present. In April, Colosio, the ruling party's reformist candidate for president in the November elections, was assassinated in Tijuana by—everyone assumes—conspiring narcotraficantes and party old-liners. This year we have all become initiates in Mexico's "adventure of disorder." Yet how festively—ruefully, ironically—Mexicans incorporate bad news.

The dancing locos draw me down to the jardín, past the Presidencia building and around to the Parroquia. In the parish church forecourt, a dozen people huddle on blankets beneath signs that say STOP THE KILLING IN CHIAPAS and VIVA SUBCOMANDANTE MARCOS. Their fast, in full view of the jardín, moves into its second week. Abandoning the parade, I turn off my camera and pass through the church gate. I drop a donation in the basket and step over a ring of flowers, lit candles, and water bottles surrounding the protesters. Elenita is curled asleep on a blanket, oblivious to the parade, wasting down to her earnest marrow. Her shiny face wears a worried frown. Just as well she slumbers, I think: the locos' wacky take on current events wouldn't amuse her.

"Santa Elenita," Carlos has taken to calling her these days, and not entirely in jest. Last November she'd arrived back in San Miguel with a welt on her cheek raised by her Oaxacan rug-maker lover. She and Carlos had reconciled, and begun refurbishing their folk art store with beautiful weavings and lacquered wood trays, bright new Huichol peyote paintings, and deep-toned ceramic hand-painted plates from the nearby village of Pantoja. I'd see them walking home along Calle Recreo hand in hand, Carlos sober and revivified, Elenita's fervent grad-student smile restored. Then on New Year's Day, the Zapatistas invaded San Cristóbal.

Everybody was caught off guard. I'd heard rumors through the Mexican branch of PEN, the international writers' and human rights group I work with, of unrest in the south. A few years ago I'd visited the cool, smoky Chiapan mountain forests where barefoot Mayans, descendants of the temple builders of Palenque and Copán, still live in near-indentured servitude 450 years after the Spaniards arrived. The previous year had ended with President Salinas negotiating NAFTA, the trade deal that promised to deliver Mexico into sunny, permanent First World affluence. Loafer-clad Mexico City residents were driving new Mercedeses up to San Miguel for weekends, jabbering into cellular phones, unleashing their spoiled children upon the jardín. New international factories lined the Querétaro highway, and up along the border the *maquiladora* plants mushroomed. The United States had even nominated Salinas to be president of the World Trade Organization when he leaves office at the end of this year. So what if drug cartels sported their own fleets of planes, seventeen of Mexico's thirty-four governors were interim appointees because of voter fraud, and Salinas asked ninety-three private businessmen to contribute $25 million each to the upcoming electoral campaign? Though it's only June, the writer Carlos Fuentes has already called this Mexico's "Year of Living Dangerously"—and it's all on display today in the political theater of Día de Los Locos.

I envy Elenita and Carlos's passionate activism, but Article 33 of the Mexican constitution forbids foreigners from participating in Mexican politics at risk of expulsion or jail. Masako and I, bearers of alien blue passports, live here entirely at the discretion of our hosts. We have no guaranteed rights worth the name. Our existence in Mexico is as fragile as this year's disturbances or some xenophobic politician's anti-gringo campaign. We come from a country that proposes to build a wall across the border to keep Mexicans out—and a state, California, with an issue on the ballot denying "illegal aliens" (read "Mexican workers") even minimal social services. This year is a reminder that Mexico could end anytime for us: come the revolution, even the new *escritura* document that says we own the house on Calle Flor turns to confetti. During the remodel last summer, when work was suspended and the house's fate uncertain, I'd asked Masako, "What if we lost it all—Mexico, the house? Would you regret we'd done it?" "Not a day, not a dime," she said. I feel the same.

The stunning advent of the Zapatistas has recharged Elenita, Carlos, and countless Mexicans. Subcomandante Marcos's cryptic Internet emissions from the jungle are pored over like tea leaves in *La Jornada,* Mexico's hip daily. President Salinas appears suddenly vulnerable, tainted. This spring Carlos and Elenita attended a conference in Chiapas, organized local support in San Miguel. Now Elenita fasts for peace here at my feet with all the ardency of those singing pilgrims who flock to nearby Tlacote for the healing waters. Will Carlos, a more worldly man at heart, be able to stay the course with her this time? As the last ragged remnants of the Locos parade move up Calle Correo like the wandering theater troupes of Europe's medieval plague years, I reach down and touch Elenita's hand. She opens her eyes, smiles bravely up. Raising her arm, she makes a feeble fist.

*"Viva,"* she says.

*"Viva,"* I say back.

A few years ago, a poet friend who edits a U.S. culture and arts magazine asked me to write a piece on Mexico. A rash of stories about road hijackings had knocked Mexico off the tourist circuit for a season or two, and friends in the States, unreasonably afraid for their safety, were deferring visits. San Miguel remained only seasonally busy, the hotels and restaurants seldom full. Nestled concentrically within house, town, region, and country, we felt safely inured from the outside world's interest. Still, there were signs of a shift: beauteous Leda, a full-fledged real estate broker now, would tell us of homes selling for shocking figures—not just to Americans but to Italians, Germans, and Mexicans fleeing the besieged capital. New flight routes from Houston and Los Angeles landed visitors a little over an hour away, bypassing the four-hour trip from Mexico City. Around the jardín, the mutation of little *taquerías* and grocery stores into shops and cafés drove us ever further to the outskirts to buy basics.

I was ambivalent about writing on Mexico. I'd kept notes and diaries but had never written publicly about our life here. I considered Mexico my refuge, not my subject. The high white walls of my studio served as ground for a shadow play of fictional figures and forms drawn from other places, other pasts. I felt I didn't know enough yet to write of this country. And as a subject, Mexico presents problems both of unfamiliarity and overfamiliarity, its resonances to English readers well mined earlier by Traven, Greene, Katherine Anne Porter, Lowry, Harriett Doerr. Now late-century Mexico—cultured, layered, profound—had become the literary territory of the cheap margarita thriller, the drug caper, the hedonistic beach romance. Yet we were here, living its true thrill.

For Masako, it had been different from the beginning. Mexican light, color, customs, and culture erupted in her art early, not just an influence but its very subject. A large survey show at the Bellas Artes of her Mexican work will consist of work drawn entirely from this culture and the fullness of her life in it. Inexorably Mexico pressed in upon my work, too: once a distant place, Mexico was now my present and, increasingly, my past—the old home the faraway place.

The editor wanted me to write about life here in the region where we live. At the time, San Miguel de Allende, Guanajuato, and Querétaro ranked a page or two each in the guidebooks, day stops or overnighters on a tour of the "silver cities," the subject of an occasional tourist piece in a Sunday travel section, the "charming little town hidden away in the Mexican mountains." If our very presence here makes us instruments of gentrification, why worsen it by speeding that process, labeling the ineffable, divulging a site of private power? Don't put a gloss on it, the editor said. Just tell what life is really like, the good and the bad. Tell the truth a good fiction writer knows.

October 4. I'm sitting in a chapel of Las Monjas, listening to a nun behind a partition chant a novena. Three nights ago, during the Fiesta of San Miguel known as the *alborada*—that paroxysm of revelry climaxing the September celebrations—Barbara Faith Covarrubias, a writer I know, became suddenly ill. Alfonso, her husband, rushed her to a local hospital. She had a perforated colon— an ordinary emergency any reputable hospital handles with zero mortality rate. But the anesthesiologist was off at the fiesta, the hospital didn't have Barbara's blood type, and she bled to death in extreme agony.

Alfonso, an ex-bullfighter, sits lean and straight-backed in the pew across from me, looking ghostly, shattered. The nun murmurs offstage. At some point we all drop to our knees. A novena—from the word meaning "nine"—will be chanted each day for nine days.

I think about Mexico's año loco, which continues in earnest. In August, a colorless successor to the slain Colosio ascended to the presidency. In Chiapas, Zapatistas and government soldiers enact a Mexican standoff. Elenita's fast ended, but so did her marriage to Carlos, and now she is somewhere south with the rebels while he tends to the store. This morning's Mexico City paper had an ad for a gold bulletproof Mercedes, another for a "risk mitigation" service offering protection against kidnappings and abductions. Distant thunder to us here in the provinces, with our sunlit days, rooftop reveries, and private cultural obsessions: but Barbara Faith Covarrubias's death is not.

I'd met Barbara and Alfonso at a PEN conference in Prague last summer. Barbara, a longtime American resident here, wrote romance novels—very successfully, I was told. I'd never met a romance novelist. We spent an afternoon wandering through Prague together. She was smart, modest, and kind; Alfonso gentlemanly, elegantly Mexican. It turned out she had tens of thousands of readers in the Eastern bloc; when she'd arrived she'd been met by a limousine and a publicist sent by her publisher. Now rising from my knees in the nunnery, I recall their saying later that Prague was a high point for them, a treasured memory.

After the novena, we gather in the sunlight outside the chapel. *"Así es la vida."* "It was her time." *"Qué triste."* Mourners' words thread the air; grief is the same everywhere. *"Pobre Alfonso."* "An unnecessary death," someone says.

Was it? Is there such a thing? Isn't it blasphemy, here in the nunnery, to question God's design? But must the niños die from dehydration, the politicians from drug bullets? Why does Mexico, festive and abundant land brimming with life, always make you think about death? Maybe Barbara's was avoidable. But who is to judge the anesthesiologist out celebrating his town's founding patron, or the tiny local hospital with its inadequate blood bank? It was Barbara Faith Covarrubias's misfortune to have become afflicted on the night of the fiesta of San Miguel. Fate, not faith, won this round.

Alfonso, bent with grief, looks lost and small in the sunlight. I shake his hand, hold it. Above us, a nun tolls the bell.


**M**id-December. The day before we fly to California for the Christmas holidays, the peso collapses to half its value. Mexicans blame former president Salinas, now believed to have been connected to the political murders and the narcotraficantes. Salinas has fled to Canada, Havana, Dublin—nobody is sure where. In Mexico City's downtown Zócalo we witness an angry demonstration against California's anti-immigrant Proposition 187, which passed on last month's ballot. On the plane I sit next to Yoko, a Japanese girl who works in quality control at a Nissan plant in Mexico.

"In Japan," she says, "if something falls down on the production line, workers rush to analyze the cause, take blame. In Mexico, it's *'se cayó'* (it fell) or *'se rompió'* (it broke). Nobody admits responsibility."

"What do you do, then?" I ask her.

"First you approach the worker to the right and you ask is everything okay. Then you approach the worker to the left. Finally you agree with the worker who made the mistake that maybe something happened—'*se cayó.*' But you never blame."

"Pride, machismo," I say.

Yoko nods. "Every culture is different."

How true, I think, as we zoom up the freeway from LAX in the back of a green taxi driven by a garrulous Nigerian UCLA student, a bright wind sweeping the basin, the palm leaves glittering silver in winter light. Recent years have not been kind to the city: fires, freeway shootings, the Rodney King police beating and riots. In January the Northridge earthquake collapsed apartment buildings, severed arterial freeways, sent a motorcycle cop hurtling into space. In Venice we walk a Diebenkorn palette of sunset sky, water, sand.

Life at sea level. We see friends and movies we've missed, drink in a little of the old obsessive pace. We experience unaccountable urges to buy things. We talk with editors and art dealers. Mexican cultural influence is everywhere, even if nobody wants to go there. The global monoculture advances, knitting our two worlds closer together: earth as one vast bazaar. Masako now buys *Art News* in San Miguel, while Californians eat off pottery from Dolores Hidalgo.

At a family Christmas gathering, we distribute Mexican folk toys among new nieces and nephews, answer questions about our life "down there." Daughter Maya is making good bucks at her job; finally we can laugh about the typhus episode two years ago. She talks of coming again soon.

The next day, speeding north up Highway 101 to visit Masako's family in San Francisco, we pull over among artichoke and lettuce fields at Mission San Miguel Arcángel, built by that same Junípero Serra whose first churches we'd recently visited only a few hours from San Miguel, in the Sierra Gorda mountains. We wander through a cactus-filled courtyard and Indian-painted chapel, drinking in familiar shapes and moods. Everywhere we see a Mexican California, sense the poignant relationship between the two lands. (The governor behind Proposition 187 knows full well that if Mexican workers went on strike for one day, California would simply grind to a halt.) Where does one country stop, the other begin anymore? Where is the border between experiences? Our journeys back and forth seem like trips across town now. We live in transnational space, airports our waiting rooms, our suitcases always half-packed.

Dropping down off the Bayshore into downtown San Francisco, we talk about what we'll do when we get back to San Miguel on Friday. We'll make dinner for Juan Carlos, who in a single day lost his shoe export business in nearby León when the peso collapsed two weeks ago. Afterward we'll climb the stairs to the new roof and talk among the stars until it gets too cold. Then we'll summon a mesquite fire against the chill and toast fate's vagaries, glad to be reaching the end of this año loco.

# $S$*abor*

THE WEATHER MAPS OF U.S. NEWS
programs often portray Mexico as a blank—
as if weather, not to mention life itself,
simply stopped at the Texas border. But
Mexico's lustrous coasts, stubbly deserts,
furry jungles, and ragged mountains, its
high peaks and dank lowlands, are beset by
a living weather of withering heat, biting
cold, hurricanes, and droughts—not just
that benign sun so tonic to northerners.
Here on our mile-high *altiplano,* defined by
the two great Sierra cordilleras running
down either side of the country, hailstones
big as golf balls drop suddenly out of hot,
dry May skies, ripping holes in the trumpet
vine on the walls of Masako's studio, shred-
ding the leaves of the spider lilies outside
her window. Howling winter winds shake
the jacaranda trees as if for some offense

they'd committed. On summer afternoons, tropical thunderheads gather along the horizon like bad thoughts, then sweep in to pound the town with deafening rains, stripping paint off walls, turning the steep lanes into coursing streams within minutes. Hilario says his father used to set his watch by these daily summer rains. Though they're less regular now, we still plan our afternoons around the rain—as on this mid-August 1996 day, when friends are coming for lunch.

The intimacy of weather and land extends to nearly everything around us. We'll eat today from plates and bowls thrown and glazed at the Vásquez kilns in Dolores Hidalgo half an hour away, using Talavera techniques that first came from Spain to the Mexican town of Puebla. The blue and green drinking glasses are hand-blown at the factory down by the train station. We'll dine on a table made of an old door from an abandoned nearby hacienda, beneath a chandelier forged in an ironmonger's shop in town. We'll sit on chairs hewn from local mesquite trees and leather tanned here. The muslin tablecloth comes from a factory outside of town, the hand-loomed cambaya cloth napkins from our trip to Michoacán.

We'll eat fat green chiles from a nearby farm, brought on a food truck to the Parque Juárez every Thursday. The squash blossom flowers that Masako—and Mercedes, who is helping us today—are making into soup in the kitchen were brought to our door by laughing girls. The dark Oaxaca-style *mole*, with its countless spices, will be served over chicken bought from the lady whose gringo husband runs the ice cream store and changes money at a better rate than the banks. After lunch we'll climb the stairway León built of stones from a riverbed a few miles from here, mortared by the descendants of masons who built the old Chichimecan pyramid on the other side of the dam off the Guanajuato road.

This sensuous texturing of time and history into the everyday provides the undercurrent of pleasure in being here: a voluptuary of moments. Use and beauty combine into what Octavio Paz has called the "fiesta of the object." *Sabor,* that inclusive Spanish word meaning flavor—not just in food but in all things: music, art, speech, dance—suggests a sensory profusion understood to show generosity of heart and imagination. Walking from kitchen to dining room to patio to studio to garden, each object my eye lands upon is coded into time, memory, and experience: a living history that twines around us more each year, like the jasmine, sisus, moneda, and bougainvillea vines that embrace the garden and patio walls.

The occasion for the lunch is the arrival of a writer friend to stay in the casita for a week. We'll introduce her to friends: two Mexicans, two Italians, a French woman, another American.

Entering the garden to pick spices, I dodge orange and black monarch butterflies floating on invisible currents. A hummingbird stabs at a trumpet vine bloom. After the roof remodel, birds stayed away for a good year; but now woodpeckers hammer again at the avocado trunk in the mornings, and clouds of chirping finches alight in the chirimoyo late afternoons. I lean down into colliding aromas of spices, where a rosemary plant aspiring to become a tree crowds chile, basil, thyme. Hilario considers arugula a weed and keeps tearing it up; Masako replants it; he rips it out and replaces it with chile. I pluck off a young arugula sprig before he can get to it. After lunch we'll make mint tea from the fresh leaves I pick.

Fecund Mexico. So many foods come from this part of the world. What did Europe eat before Columbus? Turnips, game, gruel? People have inhabited these regions for at least 20,000 years: the date keeps being pushed back. Recent discoveries in a cave in Oaxaca place an agrarian society in southern Mexico as early as 8000 B.C.: the evidence included human bones, and the rind and seeds of that same yellow-orange squash blossom, calabaza, we'll serve for lunch today in a soup.

No need to pick cilantro, because this morning the chattering girls came to the door with piles of it atop their baskets of cactus, fresh blue corn tortillas, and chopped salsa of tomatillos, onion, avocado, lime.

I slide under the jacaranda's canopy of shade onto the old stone seat in the corner, brushing aside the stray chirimoyo limbs that keep evading Hilario's machete. Is it his eyesight? Middle-aged now, he's still too macho to wear the reading glasses Masako brings him from the States. Since the incident with the maid Lucrecia, he has his affairs elsewhere, if at all. He still goes on religious peregrination to San Juan de Los Lagos every January but only walks partway now, taking a bus the rest of the way. His eldest son is becoming an engineer; his children move into the middle class. Hilario feels left behind, gets discouraged at times, drinks. Once I came back from a trip and found him asleep on Masako's studio bed with a bottle of tequila, the television on. I asked him what he was doing. "Burglars in the neighborhood. I stuck around to watch the house," he muttered, inviting me to share the fiction. I nodded, helped him get himself up and on home.

Ever since that day when the woman who worked here thirty-five years ago came and told me her history of the house, I picture a tall, tan mare tethered to the iron ring in the wall above my head. This bench in the garden is the one we sat on when we first saw the house, and I climbed the back stairs to the roof and we decided to buy it. Now a sisus vine winds along the old stone wall, entangling the iron ring, and violets, irises, roses, and spider lilies bloom where there was dry dirt.

A knock on the front door, followed by Clarisa's hearty voice. She stops by regularly these days to show off her second child and do embroidery work with Masako. Clarisa and Marisa were just kids when we moved in here and they helped us out. Time shifts the cast of characters. Those who will come to lunch today are different from those who came a few years ago, as they were from those we first used to see. Mina never came back to Mexico after Paul died. Arnaud is back in Port-au-Prince, the gray eminence of Haitian letters. Since Maruja and Billie moved their store off the jardín to another part of town, we see them less. Elenita, who left Carlos to join the Zapatistas, now lives alone in Guadalajara, I hear. Alfonso Covarrubias, the ex-bullfighter, died almost exactly a year to the day after his wife, Barbara, died that terrible night of the fiesta. He'd never recovered. During that last year I'd see him wandering the streets, blank-faced, a ghost already.

One day recently I passed René's store and saw him through the window, reading. I went inside and we talked a while. René has settled in, his notoriety fading with the years. Still the story is told around town of the man who was killed twice, and in its variations it curls and twines and shoots out as many different branches as the vines running along this old garden wall.

In the greater world, ex-president Salinas is on the lam in Ireland, his brother Raul in jail for drug trafficking and illegal enrichment—while Subcomandante Marcos and the Zapatistas, dug into the Chiapan jungle, remain the country's uneasy conscience.

Sometimes, passing the dry cleaners up the street, I think of the Corto Maltese, the restaurant with the great salsa bands that first summer of 1985; and of Paolo, its shadowy proprietor, the former Red Brigades soldier hiding out from the police who simply disappeared one day—back to France, we learned later, to serve out his sentence. Last week I was in a bistro a few blocks off the jardín run by Danielle, a French artist who'd moved here that same summer we did. She came over to my table.

"You won't believe this," she said. "I found out what happened to Paolo."

"Tell me."

"Last summer I was in France, on a train from Paris to Lyon. By sheer coincidence, sitting across from me was a Mexican woman I used to know here in San Miguel. Do you remember Macarena?"

I did, actually. "Hennaed hair. Flamboyant. Extravagant laugh."

"Yes. She had a clothing shop in the arcade across from the Bellas Artes for a while. Well, we started talking. She asked me if I remembered Paolo, and I said of course. We used to dance at his restaurant, the Corto Maltese. Macarena reached in her purse and pulled out a novel she was reading. It was one of the *Romans Policiers* series, a mystery, by Gallimard, the French publisher. In fact wait, I have a copy in the kitchen. . . ."

Danielle disappeared in back, then came back out with a book in French, the author's name something like "Leonardo Lionni."

"Turn it over," she said.

I did, and there was a picture of the author: unmistakably Paolo. He looked the same, but with a jacket over his black T-shirt. I looked up at Danielle, incredulous.

"Apparently," she said, "while Paolo was in jail, he began to write to pass the time. When Gallimard bought his first

novel, an arrangement was made with the French government. You know how we are in France. Literature redeems,
like with Jean Genet. So they pardoned him. Now Paolo—
who knows his true name? Even this name Leonardo Lionni
is a nom de plume, Macarena says—is a successful author in
France, his books translated into many languages. Can you
believe it?"

"Amazing," I said. "And what about Macarena?"

"She opened a little boutique in Paris on rue de la
Huchette selling Mexican and Guatemalan clothes—serapes, huipiles, sandals. Apparently she does very
well."

In this town full of stories, I become, as years pass, a re-
pository of lore. Maybe I become lore myself: the gringo
writer who lives in that old house on Calle Flor, sometimes
seen standing on street corners staring at blank walls, or gazing up at an empty blue sky. Or Masako, the japonesa artist
and photographer with the beautiful long hair she makes art
from, the one with the gringo husband.

When we first moved here, the few foreigners around
were young transients, old retirees, aging bohemians. Now
boomers arrive in droves, buying up the old houses, starting
businesses. We have two Internet servers now, a dozen realty
offices, boutiques, video stores. Movie stars sneak in and out
of town to visit or take art classes at the Instituto Allende.
You can buy portobello and oyster mushrooms, Bulgarian
yogurt, French brie. There's a face-lift clinic outside of town.
San Miguel de Allende is touted in the magazines as a place
to visit.

In old towns like this one, history, religion, and ceremony
soften the effects of change. Mexicans, unlike North Americans, consider technology a convenience, not a faith or a
metaphysic. Foreigners still number little more than 5 per-

cent of the population. ("One good kidnapping," Carlos joked the other day, "and they'll scatter like pigeons.") Inside the Parroquia, throngs gather for daily Mass as they always have. In the jardín, the balloon sellers roam, there's a poster for the Sunday bullfights, and ice cream is still sold out of tubs on a cart borne by a dray horse. Tonight after the rains, hundreds of teenagers will gather for the paseo, that timeless mating procession. On Tuesday the traveling market, bigger than ever, will unfold its wares.

In Heisenberg's physics, we alter a phenomenon by the act of our regard. In writing about this country, this town, this house I love, I sacrifice part of it. There is eco-tourism, but no equivalent restraint on cultural tourism. Inevitably, historical sites like this will be preserved as commercial "living museums." We will visit a place called "China," in quotation marks, or go out into "nature." We will visit "Florence" in situ, once the site of a Renaissance city of the same name. What was formerly the town proper becomes the "old town," surrounded by the "new town." Over the hill east of here, just beyond the highest view from the roof, a new shopping center grows to accommodate the housing developments erupting around it; while down here in the old town center, a place called "San Miguel"—an inordinately pretty, quiet, Mexican town of cowboys, storekeepers, and refugees from Mexico City and parts more distant—things are the same but not. The romance of the Other—part of what first landed us here—dims: in California I speak more Spanish; here, more English. My two environments cross, come to mirror each other. Last week I went to a party where there were more gringos than there used to be in the entire town. Sometimes I wonder: Will a plague of our own kind drive us on?

Still, when morning light spreads down these garden

walls and the great bell of La Luz rumbles across the air, when reddish dusk steals through the streets and lanes and the moon rises over the mirador, what I loved before here I still love. If the water doesn't run out (for unlike the soil that washes down to the plain below, then is brought back up as loam by the burros, water never returns), maybe I'll end up here, another old gringo sitting in the sun.

Sometimes I think of Neal Cassady, whose Road of Excess ended not at William Blake's Palace of Wisdom but facedown on the railroad tracks outside of town. Maybe there's no home really, only road's end.

Limes. I almost forgot. We'll need them for salad dressing and *agua mineral.* Our Mexican friends will squeeze that universal curative and flavoring on everything—soup, vegetables—and so will we. I get up and cross the garden, pass through my studio into the patio, and mount the stairway León built to the roof. I tear a dusky sprig of sage from the terra-cotta pot against the peeling wall, twist off three green limes from the tree in the pot. When we first finished this roof and stairs with Epifanio, we thought we'd never build again. Lately we talk of restoring the house closer to its original form, much as the woman who used to live here described it. Last week I saw Epifanio on the street and we talked about doing some more work, though when I mentioned the encounter to Masako she frowned.

Thunder from the west. In an hour or two the sun will disappear. The first fat drops will freckle the stones, followed by battering rains. After lunch we'll leave the *comedor* and come up here on the roof, let the storm rage around us. Then our friends, growing drowsy, will leave for siestas. By nightfall the mountain sky will thicken with stars, the moon etching shadows on the stones.

I descend the stairs bearing my fruits and spices. In the kitchen, the simmering aroma of dark *mole* lies on the air as Masako and Mercedes fuss over the pots, salsa music spinning from XESQ, Radio San Miguel.

A knock on the door. Friends arrive.

# Chapter 20

# T he Embrace

EXTERIOR, ROOFTOP, DUSK.

The town, cantilevered up its hillside, blushes red. Earth and stone walls grow inflamed, as if heated by some inner forge. The Parroquia's sandstone spire thrusts heavenward, a compass point.

New Years Day 1999. *Qué milagro.* We're still here—the house, the town, Mexico. The seasons ravish us: migrations of swallows, bats, swifts, ravens—and these keening, white-eyed, glossy black grackles, spiraling toward their nests in the jardín. A squadron of snowy egrets crosses them from the north, en route to the Parque Juárez to settle for the night in the tops of the pecan trees.

It's still my sweet spot, up on this roof. Up here, I resolve the world.

Firecrackers from the direction of *el*

caracol announce a fiesta. Maybe there'll be *castillos* tonight, wooden fireworks towers. In the street below, our little neighborhood Hercules, balancing heavy buckets of hot water and corncobs on his gnarled shoulders like scales of justice, passes by, booming out in a Plácido Domingo baritone: *"Elotes! Elotes!"* (Corn on the cob, corn on the cob.)

On Christmas Eve we watched worshipers line up during Mass at the Parroquia to kiss a pink plastic doll beneath a huge banner that reads: *María Guíanos al Tercer Milenio* (Mary Guide Us into the Third Millennium). Last night we stood up here eating grapes and making wishes, one for each tolling midnight bell. Today all the ambulances gathered in front of the Parroquia and turned on their sirens while the priest blessed them. A few yards away a demonstration marked the fifth anniversary of the Chiapas uprising.

Already they're selling cakes in the bakeries for Three Kings Day, and next week the mariachis will serenade the Virgin of Guadalupe in her niche under the portales. On January 16, Susana will bring her two cats and new puppy to San Antonio Abad church for the blessing of the animals. Then comes the pilgrimage to San Juan de Los Lagos, which means we won't see Hilario for some days.

Fourteen winters ago, two soul-weary, peripatetic Americans stumbled into a country and a town they knew nothing of. More than ten years now in this house on Calle Flor. Each year feels like starting over. The last one began with *la helada,* the century's worst frost, killing trees and plants and flowers, turning gardens black. Everybody blamed El Niño. The farmers were hit worst as always, and we all sent food and blankets to the campo. The magenta bougainvillea in the corner of the patio, the one whose color Masako had been so adamant about, died; when Masako and Hilario came home with a new one from Candelaria they announced resolutely: "This one will make it." So far it has. The jacaranda in the garden sprouts pale new green leaves but will flaunt no purple blooms this year.

On September 29, the night of the Fiesta of San Miguel, a dam broke above the town, sending down a wall of churning, muddy water, turning the streets into raging rivers. Houses were swept away. Ambulances and fire engines rescued people from mud-clotted homes down by the arroyo while police roamed the town shouting *"Emergencia!"* Carlos's aunt Lucía was swept to her death trying to fish a gas tank from the torrent. The fiesta went on anyway—the brass bands, the parade of papier-mâché figures up Calle Canal, the Indian dancers from every part of Mexico.

One morning in October I heard a loudspeaker blasting a piece of dance music over and over. Unable to work, I left my studio and walked outside. The next block of Calle Flor was dressed like a carnival set. Coming closer, I saw Arriflexes, dollies, viewfinders, makeup girls, throngs of extras. A director was shouting in Spanish and English through a bullhorn. "What's up?" I asked Fidelio, who runs La Piñata, the restaurant on the corner. "They're shooting a Julio Iglesias video." Here came Julio himself, dancing down the street, mouthing to the soundtrack, surrounded by half-clad beauties in wet T-shirts. This is where we came in, I thought: refugees from L.A., where every block alternates as a movie set and you're always tripping over cable wires.

A few days ago I was having breakfast in La Piñata when Fidelio said, "Look! There it is!" We all gathered around the old television set above the tables and watched the MTV video of Julio and the girls, singing and dancing against the Pompeiian red walls outside La Piñata door on Calle Flor.

It's all showbiz, I guess—though the neighbor across the street, the old colonel, simply says in reference to all this madness, *"Así pasan las cosas."* He uses the expression casually, as Americans might say "that's life," or "shit happens"—though its poetry always floors me, with its healthy resignation to fate, its recognition of how the world really works. *Así pasan las cosas.* Things come, they pass on—freezes, floods, even Julio Iglesias.

Yesterday afternoon Masako burst through the front door, an astonished look on her face. She'd run into our perennially cool and distant next-door neighbor, Señora Fernández, on the corner of Calle Pila Seca. During the time of the roof remodel, though we'd plied Señora Fernández with bouquets of flowers and repainted her walls, relations had turned even chillier. Yesterday Masako greeted her, her husband, and her daughter with a cheerful *"Feliz Año,"* as one does. Señora Fernández returned the greeting, then spread her arms wide and enfolded Masako in a warm embrace. Her daughter followed, then her husband.

Telling me of the *abrazo*, Masako teared up. So did I.

This morning, just outside my door, I received the same treatment. Does this mean we're accepted at last along Calle Flor?

E xterior. Rooftop. Night. The sky darkens. A warm wind shivers the avocado tree. The Parroquia's lights seep on. Must be a wealthy wedding in the church. Or the Texas woman down on Calle Quebrada has made a donation to Urbano the priest so she can herd her guests to the balcony for the light show.

I turn away, climb down León's stone stairs to the old house. In the morning I leave. Affairs beckon across the border.

*Ojalá*, God willing, I'll be back.

# Acknowledgments

THANKS ABOVE ALL TO MASAKO, *mi compañera de viaje.* My gratitude for their professional help to Charles Conrad, Liz Calder, Rosemary Davidson, Shona Martyn, Bonnie Nadell, and Becky Cabaza; for Mexico help to Anita and Karl Anton von Blyleben, Víctor Cuevas, Carmen Delgadillo, Beverly Donofrio, El Colibrí, Jesús Espinosa, Robert deGast, Carmen and Pedro Friedeberg, Victor Heady, Gina Hyams, Café La Parroquiana, Lucina Kathmann, Mama Mía, Carmen Masip, Mary Marsh, Sue McKinney, Robert Sommerlott, Deborah Turbeville, David Wright, and Cilla Zweig; for literary inspiration to Carlos Fuentes, Carlos Monsiváis, Elena Poniatowska. *Un abrazo* to Chick Strand.

TONY COHAN is the author of the novels *Canary,* a *New York Times* Notable Book of the Year, and *Opium,* a Literary Guild selection. His essays, travel writings, and reviews have appeared in many books, magazines, and newspapers, including the *Washington Post* and the *Los Angeles Times.* His work as a lyricist with pianist and composer Chick Corea and others can be heard on a number of albums. He divides his time between Venice, California, and Mexico.